Negotiating
with
GIANTS

Get what you want against the odds

Peter D. Johnston

NEGOTIATION
PRESS

Cover design by Tim Miller.
Author photograph by Robert d'Estrubé.
Layout by Connie McCann.

Selected as a Winner by the international jury at the 2009 Indie Book Awards (**www.IndieBookAwards.com**). *Negotiating with Giants* was recognized as one of the best independently published books across four distinct categories: Business, Social Change, Motivational and How-to. Publishers and their books are eligible for these awards if they are independent of the largest global publishing groups. To find out more, or to order books, please visit **www.NegotiatingWithGiants.com**.

This publication is designed to provide accurate and authoritative information with respect to the subject matter covered. It is sold with the understanding that the publisher and author are not engaged in rendering negotiation, legal, accounting or other professional services through this book. The guidance provided in these pages is general in nature and therefore readers should always seek relevant professional advice that is specific to their situation and appropriate for the country, province or state in which they reside or operate professionally. Please refer to the section labeled *Chapter Notes* for further information about this book's contents, sources and applications.

Printed in Canada.

ISBN: 978-0-9809421-0-1

For more information, please contact:
Negotiation Press
15-1594 Fairfield Road, PO Box 50043
Victoria, BC, Canada V8S 5L8

Distributors in Canada include Sandhill Book Marketing and North 49 Books.
Distributors in the United States include Baker & Taylor and Bookazine.

10 9 8 7 6

CONTENTS

INTRODUCTION: THE COIN

THE COIN SHIMMERED.

It sat in the middle of my open palm as I stood sweating in a hidden-away jungle retreat south of Manila.

The rules of the game were straightforward. To claim this golden coin, all I had to do was clench my outstretched fingers into a fist as soon as the elderly Filipino priest in front of me made the slightest move to grab it. If I defended the coin, it was mine.

He faced me, his eyes serene and twinkling, his large palm open, hovering just under my hand where the coin lay exposed.

"So, Mr. Pete Johnston, who holds the power here?" he asked with a warm smile.

I laughed. Our Harvard-based team had spent a week in the Philippines working with senior government officials on extreme power struggles and related negotiation challenges that had plagued their nation for years. This respected local man of the cloth participated in some of our highly confidential, closed-door sessions. He knew his question was relevant.

"Father, I only have to close my hand. You must bring yours all the way from underneath mine so you can grab the coin before my fingers defend it."

"And so?" he asked again.

"The power is mine," I answered.

He continued to smile. "So it would seem," he confirmed.

We began the game, our eyes leveled at one another as I stayed on the lookout for the first hint of movement from his hand. A minute later, the coin disappeared from my palm, and somehow ended up in his. Baffled, I insisted we play again. How could I have missed seeing his hand coming? He'd lucked out. I gave my head a shake. Now I was really going to be on my guard. The power was mine, and soon the coin would be too.

The coin disappeared from my palm again. And again, and again, and again. I watched helplessly as this ageing priest kept snatching it with apparent ease.

Mercifully, he suggested we sit down. When we'd finished chuckling, I listened as he spoke in quiet tones, explaining his game to me, a game he said was as old as Asia itself.

The game's secrets were deceptively simple. He approached me knowing I'd had a long day and would be tired. He had me play a game I wasn't familiar with, but one he knew well. He put me in a defensive role—he'd be the one deciding when to attack. He focused on the coin alone, centering himself both mentally and physically right over it. He led me to believe I held all the power, falsely anchoring my expectations. He didn't rush in. He waited patiently until the time was right, when I blinked or my mind strayed. Lastly, he did *not* go after the coin. As the attacker, his strategy was to go after the plump flesh surrounding his target, quickly pressing down with his fingers as they encircled the coin. The downward pressure popped the coin up and into his hand, making it look easy.

As the priest unveiled his insights, it became clear why this ancient game mattered. He knew our team was up against a ruthless giant in one of the negotiations we were working on with his government, but somehow our standard advice didn't seem to adequately recognize the forces on the other side of the table.

This quiet, wise-man's game wasn't just a game: it was a philosophy, a strategy, and a plan for getting what we want from those who tower over us and hold overwhelming power in their hands—our giants. This wasn't the first time I'd thought about how negotiating with giants involved unique and sometimes deadly challenges. But it was the first time I'd thought in any detail about the different approaches these negotiations required, and how power can appear to be in someone's hands when it really isn't.

I thanked the priest for sharing his game, unaware that our brief interaction would stay with me for more than a decade, up to this moment. What began that evening was a fascination, which would increasingly become the focus of my advisory work, teaching and research.[1]

I would go on to join discussions with academics at the Harvard Negotiation Roundtable as I started exploring negotiations with giants today and throughout history. I'd work on giant negotiations for entrepreneurs, musicians, athletes, prisoners, patients, consultants, foundations, fired executives, cheated spouses, weakened unions and developing nations—negotiating on behalf of these smaller clients whenever helpful. I'd continue my distinct work with giants as well, supporting Wall Street firms, venture capitalists, international bodies and corporations such as Microsoft, Intel, Suez and HSBC, furthering my understanding of their interests, especially in dealings with smaller players.

This book is my attempt to pass along what I've learned about the toughest, riskiest negotiations any of us will encounter in our professional or personal lives, at a point in history when the stakes in many of these negotiations couldn't be much higher, as we'll soon see.

WHAT DEFINES A GIANT AND WHAT EXACTLY IS A GIANT NEGOTIATION?

Giants have always been part of our lives. Today, however, they're everywhere, and often much larger, more controlling, more menacing and much faster on their feet than ever before, with big hands that can reach into every corner of every continent.

One of those corners is probably in your neighborhood, maybe even in your own home.

Where huge dinosaurs once ruled the earth, giant nations, corporations, systems, groups and individuals now stand tall, the new rulers for this millennium. These titans gain their status through a combination of resources and social or emotional clout many times larger than our own.

By my definition, *we're negotiating with giants anytime we try to influence them to do something, or not do something, and most objective observers would rate our odds of success between zero and 40 percent, often believing it's more likely we'll be crushed.*

Our giant might be a government if we're an unhappy taxpayer, an abusive husband who controls all the money, or a massive corporation if we're a supplier negotiating a critical contract. With the worldwide growth of big business over the past quarter century—propelled by open borders, the efficiency of consolidations and relaxed antitrust regulations—even a robust smaller business with a few million dollars in sales can find itself standing in the mind-bending shadow of a corporation 50,000 to 100,000 times its size.

One of these hulking shadows belongs to Wal-Mart. Sales at the aggressive retailer totaled just over $1 billion in 1980. Now its sales are approaching half a trillion a year, placing it among the world's largest corporations—ever. Wal-Mart's home base, America, generates close to $15 trillion worth of transactions, five times their value in 1980, making the US the largest economic juggernaut in history. The top 1% of Americans who reap the greatest rewards from all this growth earn at least 90 times as much as those in the bottom 20%, triple the size of this divide in 1980. Wherever you live, the average person on the street stares up at the giant organizations and individuals surrounding them, wondering how to move out from their shadows. For those in developing nations, this mounting size divide feels both unfathomable and unfair.[2]

THE DISTINCT CHALLENGES IN GIANT NEGOTIATIONS

Around the globe, entrepreneurs, consumers, employees, job-hunters and citizens concerned about issues such as global warming find themselves increasingly frustrated, unable to get what they want from their giants— money, resources, rights or change—and uncertain how to negotiate with our new Goliaths.

While our modern mammoths routinely play positive roles by creating jobs, producing wealth, spreading innovation and establishing new standards, they're also capable of hurting us, on purpose or not. They may damage our possessions and relationships, steal our ideas, devour our time, ruin our reputations, create one-sided deals in their favor, tie us up in court until we run out of money, or simply ignore us at their leisure, without being held accountable. Just getting to the negotiation table with them can be an enormous hurdle.

So how do you negotiate with Wal-Mart? With America's President over going to war? An improved education system for your kids? The end of state-sponsored racial discrimination? A cleaner environment? An ethical issue with an intimidating boss? An unequal personal relationship? A Super Bowl victory for a team of losers? A capital infusion if you're a start-up venture on the verge of bankruptcy? Better healthcare from your medical system? Better service from a huge phone company? The return of stolen treasure, lost rights or a canceled credit card? The survival of a city about to be destroyed? Or, in perhaps the most extreme case we'll look at, your own survival should you ever be taken hostage by an armed killer?

What I've discovered is that all the answers we're looking for are connected by *four size and strength strategies* used by successful smaller players.

OUR ANSWERS COME FROM REAL-LIFE STORIES

Negotiating with Giants tells the stories of dozens of smaller players who get what they want from their Goliaths. The lessons from their journeys can be applied to our own negotiations today, whoever our giant happens to be. I've given a name to these smaller players who achieve their success through giant negotiations: I call them Size Wizards, because they know how to make themselves bigger and stronger, their giants smaller and weaker, and their opportunities much greater than they'd otherwise be.

As I take you on a whirlwind tour of both current and historic events, we'll look over the shoulders of these Size Wizards, watching them execute the same quartet of defensive and offensive strategies. We'll learn from them, whether their lessons come from business, politics, education, health, entertainment or sports.

Among those we'll meet: entrepreneurs Jesse Rasch and a young Bill Gates; writers Harriet Beecher Stowe, Rachel Carson and Ida Tarbell; statesmen Ben Franklin and Nelson Mandela; social activists Emmeline Pankhurst and Rosa Parks; whistleblower Cynthia Cooper; Magna Carta rebel Robert FitzWalter; Internet rebel Carl Oppedahl; consumer Lucia Pacifico; coach Bill Belichick; parent Pamela MacKenzie; entertainers David Letterman and Courtney Cox; and photographer Lewis Hine.

I've gathered the stories of these Size Wizards, and others, from a wide range of sources including my smaller clients and contacts with first-hand knowledge. In some cases, I've changed the names of certain Size Wizards and any circumstances that might lead to their being identified.[3] One entrepreneur called me at the last moment, telling me his wife didn't want his name used because she feared the money they'd earned could make their children a target for kidnappers. More commonly though, these Size Wizards fear their giants. Giants are notorious for "encouraging" smaller players to keep their success stories to themselves, frequently getting them to sign "gag clauses" aimed at guaranteeing their silence—one of the reasons this book hasn't been written before now.

It feels good to be inspired by a story or a new idea, but given the stakes and immense challenges in our giant negotiations, we need more than inspiration. We need concrete answers. At the end of every Size Wizard's story, I'll share my analysis and provide bullet-point advice so you can tailor each story's unique lessons to your own circumstances. We'll plunge into these richly detailed stories after our opening chapter has revealed the time-honored habits, helping hands and strategies employed by successful smaller players throughout the centuries.

In the far-flung Size Wizard adventures that lie ahead, we'll uncover what giants care about, what makes them act, and how to: choose the best conditions for influencing them; attract our giants or penetrate giant organizations; keep our ideas safe and protect ourselves; exploit the mainstream media or our own media; structure giant deals to create as much value as possible; increase the likelihood our giants will live up to their commitments; talk to our giants eye-to-eye in the most difficult circumstances; and take advantage of *their* strengths and *our* weaknesses.

The Golden Slingshot that Gets Us What We Want

Do you remember how David defeated Goliath, killing the nine-foot-tall Philistine with a single stone from his ancient slingshot?[4] Well, it doesn't happen like that anymore. Giants in this millennium don't tend to die or go away overnight. They're going to be around for a while, or their heirs will be, long enough that if you try to hurt them, they may well find you and make you pay a heavy price. The Size Wizards don't focus on winning, or beating their giants, they focus on getting what they want.

Faced with the harsh reality of our modern-day Goliaths, we need updated weapons. Our slingshots must be golden—solid, malleable, polished and precise. We won't use stones as our ammunition. Instead, we'll use the piercing secrets of the Size Wizards to overcome the odds against us, aiming to work *with* our giants and resorting to aggressive actions only if truly necessary.

From our ground-level view as smaller players trying to satisfy our interests, history's message seems clear: along the path to uncommon success or resounding failure, most of us will encounter a giant negotiation that determines our fate one way or the other. If this is true, no matter who we are, no matter where we live—Los Angeles, London, Moscow, Johannesburg or the jungles of the Philippines—we can't prepare ourselves soon enough.

SECRETS OF THE SIZE WIZARDS

Draw on the habits, helpers and strategies used by successful smaller players.

IT'S 1912. A CHICAGO-BASED PHOTOGRAPHER NAMED MOFFETT is struggling to make ends meet.

Out of the blue, the photographer is sent a telegram by Teddy Roosevelt's presidential campaign manager, George Perkins, who tells him that the American President plans to distribute three million election pamphlets. On the cover of each one, Perkins says Roosevelt might use a photo he once commissioned Moffett to take, if Moffett is interested in the opportunity. *Finally, my lucky break!* Moffett thinks. In the telegram, Perkins asks how much he'd be willing to pay the Roosevelt campaign for nationwide exposure of his work and his studio, indicating that he'll need an answer quickly. Other studios will no doubt snare the opportunity if Moffett doesn't.[1]

Moffett needs to think fast. *What's the right amount to be paid here?* he wonders. *$100? $250? $500? And where can I get my hands on that kind of money?*

Before we find out what Moffett does with his good fortune, we'll explore the habits, helpers and strategies of the Size Wizards, all those successful smaller players who overcome the odds against them in negotiations with giants. And by the way, we shouldn't care if some of our Size Wizards are not fully aware of the steps they've taken to achieve their own success, so long as we can knowingly follow in their footsteps.

Together, we'll unravel the vibrant threads that bind these wizards of influence to one another. By the time we loop back to Mr. Moffett, with the secrets of the Size Wizards fresh in our minds, we'll have a clear idea of what to do if placed in his shoes.

SECRETS OF SUCCESS: APPLY THE RIGHT HABITS

The Size Wizards think differently about what it means to negotiate, staying away from the "negotiation table" as long as possible. Over the course of five decades, Nelson Mandela negotiated *away* from the table, even while imprisoned, to influence the outcome he wanted: a multi-racial democracy in South Africa.

If Mandela had tried to enter into face-to-face negotiations with South Africa's pro-apartheid government in the 1950s in hopes of achieving the same outcome, he would have been jailed sooner, or killed. So he negotiated from afar, and actively prepared for more formal negotiations one day in the future. When he and his group, the African National Congress—the ANC—at last negotiated their way to the table in the 1990s, Mandela would send a union leader on his behalf. Other Size Wizards sometimes decide there is no need for anyone on their side to ever speak with a giant, and no need for any written agreements, relying on oral deals or actions instead. In these ways, the Size Wizards redefine what many people think of as "negotiation," while also leading us to revisit the traits we might expect of great negotiators.

Success in most cases, at least 80% of the cases I've seen, can be traced to moves made away from the table, not at it. Before any serious discussions in person or on the phone, the Size Wizards wait until they've altered the basic size and strength dynamics in play, increasing their odds of getting what they want and avoiding the common smaller player fate of being crushed at the table, if they get that far.

Given their big resources and clout, giants would love us to cling to the widely-held view that negotiation is mainly about what happens at the table, because this mistaken belief benefits them. The Size Wizards are always aware that they are negotiating whenever they try to influence their giants in any way. This allows them to prepare and exert influence away from the negotiation table, much earlier than their giants might think.

The Size Wizards are grounded dreamers—they figure out what they want and focus on getting it. While backpacking in Bolivia one morning, a client of mine named Bruno came across an old woman by the side of the road. She was selling plump oranges. Since Bruno was heading off for several days in the countryside, he decided to buy a few. He paid the woman the equivalent of 75 cents each for three oranges, thanked her and continued on his trek.

Minutes later, after trying one of her tasty oranges, he returned to buy more from the woman, offering to purchase her 30 remaining oranges for 50 cents each. She said no. He then offered 75 cents as he'd done before. She refused. Bruno could not believe it. He kept raising his offers, finally reaching $1.50 an orange, $45 in total. The woman pulled back the scarf protecting her leathered face from the dusty road and shouted, "I said no!" She pointed at her head, indicating *he* must be *loco*—crazy. He walked away in a huff.

After 20 minutes, Bruno's confusion lured him back to the fruit stand one last time. He noted the woman still had 30 oranges, but made it clear he no longer wanted any of them. He only wanted to understand why she wouldn't sell him all her oranges for the small fortune he had offered in return. She relaxed, smiling slightly. "It's still morning," she said. "If I sold all my oranges to you, I'd have nothing else to do for the rest of the day."

This old woman knew what she really cared about, despite what others thought of her and despite having Bruno offer her so much money. This, quite simply, was her gift. I've seen sophisticated small-business owners turn down giant deals for similar reasons. They didn't want to lose the joy and meaning in their lives by selling out too early. So many smaller players never figure out their own core interests—their driving goals, needs and concerns—before dealing with their giants. As a result, they get nothing, or they get what they asked for, but it's not what they really wanted or needed.

The Size Wizards focus their imaginations, thoughts, time and resources on satisfying their most meaningful interests, not straying to try and "win" against their giants, because this lowers their odds of success. They're not just dreamers, they're *grounded* dreamers, pursuing realistic dreams that are tested, re-evaluated and adjusted. They're persistent, optimistic problem-solvers on the way to their dreams, looking first at *how* to do things rather than *what* they should do. And don't think they never doubt themselves and their dreams, because they do. That's part of staying grounded.

Surprisingly, given some of their big dreams, our Size Wizards are not huge risk-takers in going after what they want. Their risks are usually well-calculated, and well-managed if they fail. For example, most of the entrepreneurs in our stories don't gamble their way into new opportunities, they evolve into them based on previous work, and they often risk other people's money to fulfill their dreams, not their own money.[2]

The Size Wizards seamlessly weave together their negotiation activities and their core activities. In 1859, a pioneer named Edwin Drake trekked to western Pennsylvania and drilled the world's first oil well, attracting thousands of oil baron wannabes. Years later, when Standard Oil was still a small player in the industry, John D. Rockefeller faced a major decision. He could build his refineries in Pittsburgh, Pennsylvania, which was closest to the oil fields with easy access via the Allegheny River, or he could center his operations farther away in Cleveland, Ohio and send the crude oil there.

Based on logistics, Pittsburgh was the obvious choice, the city many smaller players selected. But based on future negotiation dynamics, Cleveland won out. Why? Because it had three competing railroad companies that could carry Rockefeller's oil, whereas Pittsburgh only had one, meaning Rockefeller could be held hostage there on freight rates. Cleveland's access to water for shipping in the summer gave the businessman even more leverage in his negotiations with the city's three giant railroads, ultimately resulting in low rates that would help vault him ahead of his competitors and launch his empire.[3]

Like Rockefeller, the Size Wizards think through the impact of their strategic operating decisions on future negotiations and how these two distinct sets of activities can complement each other. Here's another example: a company looking to be bought out at some point by a technology giant will want to make sure today that its chosen computer systems and core competencies can easily be woven into its targeted giant, allowing the deal to go through and the acquisition to be valued as highly as possible.

The Size Wizards do nothing to needlessly alienate a giant as they structure and execute their daily operations and related contracts, while doing everything they can to grow the value and favorable impact of these operations on their giant dealings.

The Size Wizards remain firm *and* flexible. American statesman Ben Franklin believed in being firm with people he worked for. He said, "A little sturdiness when superiors are much in the wrong sometimes occasions consideration. And there is truth in the old saying that *if you make yourself a sheep, the wolves will eat you.*"[4]

The Size Wizards, who include Ben Franklin in their ranks, stand firm in dealings with their giants, rooted in well-tested beliefs. They firmly represent their interests, promote reasonable standards to guide agreements, pursue walk-away alternatives whenever fitting, deal with difficult behaviors, and follow through on their aggressive goals. Yet they always remain flexible enough to consider other approaches that might make more sense, frequently shifting gears for unexpected opportunities or threats. Mandela himself, who finally achieved his goal of a multi-racial democratic society, firmly started out with a very different goal, as we'll see later while digging further into his story.

When the Size Wizards find themselves firmly at odds with their giant on the substance of an issue, in keeping with Roger Fisher, Bill Ury and Bruce Patton's wise advice in the book *Getting to Yes,* they're hard on the problem but show flexibility by being "soft" on the people involved, treating them with respect.[5] As smaller players who often aren't seen as credible by their giants early on, the Size Wizards disagree *without* being predictably disagreeable, even poking fun at themselves during heated discussions.

The Prime Minister of Canada, John Diefenbaker, suffered in the 1960s for being *in*flexible and disagreeable toward his American giant. The economist John Kenneth Galbraith told me about a tense meeting he and President John F. Kennedy had with Diefenbaker where they deadlocked on vital issues. At one point, a smiling Kennedy passed Galbraith a note labeling the abrasive Canadian leader a "son-of-a-bitch." As the meeting ended, Galbraith forgot to pick up the note, but Diefenbaker didn't.[6] The relationship and its impasses worsened. Kennedy hadn't behaved well, but giants are giants, and if irked, they can exact revenge. Diefenbaker wasn't re-elected and blamed Kennedy for subverting his campaign. If Canada's leader had been firm *and* flexible, he could have stayed true to his core interests while being more flexible in how they were met, remaining likeable throughout.

The Size Wizards take advantage of the context that most favors their interests. Russia's Nina Rakhmanina couldn't understand why her small home-repair business in Moscow wasn't doing better until she looked more closely at the context around her: Russian divorce rates had soared, with three out of five marriages failing, leaving many women without husbands who traditionally did all the repair work. Nina realized that she had to influence this giant market of needy women, targeting them more directly so they'd phone her and she could dispatch one of her repairmen to their homes. She decided to call her new concept "Husband for an Hour," and women loved it because apparently, that's the perfect amount of time to have a man around the house. Demand surged, Nina's rates went up and her home repair business flourished.[7]

Just as farmers always keep an eye on the weather when planting, successful smaller players remain mindful of the broader conditions affecting efforts to influence their giants. If a particular context is found to be favorable, as in Nina's case, the Size Wizards move quickly, tailoring their approach to that context. If the context isn't as favorable, they may decide to wait for improved overall conditions, or try to shape a new context that will favor them.

Context affects how we perceive our interests and choices, and provides clues as to how we're expected to act in negotiations. Common drivers of context today include: local, national or international economics and politics; growing environmental challenges; ageing demographics; industry trends; consumer needs; technology innovations; and evolving social values or ethics. Context can also relate to an immediate environment, such as your company's recent financial performance, or on the personal front, your past dealings with someone who breached your trust. When negotiations offer up many different potential contexts, the Size Wizards emphasize those most helpful to them.

The Size Wizards are very careful about their precise timing within any context. Talking to an intimidating and powerful boss about a new bet-the-firm initiative when he or she has had a lousy day may well lower your odds of success, even in a context where your firm is doing well and you've excelled. Similarly, the Size Wizards take into account prominent dates on their giant's calendar such as milestones, meetings, quarter-ends or year-ends, dates that might benefit or undermine their efforts to get what they want.

The Size Wizards are information hounds. One political party I worked with during an uphill election battle decided it was too expensive to hire professional pollsters to decipher what voters were thinking. So instead, to gather this critical information, we resorted to our next best choice: taxi drivers. But not just any taxi drivers, really well educated drivers— immigrants with degrees in statistics who could canvas thousands of passengers and hand us reliable results for honing our message and focusing our limited resources on areas that looked winnable. One aspect of the drivers' unorthodox polling made the difference: they found few "undecided" voters. Why? Unlike pollsters on the phone, these grinning cabbies could say, "Yeah, but if I put a gun to your head, who are you voting for?" Our drivers proved uncannily accurate, helping turn the election in our favor.

The Size Wizards get their hands on useful information any way they can. To understand what's motivating a giant, they'll ask a lot of questions of their giant and others, digging under staked-out positions to uncover hidden giant goals, needs and concerns that might prove useful. They look for background information on those they're negotiating with, trying to understand their individual interests and negotiation style. They also search for facts, ideas, loopholes, precedents, laws and regulations—anything to tilt the odds in their favor. They love the Internet, libraries, newspapers, books, record-keeping offices, filings with corporate regulators, as well as insights from those who've been in their shoes.

The smaller players we'll meet question their information, trying to confirm it with a second source, revisiting assumptions about people and things so they can act on reality and not on misleading perceptions. They store essential documents and notes from their conversations in safe places, even if they're poorly organized in other ways. They even paste information on their walls, including inspiring thoughts and quotes. Finally, the Size Wizards know what they know and what they don't know, allowing them to mind their blind spots, get help where needed and keep searching to fill in the blanks.

The Size Wizards never forget the one interest most giants obsess about—growth. On a blustery day in December 1903, Orville Wright shook hands with his brother Wilbur, then climbed into their aircraft at Kitty Hawk, North Carolina. Among those helping the brothers was someone history would ignore: an anonymous representative from Standard Oil. He'd supply the gas needed to get the world's first functioning plane up in the air.[8]

By this time, John D. Rockefeller's Standard Oil group had transformed itself into a global behemoth, after ruthlessly swallowing dozens of other smaller players. It now dominated international markets as well as the sale of America's refined oil products. So why did a giant that already owned a worldwide industry feel compelled to have one of its salesmen sucking up to a couple of no-name inventors? The answer lies in the single obsession that keeps many of our giants awake at night.

Without growth, most giants languish or shrink. With growth, which created them in the first place, both organizational and individual Goliaths get to retain their perks and purpose, reveling in their growing dominance, resources, riches, prestige or support.

To help guarantee this growth, corporate giants in particular find it useful if we're addicted to their caffeine, sugar, nicotine, alcohol, medications, weapons, diets, TV—and oil. When oil Goliath BP says its initials stand for *Beyond Petroleum* and it builds solar-powered gas stations, don't be confused. BP is still relying on our addiction to its vast oil reserves for long-term sales growth. The company is simply marketing itself smartly to grow its short-term sales, targeting anyone worried about the environment. To ensure no employee is ever confused about its number-one interest, BP and its corporate brethren constantly reward employee growth initiatives with bonuses and options to buy shares.

A crucial means for assuring future growth lies concealed behind a giant's visible assets in something I call their "Hidden Infrastructure"—all those invisible or intangible structures, systems and networks that enable giant influence and help a giant fend off smaller players. This Hidden Infrastructure can include: favorably constructed industries and laws; political structures driven by big donations and lobbyists; networks of high-priced lawyers and high-level contacts; connections into powerful media outlets; and the moat systems that surround giant castles, warding off unwelcome visitors through unavailable contact details, unanswered phone options and unhelpful giant gatekeepers.

In looking to attract their giants, craft deals or pressure giants into giving them what they want, the Size Wizards know that growth often serves as a critical lever of influence. Smaller players can provide their giants with new avenues for growth, like the Wright brothers did with Rockefeller. They can also threaten giant growth as competitors looking to be bought out, as activists looking to set legal precedents, or as government officials concerned about a giant's spiraling influence—precisely what led to Standard Oil being broken into 34 smaller pieces in 1911. Highlighting just how strong a force the pursuit of growth can be, all these pieces of Rockefeller's former empire continued to grow on their own, with two of them recently re-uniting to form Exxon Mobil. This newborn Goliath's *profits* in 2007 alone grew to $40 billion, dwarfing anything mighty Standard Oil ever achieved.

By developing the right habits, you build a foundation for your overall influence efforts: 1) Know that you're negotiating anytime you try to influence your giant, staying away from the negotiation table as long as possible. 2) Be a grounded dreamer, persistently, patiently and realistically focusing on the goals, needs and concerns that matter to you. 3) Weave together your negotiation activities with your core operating activities so that each set of activities is enhanced. 4) Choose a favorable context and good timing within that context. 5) Remain firm and flexible, bending only as justified by your overall interests or independent standards. 6) Be an information hound, seeking to know all relevant interests, facts and standards, always questioning your sources and most basic assumptions. 7) Never forget the one interest that most giants obsess about—growth.

SECRETS OF SUCCESS: CALL ON THE RIGHT HELPERS

Her personal story was wrenching. Stacey shared with me that she'd been sexually assaulted by her local priest as a teenager.[9] When she told her parents, they didn't believe her, especially after Father Ralph calmly denied the charge, saying Stacey was unstable. When she got pregnant, her parents still refused to believe their priest was responsible, but as Catholics, they insisted she have the child. The baby was born, no one was told and he was sent away—to be raised in a monastery by priests. Stacey hadn't seen her child since his birth, and he was now a teenager himself. After listening, I gently inquired why she'd called. "Father Ralph died last week," she said. "On his deathbed, he confessed his secret, finally admitting what he'd done to me. The Church wants to negotiate."

Stacey ended up reaching an agreement with the Church: she wanted nothing for herself but everything for her son—and she got it, including a large trust fund and a fully-paid education. She had always hoped Father Ralph would be exposed by someone he'd told about the rape, but she never expected he'd turn on himself and leak his own secret.

When negotiating with tight-lipped, foreboding giants, the Size Wizards often benefit from giant secrets being leaked to them by sources they've cultivated, or if they're fortunate enough, by completely unexpected sources like Father Ralph. These "secret" helpers are just one set of helping hands that smaller players can call upon for support. These distinct helpers come from both inside and outside our giants' castles, regardless of whether a castle is an individual Goliath's home, a corporate Goliath's headquarters or a religious Goliath's cloistered hallways:

- **Controllers.** *The decision-makers*: they control the final decisions inside a giant's castle on issues that are relevant to your efforts. They can help by sharing their interests and favoring a deal with you because you figure out how to best satisfy these interests. Giant decisions may need sign-off from several different types of Controllers, such as a senior manager, someone in finance and someone else in legal. The Size Wizards identify these players early on, knowing that true Controllers are capable of following through on their commitments. If you can't identify a Controller inside your giant on this basis, it may mean you're targeting the wrong giant.

- **Convincers.** *The influencers*: they significantly influence the decisions of giant Controllers. They can help by *pulling* for decisions that favor you *and* your giant. Inside a castle, they may be quietly convincing, not necessarily showing up on any organizational charts. Outside a castle, they might be found as consultants, lobbyists, mentors or spouses, offering Controllers information and viewpoints free from any internal bias.

- **Coercers.** *The arm-twisters*: they, too, significantly influence the decisions of giant Controllers, but they use positions of informal or formal authority to *push* giants toward an outcome. They can help by acting in a way that meets your interests, often moving aggressively and wielding accepted norms, rules or laws to achieve their ends. Informal Coercers may be found inside or outside castle walls, and commonly involve well-respected, senior contacts shared by you and your Controller—a member of your giant's board being one example. Formal Coercers are usually outside, and include judges, arbitrators, regulators and law-makers.

- **Connectors.** *The networkers*: they know people who matter to you. They can help by connecting you or your message—directly or through others—to Controllers and other helpers whenever you need a warm introduction. Some Connectors have hundreds, even thousands of acquaintances from all walks of life.[10] Other Connectors are much more specialized: executive assistants are important internal Connectors to their bosses primarily, or lawyers outside a giant's castle may help by connecting you to certain clients of theirs.

- **Coalitionists.** *The allies*: these members of your extended team share interests or a desired outcome with you. Though independent of you, they can help by collaborating with your core team, adding to your base of resources, knowledge, relationships, expertise or size in sheer numbers. Any partnership with Coalitionists will involve a total of anywhere from two players to dozens or even millions of players. Coalitionists can be found inside or outside a giant's castle.

- **Counselors.** *The advisors*: they hold insights based on their direct experiences or general knowledge. They can help by counseling you on everything from strategy and giant thinking to the types of helpers you'll need. Counselors may be inside or outside a castle. Prime candidates are current and past giant employees, professors, your former bosses, paid professionals such as consultants and lawyers, and savvy friends.

- **Cracks.** *The informants*: they have coveted information about your giant. Cracks can help by giving you a peek inside a giant's mind or castle to see things that your giant as a whole would prefer you didn't see. Cracks tend to be insiders, but may include outsiders such as former employees, suppliers or journalists. On occasion, they unintentionally release information that is not supposed to be shared. Other times, they're seeking revenge on a giant, they're looking to expose violations by a giant, or like Father Ralph, they're implicated in giant wrongdoings and want to save themselves.

Nelson Mandela often quotes the Xhosa tribal saying "*Umuntu ngumuntu ngabantu*," which translates to: "You can do nothing if you don't get the support of other people."[11] The Size Wizards look at any giant individual or giant organization—no matter how big or intimidating—and what they see are people like you and me with interests that need to be satisfied. They don't get overwhelmed by "bigness," focusing instead on the small things that make people tick. And they know that in any large organization, despite appearances, there will always be people pursuing different personal, professional and organizational interests. The Size Wizards set their targets on those helpers inside giant organizations whose interests are most closely aligned with their own.

The helpers I've outlined are the people who help us make sense of our giants and the Hidden Infrastructure that supports everything a giant does. We won't need all these helpers in every negotiation, but to be prepared, we should try to identify as many as possible. We should also remember that a helper can change roles—a Controller in one situation may be a Coercer or Convincer in another, depending on the issues.

Some of my clients begin their preparations by drawing what I call a "people map," a visual snapshot of all their potential helpers. I advise them to start with the Controller making a giant decision, and then to add other helpers they may use to influence that Controller. Beside each helper's name, they produce quick profiles, interests and known approaches for best influencing this helper—whether we're talking about approaching them in person, on the phone or through others and whether we're most likely to persuade them with facts, figures, principles, emotions, supportive gestures or intense pressure. In addition, my clients will highlight on their map those areas where helpers need to be cultivated. Ultimately, they're left with a vivid overview of what truly matters in their giant negotiation: the people, including who knows what, and who influences who.

The complexity of your own negotiations will help you decide whether you want to physically map out the different players or not. Either way, your chosen helpers will complement your strategies, or determine which strategies you'll pursue.

As you apply the Size Wizard habits we discussed earlier, you'll call on one or more sets of helping hands for support: Connectors open doors; Coercers twist arms; Cracks pass you valuable information; Counselors point you in the right direction; Coalitionists pull you forward with new resources and clout; Convincers use their influence to turn outcomes in your favor; and Controllers sign off on your deals. In the stories and examples that lie ahead, I'll point out the key helpers involved in executing the size and strength strategies of the Size Wizards.

SECRETS OF SUCCESS: EXECUTE THE RIGHT STRATEGIES

We now know the habits of successful smaller players and the wide-ranging helpers they call on for support. What remains are the basic strategies needed to apply these ingredients for success. The Size Wizards execute four broad strategies, matching up with their main challenges in giant negotiations, as set out in the following table:

Main Challenge	Dominant Size and Strength Strategy
Your giant can't be trusted with your ideas, is poised to attack, is attacking already, or may well violate the terms of a deal.	**Defend Yourself from the Start.** *Build up vigorous, pre-meditated defenses for your information, reputation, interests, deals, activities and time, quickly turning from defense to offense*—**Chapter 2.**
Your giant may not know you exist, yet you really want to influence their actions—or your giant knows all too well that you exist and their aggressive stance puts you squarely at odds with them.	**Level the Playing Field.** *Make your giant smaller and weaker*—**Chapter 3**—*or make yourself bigger and stronger to get what you want*—**Chapter 4.**
You're ready to give up. No decent agreement seems possible with a giant counterpart. It looks like you will either accept a bad deal or walk away altogether, with potentially dire consequences.	**Craft Golden Deals.** *Transform weak deals or no-deals into precious deals, often drawing on differences between you and your giant as you structure your agreements*—**Chapter 5.**
Your giant won't meet with you, won't say "yes" to you once you do meet, doesn't listen, entrenches themselves in extreme positions, or is openly hostile face-to-face.	**Stand Tall in Conversations.** *Increase your stature by what you say and how you say it, knowing that in most situations, you should only negotiate directly with giants as a very last step, if at all*—**Chapter 6.**

If you are in a giant negotiation as you read this, and you'd like to get your hands on new insights, strategies and tactics, you should skip ahead to the chapter that best meets your specific needs. You'll want to circle back to the other strategies once you've handled your most pressing issues.

If you're *not* currently negotiating, I'd suggest that you move through the four strategies in sequence, just as you would when starting from scratch in any giant negotiation. In successful outcomes, my research confirms that *one* strategy typically dominates, with at least one of the other three strategies playing a supporting role. Each of our stories is categorized by the dominant strategy driving a Size Wizard's success.

Some of you may already be Size Wizards. If so, you can broaden and deepen your range of abilities, aiming to master all four strategies in any context. Do this, and you'll be in good company—joining the likes of Ben Franklin and Nelson Mandela.

With your habits and helpers in mind, and possibly a people map, you'll execute the size and strength strategies, with one strategy usually dominating the others. Since giants can hurt us so easily, you need to think "defense" first. Once you've protected your main vulnerabilities, you're in a position to begin leveling the playing field, bringing your giant down to size or bulking yourself up. Then, and only then, you can craft golden deals that are not one-sided in your giant's favor. As a final step, you're able to go to the negotiation table, standing tall based on the best practices of the Size Wizards and your extensive preparations away from the table. Should you ever need a quick reminder of the habits, helpers, or size and strength strategies that make the Size Wizards successful, flip to the Back-of-the-Book Summary that starts on page 255.

Moffett's Mistake

We come full circle to Mr. Moffett, our photographer in Chicago, last seen pondering how much money he should pay to have his photo used on the front of President Roosevelt's campaign pamphlet.

What Moffett did not know was that Roosevelt's team had *already* used his photo.

That's right. Three million pamphlets were about to be distributed nationwide when someone noticed Moffett's credit on the photo, indicating the copyright was his. If the campaign had decided to hand out the pamphlet without Moffett's approval, it risked a $1 liability per pamphlet—$3 million in total—a boatload of money today, an absolute fortune in 1912.

Moffett was sitting pretty. The photographer had the leverage he needed to fulfill his boldest dreams before heading to an early retirement. Instead, believing he had a fading opportunity because of how his giant framed his decision for him, Moffett got back to Roosevelt's team immediately. He offered to pay the campaign a hefty $250 fee, adding further to his financial woes.

Unlike the Size Wizards, Moffett never questioned his most basic assumptions, such as how quickly he needed to respond or whether his giant was using a form of communication that met its interests, but not his. By sending a telegram, Roosevelt's team carefully avoided telling any big lies, while also avoiding the truth. If Moffett had phoned his giant (definitely an option in 1912), he could have learned enough to get him thinking strategically. Even without knowing more, he failed by ignoring standard billing practices that firmly dictated *he* was to be paid by all his clients based on the size of their expected audience. Finally, Moffett didn't pursue moves "away from the table," like drawing on the high-society types he knew through his work. They could have acted as Connectors, easily hooking him up with other helpers, including people close to the Roosevelt team, so he'd have a better idea of what to do.

Naturally, Moffett's $250 offer was gleefully accepted. In the end, the tiny credit on his photo in the campaign pamphlet did absolutely nothing to reverse his fate. Moffett would die a bitter, brilliant photographer, who simply lacked the right habits, helpers and strategies to get what he wanted from his giant when it mattered most.

2

DEFEND YOURSELF
FROM THE START

Fortify your defenses on six fronts, assuming giant attacks are inevitable.

AN ISRAELI BUSINESSMAN DEVELOPS A REVOLUTIONARY APPROACH for supplying meat to American troops stationed in Vietnam in the 1960s. His simple idea could save the United States up to 40% of what it expects to spend as it goes out to meat suppliers for bids. The problem: government officials want to know his idea before considering his bid. Should he tell them?

We're exposed to risks when negotiating with anyone, but giants are uniquely positioned to make our biggest risks, and even our tiniest risks, become a painful reality. Their resources and clout—supported by their Hidden Infrastructure—can lead them to claim our ideas as their own, attack our reputation, undermine our efforts to build value, create one-sided deals, violate deals or steal our time, often free from any consequences.

While some defensive measures are embedded in the other three size and strength strategies we'll explore, we need to kick off our efforts by focusing exclusively on the careful preparation of comprehensive, rigorous defenses. By pre-meditating our defenses instead of just reacting, we can both pre-empt and repel attacks, throwing our giants off balance and quickly shifting from defense to offense to get what we want.

In *Defend Yourself from the Start*, the Size Wizards act in these vital areas:

- They guard important information, figuring out whether or how to share it.

- They defend their reputation, immediately reversing any harmful misperceptions.

- They shield their core activities, building these operations with defense in mind.

- They protect their deals by knowing what they care about.

- They fend off broken promises by embedding compliance in their deal-making.

- They shelter their valuable time by applying simple rules.

In defending themselves, the Size Wizards emphasize elegant problem-solving, instead of aggressive legal approaches which can be time-consuming and favor giants with deep pockets. However, our wizards of influence do quietly prepare themselves on the legal front, ready to mobilize informal and formal Coercers—including judges and juries—to catch their giant's arm and twist it, gently or firmly, should their giant begin to take a swing at them.

As we'll soon see, successful entrepreneurs can be excellent role-models on defense. In fact, there are more stories about young businesses in this chapter than in any other. Just as I'll encourage business professionals to immerse themselves in the non-business stories and examples in the chapters ahead, I now encourage non-business readers to dive into some amazing stories and learn from people who aren't like you.

Among the stories to come, our Israeli businessman wins his meat contract without risking the premature disclosure of his breakthrough idea. A Texan defends his reputation in an unprecedented manner. A seismologist in a major earthquake zone minimizes the risk of ground-shaking giant attacks on his software company. A famous trumpet player uncovers the types of contractual clauses that can protect our deals and our most cherished interests. A spurned wife shows us how to handle cheating spouses—and cheating dictators. And the CEO of a small health venture dances with her rich giant, keeping one eye fixed on the clock overhead.

GUARD YOUR INFORMATION

What we know is frequently a source of value for our giants. But sharing what we know has its risks. Knowing *what* to share, *when* to share it and *how* to share it—well, that's one of the advantages of being a Size Wizard.

We'll now move between the harsh realities of Vietnam and the fantasies of Disney World to look at two different approaches to sharing knowledge in a way that meets our interests, lowering the risk our knowledge can be stolen or used against us.

STORY: TENDER MEAT

The Vietnam War is escalating in the 1960s and America is sending more and more troops to secure and grow its foothold in South Vietnam.

The US troops are young, voracious eaters. Their food must be delivered reliably, quickly and in large quantities. Meat in particular poses a challenge. Suppliers need to source and ship it from other countries where large animal farms remain secure, unaffected by the destruction of warfare. This beef and poultry has to remain frozen for long periods of time before being distributed for cooking and eating.

There are plans for huge refrigeration facilities to be constructed across southern Vietnam. These facilities will be obvious targets for Viet Cong fighters attacking from the north. Just the threat of local electricity sources being purposely cut off—ruining the meat in such hot and humid conditions—stands to inflict major costs on suppliers and the government, let alone the costs of rebuilding any facilities that are completely destroyed.

Storage costs will be exorbitant on top of the price tag for millions of pounds of meat, shipping that meat by water, and transferring it inland to new, high-risk facilities requiring 24-hour protection. To grasp how difficult it will be to protect this meat, the Viet Cong are already going after the most secure targets, even proving adept at sneaking into American military bases at night, using miles of hidden tunnels.

These are the kind of logistical challenges that bedevil four-star commanders. Deciding where, how and when to move their troops is often much easier.

The American government puts out a tender for supplying meat to Vietnam with bids to include the cost of buying the meat, building and managing facilities, and getting the meat into those facilities from the freighters arriving in southern ports.

The Defense Department receives a number of bids, with the dollar amount of these bids only reinforcing how expensive war can be when conducted overseas.

One bid is all but tossed aside.

Not for being too high.

For being too low.

This low bid is viewed as ridiculous. It's 25% to 40% lower than some of the other strongest bids. Government officials are highly skeptical the bidder can deliver as promised. They assume the meat will never arrive, or it will arrive, and no human being will want to go near it.

Defense personnel contact the low bidder as a matter of due process. They invite a young, dapper Israeli entrepreneur named Michael Schiller to explain exactly how he plans to deliver under his proposed terms.[1]

Michael is torn. He understands why officials are doubtful, yet he doesn't want to tell them how he *will* deliver good quality meat much more cheaply than the other bids. If his solution were complex, hard to replicate and protected by proprietary processes or clear legal rights, Michael might tell the Americans what he has in mind, especially if he had trusted helpers inside the Defense Department who could protect his idea.

But Michael's idea is so simple, so easily implemented by any half-wit in the supply business, that the Israeli knows it may be stolen from him if he shares it in the wrong way, or at the wrong time. His idea could then be passed along to an existing preferred supplier who would be awarded this lucrative contract.

When an impasse is reached in his discussions with the government, Michael worries his small company is about to be passed over. Feeling the pressure, he suggests a solution, one that should protect the value of his idea while also giving the US government the confidence it needs to award him the contract.

Government officials finally agree to award their contract tentatively to Michael based on his low bid, with the immediate ability to revoke his contract as necessary. As part of his winning bid, the entrepreneur posts a bond worth millions of dollars, money he has collected from financiers in Israel who believe in him and his idea.

If his idea is judged as nonsense or completely impractical by a mutually-agreed third party, then he forfeits these millions. With these stakes and these terms, should he lose the bid, Michael will probably lose his business as well.

Tension fills the air as he sits with dubious Defense officials and lays out his plan. His solution: don't store and refrigerate the meat in Vietnam. *Brilliant*, officials must think. "So where do we put it?" they ask, visions of Michael's bond money dancing in their heads.

Michael explains his company will buy or lease dozens of old freighters with freezers, many more than would otherwise be needed. These freighters will both transport *and* store the meat, keeping it frozen and well-protected just off the shores of Vietnam. Meat will be delivered ashore on a just-in-time basis to feed hungry troops. Other freighters will ferry back and forth from their supply sources, replenishing the storage freighters.

Jaws hit the floor.

Floating refrigerators!

The implications of Michael's idea are clear. There is no need to make an investment in expensive infrastructure on the ground that would be used for a matter of years at most, if facilities lasted that long while under attack. Freighters storing meat could be more easily protected on all fronts, and would be a much cheaper alternative. At the end of the war, they could be sold, returned if leased, or used for other purposes. They wouldn't be a wasted asset like the land facilities being proposed in competing bids.

Why did no one else think of it?

Maybe the giant suppliers bidding against Michael became unintentionally anchored by more traditional solutions mentioned to them by Defense officials. Maybe these giants did think of Michael's idea, but they didn't want to propose a less capital-intensive plan that might lower their overall profits on the project. Or maybe no one else felt the desperation sometimes required for developing a breakthrough idea.

Michael Schiller may have suspected that if his bid were just 10% lower than those of American bidders, he wouldn't win as a foreigner. Any number of domestic players could argue that their higher prices were justified by their well-established reputations for quality and reliability. But up to 40% lower? Michael knew that this kind of discount would be untouchable and tough to ignore on such a large contract.

How could he achieve such a discount? Starting with an extreme goal in mind like 50%, Michael may have forced himself to figure out an answer, finally settling on one that came up just short of his target. Extreme problem-solving like this is used by many Size Wizards. The entrepreneur's direct experience in Israel could have also offered up clues to a solution for Vietnam. Whatever the explanation for his floating fridge concept, Michael saves the United States loads of money while earning himself a fortune.

Two simple ideas lead to his success: one solves a big American problem, and the other solves his own problem over how to share his idea credibly, without having it stolen.

GUARD YOUR INFORMATION

Giants can render a deal with you worthless or much less valuable by stealthily gaining access to intellectual capital you hold, including your ideas and competitive secrets. Sensitive information like your client lists, sources of financial support and walk-away plans are also potential and vulnerable targets.

Michael Schiller had no formal legal protection on his refrigeration idea because you cannot patent, copyright or trademark an idea alone.[2] So he reverted to a process that gave *him* something to lose, beyond the contract itself. This process involved a formal Coercer—an arm-twisting helper—in the form of a third-party arbitrator, as well as collateral and the contingent awarding of the meat contract to him, all of which made it less likely his idea would be stolen. The Controllers here—those decision-makers inside his American giant—agreed with the option he put forward because *they* had nothing to lose and everything to gain in terms of how well their interests could be satisfied. When Michael's idea was so simple, and there were no helpers lined up inside the Defense Department to support him, he needed a solution such as the one he used.

Michael couldn't further develop his idea without winning the meat contract. In many situations though, the more you can turn an idea into a reality, the better off you'll be. Why? First, your idea in an advanced, applied form is distinguished from thousands of other new ideas and will attract greater attention for its perceived value. Second, if after sharing your idea, you need to move forward without your giant, either on your own or with another player, you'll have a head start. Third, the more you've thought about your idea and its applications, the harder it is for your giant to simply steal it, assuming you don't share too much information quickly. Finally, many giant organizations do not excel at developing new ideas so they'll be more inclined to partner if you've already saved them a lot of time, internal hassles and risk-taking.

Nothing we've mentioned so far relates to legal maneuvering, which can also be helpful, but should not be relied upon. Legal protections are often less effective because of a giant's ability to steal your ideas anyway—without your ever knowing—or if you do challenge them, they can fight you in court, costing you time and money.

At a minimum, formal protections such as copyrights, trademarks and patents act as polish for your shield so your giant is put on notice that a collaborative approach might make more sense than going into battle.[3] At best, when combined with other strategies, legal steps can prove decisive. To support these legal steps and your ability to influence others more generally, be sure to carefully document the development of your ideas with any physical evidence, dates and witnesses.

Ideally, giants would sign meaningful Non-Disclosure Agreements (NDAs) saying they will not disclose or use what they learn from you. But many giants won't sign these agreements, initially at least, worrying they might be exposed to ideas they already have or could develop independently in the future.[4]

Here are some other ways to protect your information:

- **Tread cautiously early on.** With most giants, as a guideline, even if you have helpers or a solid Non-Disclosure Agreement in place, you should only provide information at the outset that can attract their interest without giving them any highly proprietary information that could be stolen or misused.

- **Decide what you'll share before any meetings.** Face-to-face, giants can test you with questions you shouldn't answer. Prior to going into meetings, map out what you will and won't say and how you can appear helpful without risking unhelpful disclosures. List the pros and cons of sharing material pieces of information.

- **Use proxy information.** Think about "proxy information" to give your giant—filtered, high-level information that positively and accurately reflects your efforts, but doesn't reveal too much. As examples, in business, if asked for confidential profit margins, say something like "above industry standards." If asked who else you are talking to, say "several leading players." If asked about a proprietary technology, relay testimonials from respected non-giants who have seen it.

- **Just say *no*.** Worst case, you can always say, "I'm sorry, that's confidential. We'd be happy to share more as our talks progress." If all goes well, you'll incrementally share and receive proprietary information as you develop a more trusting relationship, putting a strong Non-Disclosure Agreement in place at a later point as required.

In contrast to holding your cards closely, you can sometimes go to the opposite extreme, protecting yourself by blatantly sharing proprietary ideas. The Walt Disney Company learned how effective this approach can be for smaller players.

Architect Edward Russell and retired baseball umpire Nicholas Stracick had an idea for building a massive sports complex at Disney World. They took their idea to Disney in 1987, choosing to fully expose their concept and how it would be executed. They did this rather than hint at their idea or unveil small pieces of it, which risked allowing Disney to fill in the blanks without more of their input.

At the time, there didn't seem to be interest from Disney, so Edward and Nicholas moved on. Four years later, Disney came up with a great idea: that's right, you guessed it, *a massive sports complex* at Disney World in Orlando, Florida.

The two men hired attorney Willie Gary as a Counselor, and after the complex opened in 1997, they launched a suit.

In August 2000, a jury—playing the role of formal Coercers on behalf of our architect and retired baseball umpire—awarded the pair $240 million in damages, convinced that Disney had stolen their plans. Disney maintained all along that the complex was created in-house.[5]

How could the jury be so sure of its findings?

As Edward and Nicholas departed their 1987 meeting with Disney executives, they chose to leave behind all their plans, including a model of the sports complex labeled "Sports Island." This forget-me-not apparently impressed the jury. So much had literally been put on the table during the Disney meeting, the company could not credibly deny using the sports complex idea, whether it actually stole the idea or not.

Disney went on to appeal the jury's decision, and before long, a confidential settlement was reached out of court with Edward and Nicholas.[6]

So we've now seen two different ways the Size Wizards protect their information.

Guard it carefully, only sharing sensitive information after you've legally claimed it as your own, had a Non-Disclosure Agreement signed, veiled it with proxy information, or put a protective process in place like our Israeli entrepreneur Michael Schiller did.

Your other choice: go ahead and explicitly share confidential information, documenting this any way you can (I've overtly used my cell phone camera to capture some meetings for posterity sake). Despite the Disney case, the pay-off from this transparent and riskier approach rarely comes from court proceedings. More commonly, it's faster, less expensive, and because it clearly leaves you vulnerable, can make it harder for your giant to play games and easier for your helpers to support you, especially Convincers and informal Coercers. This approach works best when your information is *not* highly proprietary, is *not* easy to present in pieces or proxy form, and *cannot* be covered by a Non-Disclosure Agreement.

Guard your information—either by protecting it carefully or sharing it openly.

PRESERVE YOUR REPUTATION

My mom always said, "Pete, a good reputation means everything."

Over time, I discovered that the value of a reputation depends on what we do, on what aspects of our reputation are meaningful, and on whether it meets our interests to have a "good reputation" or a "bad reputation." Our reputation can relate to our genius as a scientist, our severity as a judge, our revenge tactics as a mobster, or our feats as an athlete. Whatever our reputation, it tends to represent an overall track record, but often is defined by our most vivid achievements or failures. Finally, reputation depends on who is being asked, and can involve trade-offs. A retail consumer might love us for our store's "low prices," while our suppliers could hate us for "being cheap."

Regardless of whether our reputation is deemed good or bad, we want to make sure it serves our interests with those who matter most to us. In an era when the Internet can spread word of our deeds instantaneously, we need to know what our reputation is and use it to our benefit, or begin to shape it to meet our interests.

For my mom who lives in Canada, "a good reputation" means being perceived as honest and full of integrity, qualities she believes are vital for self-esteem and opening doors to new opportunities. As we get to know a man named Vic Feazell in Texas, we'll see that he thinks about reputation the same way, and we'll learn what he has to teach other smaller players about protecting this form of reputation when it's attacked unexpectedly.

STORY: MASS DECEPTION

District Attorney Vic Feazell is perplexed.

A drifter named Henry Lee Lucas stands accused of hundreds of murders, three of which occurred in McLennan, the Texas county Vic serves for the state government as its prosecuting attorney. Usually, arrests are good news, but something about Lucas and his 1983 arrest in Texas unsettles Vic.

With some digging, the District Attorney learns through driving records that the suspect was not in Texas when the three murders occurred in McLennan County. Vic also learns that even though Lucas has a criminal past, his profile isn't that of a serial killer.

Yet an elite team of state law enforcers called the Texas Rangers is pursuing the case with zeal, crisscrossing the United States as they link more and more killings to Lucas. Each day brings new confessions from Lucas. The FBI gets involved, as do senior police officials across the nation, all hoping to benefit by closing some of their outstanding murder files while boosting the public's confidence in their abilities.

As Vic asks questions back in Texas, the former Baptist preacher who's in his mid-thirties is warned away from the Lucas case by state and federal officials. He moves up the command chain in Texas, but no one does anything except further pressure the young District Attorney to stay off the case.

Vic takes the case before a grand jury and it finds that Henry Lucas is not the killer he says he is. Lucas is guilty, however, of committing one of the greatest hoaxes ever played on law enforcement officials. An ongoing diet of tranquilizers, steaks and milkshakes fed to him by Texas Rangers, combined with first-class travel arrangements and seeing his picture in the media every day, apparently encouraged Lucas to make his unlikely confessions.

Law officials are embarrassed, especially in Texas. Vic has turned them from heroes into chumps. This isn't the first time the District Attorney for McLennan County has put an unwanted spotlight on questionable law enforcement tactics. Vic has openly criticized local police on other occasions for being too aggressive in their pursuit of suspects.

Vic Feazell will soon come to believe that Texas in the 1980s shares a strong connection to France in the 1700s, when the French philosopher and writer Voltaire said, "It is dangerous to be right when the government is wrong." [7]

According to Vic, rather than applauding his role in exposing the Lucas hoax, senior law enforcers at different levels of government plot their revenge, sending a message to him and others that it's not okay to deflate their reputations and efforts. Untraceable and damning rumors begin to circulate about Vic. People close to him are targeted with threats. Wire taps are placed on his phones, his income-tax records rifled through.

In 1985, a well-respected local television station in Dallas airs a series about Vic saying he's under investigation by the FBI and state officials, clearly insinuating the District Attorney is both inept and corrupt. It suggests he's been taking bribes from defense attorneys in return for going easy on their clients. Freeze-framed pictures of Vic, mustached with a white wisp in the middle of his black hairline, make him look sinister.

Vic declined to be interviewed by WFAA Television for its series, explaining, "I'm not going to pick up a rattlesnake and handle it." [8] He could have tried for a legal injunction against the station airing its stories, but the legal system wasn't showing signs of support for anything he did at this point.

Six weeks before the election for District Attorney in 1986, Vic is taken into custody along with his wife. More than a dozen agents comb their home, even emptying out cereal boxes to find incriminating evidence. None is found.

Regardless, a federal grand jury indicts Vic on multiple counts of bribery and other related charges. Vic doesn't have much money. Of course, being indicted puts his re-election at risk, if not ruling it out, meaning he might not have any income as he keeps trying to counter the nasty rumors, threats, invasions of his privacy and legal charges.

He is on the verge of ruin. Someone puts out the word he may kill himself.

Instead, Vic embraces the charges against him. Under indictment, and awaiting trial, he runs for re-election, making his arrest the central issue. His insignia: a pair of handcuffs broken in half, symbolic of his wrongful arrest. He lets voters know that doing his job properly has obviously ruffled feathers and now powerful giant forces in federal and state policing agencies are out to get him. He maintains he'll be vindicated.

Vic Feazell wins re-election, supported by two out of every three voters.

At his trial, he teams up with another lawyer, Gary Richardson, to defend himself. Together, they explain the conspiracy. The jury sides with Vic, clearing him of all charges in June 1987.

"I know what kind of pressure and trouble people face when they stand up and speak their minds," Vic says later. "I am pleased to be a free man today. If the federal government had its way, I would just now be finishing the first year of an 80-year prison sentence." [9]

Vic isn't done. With the giant government justice system off his back, he turns from defense to offense, pursuing a libel suit against his other giant—WFAA Television. His suit targets the station, its parent company Belo Broadcasting and the reporter who hammered him. Neither Vic nor Gary Richardson has handled a libel case before. Returning to court, the pair contends that the reports aired on WFAA gave a credible voice to false rumors and statements, leading to Vic's indictment. The District Attorney wants recognition and financial compensation for the negative impact on his reputation.

Vic has his work cut out for him. To prove libel under US law, you have to show that something written or broadcast about you is false and harmful to your reputation. If you're a public figure like Vic, however, the law sets an even higher standard to ensure that citizens and the media are not unduly muzzled in voicing concerns about your performance. As such, Vic must also prove that WFAA demonstrated "actual malice," meaning the station was either reckless with the truth, or knew that its statements were untrue before airing them.

To clinch their case, Vic and Gary uncover video clips that WFAA chose not to air, making it clear that its reporter purposely excluded parts of interviews more favorable to Vic. In court, they also present an emotional video put together in 1984 as a tribute to Vic, portraying him as a public hero. When this video ends, several jurors are in tears. [10]

The verdict in 1991 is swift. WFAA Television is guilty of libel. Vic stands up in court and thanks jury members for restoring his reputation. In his charming southern drawl, he offers to buy them drinks at a local hotel. Most will accept.

His credit cards maxed out with debt, he is awarded $17 million for damages inflicted on his reputation, and another $41 million for punitive damages against WFAA, including $1 million attributed to reporter

Charles Duncan specifically. The total of $58 million is the largest amount ever granted to an individual by an American jury in a case involving a media organization accused of libel.[11]

WFAA Television says it will appeal the decision. Vic says he'll consider taking $56 million instead of $58 million, if they pay up right away. A confidential out-of-court settlement is reached. Whatever payment is agreed, Vic won't have to rely on his salary again. He keeps working though, in a private law practice, to promote and defend the interests of other smaller players in Texas dealing with over-reaching Goliaths.

The alleged law enforcement conspiracy against him has never been proven.

In the end, suspected mass murderer Henry Lee Lucas is convicted in Texas of just one murder. Even this single murder conviction seems so questionable that Governor George W. Bush shows leniency and commutes the Lucas death sentence to life in prison—the only time Governor Bush will ever issue this reprieve for any death row prisoner.

PRESERVE YOUR REPUTATION

The best defense for smaller players taking on angry giants that might try to hurt their reputation for honesty and integrity is the same one that proved central to Vic Feazell's case in Texas: the truth.

Despite everything thrown at him, the District Attorney never forgot to stay truthful in his actions and words, remaining aware at all times that he had to stay "clean" if he were going to be effective in his ongoing criticisms of federal and state law enforcement officials.

The truth, if well presented and directed, is a powerful, influential and widely accepted standard. Vic always knew that his informal jury would be the public at large as electors, with his "peers" acting as a formal jury of Coercers if the issues in play ever reached a courtroom, which they did. These juries could focus on the facts, without being blinded like his giants by sensationalism or revenge.

If you've made mistakes that leave your reputation vulnerable, go back and do your best to fix the most obvious ones before you get involved in potential conflicts with a giant. Many giants will leave no stone unturned in efforts to defame your reputation, trying to undermine the credibility of your pursuits, or as Vic would attest, attacking you for what you've already done.

Here are some other things the Size Wizards keep in mind about reputations and protecting themselves:

- **Understand defamation and who bears the burden of proof.** *Defamation* arises when your reputation comes under attack unjustly, causing damages. Where *libel* is the written or broadcast form of defamation, *slander* is defamation through word-of-mouth. Slander is much more difficult to tackle legally because it leaves fewer traces and damages are harder to measure. In the US, *the onus is on those defamed* to prove that something said about them is not true. In Great Britain and former British colonies such as Australia and Canada, *the onus is on those accused of defamation* to prove that what they said is true. This reversal in the burden of proof underlies the nastier nature of the American media.[12]

- **Know the role of credibility.** The greater the credibility of a person who is defaming others, the higher their chances of being sued and seeing large penalties applied against them. Judges and juries don't worry as much about defamatory statements coming from sources whose own credibility is widely in doubt. Nor do they award as much to those defamed if their reputations are already questionable.

- **Be vigilant about what's considered fair comment.** In the interest of free speech in most Western nations, if you want to speak out about matters of public concern and giant public figures, you can be critical so long as you're not saying things you know to be untrue while intending to cause harm. When speaking about *any* giant, but especially a non-public giant, you can help protect yourself against defamation charges by stating irrefutable facts, then explicitly identifying anything else you say as being your opinion only.[13] If your giant doesn't toe the same line in speaking about you, they should be put on notice immediately, either by you or your lawyer.

- **Watch out for blogs, emails and websites.** You can be nailed for libel should you use any of these forms of electronic communication inappropriately. If you're criticizing your employer through a blog, look out: your comments may be grounds for dismissal. Blogs, emails and websites offer the potential for large worldwide audiences, meaning more damages against you if your own material is proven defamatory, or more money in your pocket if you're the one being libeled.

If you're defamed, consider swift non-legal responses at first to limit or undo any negative impact. These responses might involve a formal letter, an email, a speech, a press conference or a phone call to counter untruths. Sometimes, ignoring accusations in the beginning can make sense to see if they're picked up by others and spread, or whether they die off on their own. Addressing them prematurely might only fan the flames, so you'll want to monitor reaction through your helpers.

Finally, capturing relevant words and actions with dates, and having others do the same for you, is another way to bolster the defense of your reputation. Unless, of course, you've been in the wrong, in which case you may want to "muddy the waters," acting legally, but leaving few, if any, clear traces as to what actually happened.

Preserve your reputation—by moving quickly to set the record straight, sticking to the verifiable truth and not inappropriately attacking the reputation of your giant.

SHIELD YOUR CORE ACTIVITIES

It's Friday. I'm grabbing a coffee at a small café near my office when Mae, the owner, pulls me aside. She says a big coffee chain is moving into the mall and she's worried they'll cut into her business or somehow steal her perfect location.

I ask Mae a few questions, and find out she's had several new patrons lately, dressed in suits: not her kind of clientele. I tell her it's quite possible she'll be hearing from health inspectors soon, alerted by whoever the suits are working for. Their employer could be the coffee chain, or the mall's managers who stand to make much more money from a slick, high-end chain than from the long-term lease on Mae's home-style shop.[14]

As we walk through her restaurant and kitchen, Mae sheepishly points out a half-dozen fix-ups she's been putting off, including some torn linoleum flooring and peeling paint. I advise her to make these improvements right away, both to fend off the inspectors and to defend her customer base. She smiles, "Okay, okay, I'm on it." Over the weekend, Mae and her staff make the place look almost as new as when it first opened 25 years earlier. Two days pass. Health inspectors show up without warning, apparently shocked at how pristine their target is. "Well, what did you expect?" Mae asks, with mock indignation.

Mae went toe-to-toe with that coffee giant, and she did just fine, later retiring from business on her own terms. When we're dealing with giants, our core activities can be a vulnerable target and we have to plan accordingly—whether we're a restaurant owner or a trained seismologist starting up a daring venture.

STORY: RISKY BUSINESS

Sheldon Breiner understands calculated risks: the seismologist built his home just yards from the San Andreas Fault in California—beautiful location, obvious pitfalls.

To reduce the downside of living at the center of a major earthquake zone, Sheldon protected his house by reinforcing its foundations with massive concrete piers.[15]

This aggressive, yet protective approach to living can also be seen in the maverick scientist's business dealings. After earning some money through innovative technology that makes oil and mineral exploration less precarious, Sheldon focuses on another new technology, one he hopes will help him find gold in Silicon Valley.

The 50-something Stanford graduate likes Apple's Macintosh software, designed to run exclusively on the Goliath corporation's own Macintosh computers. So in 1989, Sheldon starts up a company called Quorum. Its goal: to get Macintosh's leading-edge software applications operating on

Apple may think Sheldon Breiner is being taught a hard-earned lesson, and will go away with the giant's fist poised for a final blow. But the executives at Apple are the ones about to learn a lesson.

Sheldon's company sues the Goliath known for suing.

Quorum asks the courts to decide if its products infringe on Apple's intellectual turf, making the case it is being wronged by Apple's attempts to intimidate a smaller player. By launching legal action, Quorum gains the upper hand, catching Apple by surprise.

Almost immediately, Apple caves. The towering corporation wants a deal.

Poor communication inside Apple may have led senior management to assume Quorum had done something wrong when it hadn't. Perhaps Apple executives realized antitrust issues loomed if they continued to act this way. There may also have been internal concerns over Apple getting involved in yet another costly suit. Or maybe Sheldon Breiner called their bluff, and they knew it.

Two months later, it's announced that Quorum will be allowed to continue marketing its products without any threat of legal action from Apple. As well, Sheldon Breiner's company is accepted back into Apple's Developer Program, with full rights and privileges. Other aspects of the agreement remain confidential.[18]

SHIELD YOUR CORE ACTIVITIES

Sheldon Breiner extended one hand to promote partnership. With his other hand, he held a shield crafted from carefully documented steps and breakthrough software ideas that explicitly avoided infringing on his giant's intellectual property. This shield, designed from the start as a defensive tool, was easily turned into a weapon when Sheldon and his legal Counselors took their case to a judge who had the authority to act as a formal Coercer.

Should Controllers—a giant's decision-makers—wish to discredit us, our core activities are an obvious target. As smaller players, the following defenses need to be ready, particularly if we plan to become aggressive:

- **Play by the rules.** Whether you're a non-profit or a for-profit entity, your regulatory and tax filings, policies and operations need to be in order and consistent with your mandate. If you're an employee of a giant, your hours, results, ethics and expenses may come under scrutiny. If you're a restaurant owner like my friend Mae, your facilities must satisfy the standards of local health authorities. Or if, like Sheldon Breiner, you're viewed as a potential competitor by a giant corporation, the onus is on you to stay *clearly* on the right side of the law. Always document your performance and have your helpers do the same.

- **Keep important players onside.** If you manage a small organization, key employees may be approached to work for your giant. Take care of these employees in advance, locking them in for a set period. As necessary, create a more intimate, flexible work environment with opportunities that are tough to match in a larger, more hierarchical organization. Also, make sure any important external allies, including clients, feel well appreciated for their support.

- **Develop invisible defenses.** To make "invasions" harder, embed takeover defenses in your core activities. Public companies sometimes use a "poison pill" which can multiply the number of shares held by existing shareholders, making a takeover too costly for outsiders trying to buy up control. Applying a different tack, PeopleSoft countered giant Oracle's takeover attempts in 2003 by putting big refunds into its client deals, which could only be triggered *if* the takeover went through, making the software company less attractive financially.[19] Similarly, smaller nations under siege threaten to sabotage their own infrastructure.

- **Name their game.** Sam Bull learns from a store owner playing informant that Sam's start-up potato chip company is being sabotaged by a competing food giant. According to this retail Crack, managers from the giant have urged health inspectors to harass Sam's burgeoning production plants. These managers are also going store-to-store in his strongest region, bad-mouthing his product, quietly paying owners cash to remove Sam's healthy chips from their displays—even buying entire displays and burying them in landfills. Sam calls several members of the media, sharing the facts as well as his opinions, while naming his giant and saying he'll take legal action if their brutal game continues. His story makes the news. Overnight, the tactics stop. Sam's company regains its footing and continues to grow. It's ultimately purchased for $10 million—by the very same giant that tried in vain to undermine it.[20]

- **Show their game.** Scottish farmer David McCreary finds his sheep mysteriously disappearing from their pen at night. Others die less mysteriously, with bullets in their sides. David suspects his powerful landlord, Jack Fraser. Fraser's been trying to get out of a three-generation lease with the McCreary family ever since he realized he could earn more money from German visitors wanting to shoot deer on the property. Angry and scared, David sets up a couple of hidden, high-quality video cameras near the entrance to the pen. Finally, he captures the killer on tape. It's not Jack Fraser after all, it's a local policeman who, as it turns out, was hired by Fraser. The landlord is ruined, disowned by his own family. To this day, David and the McCreary clan still rule over their sprawling sheep farm.[21]

A strong defense of your core activities, ideally pre-meditated, positions you to protect yourself against attacks while also allowing you to counterattack credibly. The Size Wizards not only think about *what* they're doing to build their defenses, they also think about *how* they're building them, trying to minimize the risk of irritating their giant or triggering new attacks. If our defenses aren't fully prepared, rapid responses can be critical to set things straight and fend off further attacks.

 *Shield your core activities—by sticking to the rules, keeping key contributors happy, installing invisible defenses, naming their game or showing them on the attack.*

PROTECT YOUR DEALS

An acquaintance of mine made a large down payment to rent a beautiful apartment in a mansion. Whenever I bumped into Mike, he raved about the place he would be moving into a few months later. It had hardwood floors, a fireplace, floor-to-ceiling windows, and shared access to a tennis court and swimming pool. On top of all this, the rent was really reasonable. I joked with my wife that maybe we should be moving in with Mike.[22]

The big day arrives. Mike shows up at his new digs with his moving van and finds a strange scene—several other vans around the house, people waving their arms and police officers trying to calm everyone down.

Mike discovers that the "landlord" who took the down payment from him and a number of other "tenants" was really a tenant himself. This impostor promptly skipped town on moving day, leaving everyone without their cash or a place to live.

That day, Mike learned a tough lesson that's a reminder for the rest of us: we need to vigorously and systematically protect our deals, which includes knowing whether our counterpart has the authority to do what they say they're going to do.

STORY: MUSIC TO THEIR EARS

Jazz legend Herb Alpert plays a trumpet exquisitely. Arguably, he and his partner Jerry Moss play giants even better.

Since 1989, giants have doled out close to one billion dollars to Herb and Jerry because the two of them know how to protect the value of their music by putting unconventional and shrewd terms in their deals. These terms actually increase the overall value they pocket just when that value seems most vulnerable, contributing to a fortune they could hardly have imagined when they first started out.

In 1961, Herb meets Jerry, a tall, gregarious promoter. Both in their mid-twenties, they scrounge together $100 apiece to form a partnership. Not long before, Herb, who's married with a young son, had almost given up on his music career to pay the bills, at one point working as an athletics instructor.

After selling a couple of Herb's songs to a record label, the new partners start their own label, rigging up a recording studio in Herb's Los Angeles garage. They each take the first letter from their last names, calling their creation "A&M Records." One day, during a break from recording, they travel across the border to Tijuana, Mexico to see a bullfight. While there, they're inspired by a Mariachi band. When they get back to their garage studio, Herb records a second trumpet on top of another trumpet track of his, but slightly out of sync, producing music with a lively Mariachi feel to it. The duo mixes in bullfighting sound effects and "The Lonely Bull" is born, recorded by "Herb Alpert and the Tijuana Brass." The song is a hit, quickly climbing America's Top 10 charts.

The Tijuana Brass? Okay, as it turns out, there really isn't any Tijuana Brass backing up Herb. Before going on tour, Herb and Jerry have to throw together a real brass band since laying down multiple tracks to make Herb sound like a band just won't work in a live setting.

By 1966, Herb and the Tijuana Brass sell 13 million albums in a single year, and claim five of the top 20 albums in the US—an unparalleled feat. Their success creates cash flow that A&M Records will use to attract other artists to its new recording studios on Sunset Boulevard. Performers such as Carole King, Cat Stevens, SuperTramp, Janet Jackson and Sting come into the Herb and Jerry fold over the years, making A&M the world's largest independent record producer.[23]

By the late 1980s, giant PolyGram Records, owned by Philips Electronics in Holland, approaches A&M as the recording industry consolidates. Aiming to lower its unit costs and raise its revenues through combined production, marketing and distribution clout, PolyGram offers around $500 million for A&M, including all of its recordings, talent contracts and operations.[24]

Herb and Jerry decide it's time to cash out. However, they want to protect the integrity of their creation. So before saying *yes* to PolyGram in 1989, these two sophisticated smaller players insist on a unique clause to ensure their label and its operations will remain separate and distinct within the growing PolyGram empire *for at least 20 years*. They also hang onto their publishing arm, Rondor, meaning they'll get royalties on A&M recordings whenever a song is played and Rondor holds the copyright.

Jump ahead nine years to 1998. The Seagram liquor dynasty, which now owns the Universal Music Group, swallows up PolyGram, including its A&M acquisition. A&M's employees are fired, its studio on Sunset Boulevard is closed and its assets are merged into those of Universal Music. One of the world's best-known labels is reduced to re-issuing old hits.

Now wait a minute, you may say to yourself, *what about that deal back in 1989 to maintain A&M's integrity for 20 years*? Well, that's exactly what Herb and Jerry are thinking. They launch a $200 million suit against Seagram for damages resulting from the violation of their 1989 deal with PolyGram. The responsibility for protecting A&M's integrity transferred to giant Seagram when it bought PolyGram along with its outstanding obligations and commitments.

"Surely this dispute doesn't have to be resolved in the courts," Seagram's CEO and new reigning family monarch, Edgar Bronfman Jr., must say to them about their suit. Bronfman then suggests another way to resolve their differences: sell him their remaining Rondor publishing assets as part of a package deal that will also settle their suit.

Herb and Jerry are persuaded. There is nothing they can do to bring A&M back to life, so they might as well be compensated. In August 2000, Seagram agrees to pay them $400 million, a nice bookend to the $500 million they received in 1989 from PolyGram—and directly related to the protective terms in that deal. Seagram's payment to Herb and Jerry is composed of $12 million in cash and Seagram shares valued at $388 million.[25]

If you're starting to think that Herb and Jerry are pretty smart—just wait. They implant yet another defensive shield in this new deal with Seagram. Their $388 million in Seagram shares is to be protected against any drastic decline in value. If the shares ever lose more than half their current value, falling below $37.50 for ten days running, Herb and Jerry will receive more shares and cash to make up the difference for *all the value* they've lost.[26] An annoying 30% decline in Seagram shares gets them nothing. More than a 50% decline, however, signals that something cataclysmic is going on and gets them back every cent they expected to receive. The deal carries over to any new entity Seagram joins or transforms itself into.

Herb and Jerry benefit here from being long-time insiders in the entertainment business. I'd guess they suspect that corporate valuations are over-inflated, especially with the looming crisis in pirated music via the Internet and recent fault lines in the stock market. So they want price protections. From Bronfman's perspective at Seagram, Herb and Jerry's request for these protections isn't a deal-breaker. It's impossible for Bronfman to believe that his fast-growing giant could ever see its share price plummet.

Indeed, just months later, Bronfman will use his corporation's growing value to close a monstrous deal with Vivendi of France. The two Goliaths agree to merge into a pan-Atlantic entertainment empire, second only to AOL Time Warner. As part of this French merger, Seagram's shareholders swap their shares on roughly a one-for-one basis into the shares of a mega-giant to be called Vivendi Universal. With the Bronfman family as its largest shareholder, Edgar Bronfman Jr. becomes vice-chair of this new entity.

Herb and Jerry's proceeds from the sale of the Rondor publishing group have been dramatically transformed. Suddenly, they hold millions of shares in a far-away French corporation that began as a water utility, with a CEO who some say fancies himself as a modern-day Napoleon, this time intent on dominating world entertainment.

Vivendi Universal's shares begin to tumble. Below $70, below $60, below $50, below $40, finally falling below $37.50 for ten straight days in early 2002. As strange as it may seem, Herb and Jerry are likely cheering in the end, thrilled to experience a severe loss.

Under the terms of their original deal with Seagram, they can now sell all their existing Vivendi Universal shares, which they do, pocketing an estimated $180 million. Months later, a grimacing giant announces that Herb and Jerry are to be paid an additional $100 million in cash from Vivendi Universal's coffers. As well, the pair is granted 8.8 million new shares—valued at $110 million—twice the number of shares they first held.[27]

Herb and Jerry's total profits from the Rondor sale and the settlement of their suit against Seagram are once again worth $400 million, including the cash they received upfront, and possibly much more if Vivendi Universal's share price continues to rebound from its lows.

Unfortunately for Edgar Bronfman Jr., his family's shares in Seagram had been converted into Vivendi Universal shares *without any price protections*. The Bronfmans, who worked so hard for generations to build the value of their liquor company, gave up their bottled jewel in the merger—and billions of dollars representing most of their wealth.[28]

PROTECT YOUR DEALS

The Size Wizards defend themselves against gaps in the terms of their agreements as well as clauses planted quietly by giants that will later haunt them. Like Herb and Jerry, they make sure their most important interests are protected, clause by clause, drawing on wise legal Counselors. Had Edgar Bronfman Jr. taken similar precautions, his family's legacy would have been shielded.

Before capturing your interests in any final agreement, take some time to remind yourself of all your interests, writing them down and prioritizing them if possible. This list can act as your guide as you develop or review written deals. Ideally, your side will draft deals to make sure your interests are satisfied, but giants often insist on drafting or using their standard templates. This may be fine *if* it saves you money, your giant fully understands your interests and they're completely open to your feedback. All formal deals should be checked out by your own lawyer to confirm your interests are being met.

Going over every single type of clause you should use to defend your deals isn't practical here, nor would it be a good idea given how unique each deal can be. However, going through a quick checklist like the one below, fleshed out and tailored to your situation, can help ensure your deal is comprehensive and protects you from common oversights:

✔ **Counterpart authority.** You need to be sure the parties to your agreement have the authority to enter into *this* type of deal. My old acquaintance Mike wouldn't have been ripped off by that con-artist tenant if he'd simply asked to see the title to the house. With giant individuals, groups or governments, you should gently raise the issue of signing authority if you're at all concerned. With giant corporations governed by common law, it's safe to assume your counterparts have the right to bind their organizations—unless you're signing a $50 million deal with a kid working weekends in the mailroom.[29] The bigger concern you'll want to tackle early on is whether your corporate counterparts have the full backing of their organizations to get your deal done.

✔ **Key interests and issues.** What is the agreement trying to achieve for those participating? Do the headings or issues as listed cover off your main interests? Herb and Jerry added the issue of "A&M's Status after the PolyGram Purchase" to reflect the interest that their musical creation remain intact. Does the deal meet the interests of parties not at the table, who might otherwise try to block it? Do any existing deals overlap with the issues covered by your new deal and need to be folded in or retired?

✔ **Responsibilities, risks and rewards.** Is the agreement clear about who will do what and when, who will assume any risks incurred, and what the parties gain? Herb and Jerry focused on a risk beyond their control—a big drop in the price of shares they received—gaining Bronfman's commitment that he would assume this risk. Who's paying the legal costs for your deal, or for any liabilities that arise?

✔ **Agreement term.** How long is the agreement to last? Is anyone allowed to exit early? Do the deal's responsibilities or benefits transfer to others in the case of corporate takeovers or someone's untimely death? If some clauses are found to be legally invalid or are waived informally, what happens to the rest of the agreement? Can the deal be extended by any or all participants? You may want certain clauses to last longer than others, like Herb and Jerry's 20-year clause related to the A&M deal.

✔ **Performance measures.** Is performance easily measured, monitored and held accountable, with shorter-term deadlines and regular check-in points rather than longer-term ones? Are there incentives in place for successes and penalties for failures?

✔ **Information**. Is it obvious how the parties will exchange information, both informally and formally, and who will handle this? Are special terms required to protect proprietary information, innovations, and ideas shared or developed under the agreement? What happens to these protections after the agreement comes to an end? What can you and other parties say about your deal and each other during the agreement or after it expires?

✔ **Dispute mechanisms.** Is there a defined way to settle any disputes amicably, such as mediation or arbitration? Ideally, the agreed state or national jurisdiction for any conflicts that go to court should be where *you* live or work. It's costly to travel to far-away courts where you'll likely be operating under less familiar laws and using lawyers you don't know as well. You'd prefer your giant face these challenges. That said, if you're ever looking to claim assets from your giant, you may want the jurisdiction to be where those assets are, even if it's abroad, so you can avoid going through two or more different court systems to try and get your hands on what you believe is rightfully yours.

Your ability to protect a deal boils down to covering off this checklist, and whether you can get your giant to agree that the deal you're proposing is better than their alternatives—allowing them to say *yes* despite the way you've defended your interests.

If your giant is being a bulldozer and pushing an agreement on you when your alternatives are weak, and you're unable to gain any meaningful protections, on rare occasions it may make sense to let them have their way. These ideas are explored in our second size and strength strategy, *Level the Playing Field*, where among other things we'll learn to draw strength from our weaknesses.

 *Protect your deals—by prioritizing your interests, embedding these interests in your deals, and running through a checklist to make sure you've covered off key clauses.*

Fend Off Broken Promises

I remember the day my father, who rarely drew attention to himself, first bragged about his gorgeous blue and gold tie. He said it was worth $50,000, and called it "the most expensive tie in the world." As a teenager, my eyes bulged, wondering if the tie were woven with gold. Then came the punch line: "Pete, this was a gift from a man who borrowed $50,000 from my business. Never saw him again, or my money. So, you have to figure the tie must be worth $50,000, right?" My father laughed heartily and I learned an early lesson in deal-making—and deal-breaking.

Getting anyone to follow through on a deal can be difficult. Giants present more formidable challenges given their size, strength and ability to fight battles successfully with their financial and legal resources.

Giants violate deals for three reasons: they forget or don't fully understand what they agreed to; they're not realistic about their ability to deliver; or they simply choose not to honor an agreement. To improve the odds our giants will comply, while protecting our downside, we need to create memorable agreements that are realistic and lay out clear promises, straightforward monitoring tools and costly consequences for any violations.

The Size Wizards think about compliance from the moment they begin to influence their giants away from the negotiation table, rather than treating it as an afterthought at the table, and they often call on their helpers to watch over their deals and enforce them.

In the previous section, *Protect Your Deals*, we made sure that our giant's promises were thorough enough to satisfy our interests. Now we delve into the vital issue of what we can do to encourage giants to keep their promises. After all, if our giants don't follow through as agreed, getting a deal with them may prove useless. Or worse, it can eat up our time, destroy our relationship with a giant and cause us to forgo valuable alternatives.

We begin our explorations with a determined wife. Later, we'll apply her insights on giant promises to Iraq, the Kyoto climate deal and a fired executive's dilemma.

STORY: CREATING NEW VOWS

Finding out that he has been cheating on her is devastating. What the hell is he thinking? They have two children! How could he do this to her? How could he be so stupid, leaving his secretary's underwear in his suitcase?

Susan Marx has a cheating giant for a husband. Ken Marx's giant status comes from his inherited wealth, high earnings as a banker and emotional hold on her. He is 15 years her senior, and like a father in some ways. The prenuptial agreement he had Susan sign ten years earlier dictates that if they divorce, she can count on a percentage of his earnings and savings from their married life, but none of what came before, which was substantial.[30]

When confronted, Ken swears to Susan he'll never cheat again, or lie, or drink so much, or be such a boor at times. He claims that his mother's death awhile back bothered him more than he knew and made him act out of character.

Susan is no longer the naïve 20-year-old kid who Ken swept off her feet. She's an established scientist with her own career. She's highly analytical and not inclined to be "screwed over" twice. But she still loves Ken and wants to believe in him. She's ready to give him another chance. Her gut tells her there's a high probability he can turn things around in the next year. She also knows, however, that Ken could stray from his self-improvement program, start drinking again and cheat again. If that were to happen, she believes that she and her kids would be better off not living with him.

Susan does a little research on the Internet. As she searches, she realizes her prenuptial agreement focused on money—the money she would *not* get in a divorce—while ignoring other points that might have reined in some of her husband's recent behaviors.

She laughs suddenly. Ken shoots her a nasty look from the sofa, absorbed in an NFL football game. She's reading about Catherine Zeta-Jones and Michael Douglas. The online article says Zeta-Jones, also a much younger woman than the man she married, must be concerned about issues of fidelity. Apparently, her written deal with Douglas stipulates the actress gets $5 million for "each act of infidelity" should the star of *Fatal Attraction* follow his famous character's lead and cheat on his wife. The way Susan sees it, if this is true, Catherine Zeta-Jones is a genius—and her new heroine.

She snorts with laughter again, as she reads that Jennifer Lopez is considering million-dollar fines for Ben Affleck if they marry and he cheats on her. Lopez goes even further according to one source, demanding she and Affleck have sex at least once every two days. Susan is impressed with this clause. Once a month would put a smile on her face.

Then there's the wife who formally limits her husband's NFL football to one game on Sundays. Susan glances at Ken watching his third game of the day and decides she's better off with him on the sofa. She has other priorities. Random drug testing is stipulated in another prenuptial agreement she reads about. She pictures herself leaning over to kiss Ken goodnight after pulling out a breathalyzer machine and testing him. *Awkward*, she concludes. And probably a real hindrance to the potential for that once-a-month smile.

Susan peers over at an unsuspecting Ken as he stretches out, reaching for another beer. *Boy*, she thinks, *he won't know what hit him.*

Compliance can never be 100% guaranteed when people have any kind of interest or compulsion to cheat an agreement or system, but Susan has now discovered that contractual terms can address the specific goals, needs and concerns in her relationship. She decides that any agreement to stay with Ken and support him emotionally will need to be explicit about: what he's going to do (see a therapist for at least a year); what he's not going to do (cheat, lie, drink or be abusive); and what they'll jointly commit to doing to make their relationship better (see a marriage counselor regularly).

After meeting with a lawyer, Susan takes Ken out to dinner to discuss the deal she wants the two of them to sign, supported by a professional arbitrator. The arbitrator would hear from both sides if ever there were any perceived violations, before deciding on remedies as outlined under their contract.

At first, Ken resists mightily, but he finally agrees to put a chunk of money where his mouth is, posting $500,000 in escrow from his personal assets as overall collateral for his pledges, each of which is valued differently.[31]

Ten days later, the new deal is confirmed in writing. If any violation is deemed to occur, signatures from the arbitrator and the victim of the violation can release the relevant collateral. Susan herself also becomes accountable on cheating and issues unique to her own weaknesses, like the odd extravagant shopping binge that drives Ken crazy. She places some of her own money and jewelry at risk to support her pledges. Anyone caught with another lover hands custody of the children over to the other person, along with keys to the house and minivan, and *all* assets held in escrow.

This reciprocal approach makes Ken feel better since he worries about getting older and having Susan cheat on him with younger men. He still doesn't like this "deal with the devil" but he does want his wife to stay with him. He knows that she was set on a trial separation if he'd rejected her idea of a contract.

On the first Monday of every month, the couple sits down to review their mutual commitments and talk about ongoing challenges as well as successes. After eight months and a number of positive steps forward, Ken inexplicably cheats on Susan again. He feels compelled to talk about it to his best friend, Jack, who in turn convinces Ken to tell Susan. She had quietly talked to Jack about her new agreement with Ken after it was reached, saying any violations would signal that Ken was on the verge of a breakdown. This time, Ken Marx's pleas for forgiveness are listened to with sadness by Susan. She'll forgive him in the end, but she won't forget their agreement.

Susan gets all the money in escrow, the kids and her freedom—without any debate, without chewing up her valuable time and without battling in court, though their divorce agreement will need to be filed with the local court and confirmed by a judge. She's knocked down emotionally for months, hurt more than she ever expected, but she can recover in the surroundings of her own home. Susan feels she tried her best to stay with Ken, and is confident her kids will understand everything she's done when they're older.

Fend Off Broken Promises

After being cheated on the first time, Susan Marx did everything she could to protect herself against further broken promises through the new vows she and Ken agreed to. Specifically, she drew on the three compliance guidelines that are applied by the Size Wizards to counter poor giant memories or misunderstandings, unrealistic terms and blatant cheating:

- **Capture deals effectively and make them memorable.** Susan decided an oral agreement with Ken would be tough to prove, difficult to recall and less likely to be taken seriously. The written agreement they reached was laid out in simple terms, approved by legal Counselors and overseen by a formal Coercer—an arbitrator. This agreement was revisited once a month during a scheduled lunch meeting. *As a result of this approach, it would be hard for Ken to claim he forgot his commitment, or he didn't understand what he'd agreed to.*

- **Make deals realistic, meeting everyone's interests at least adequately.** Ken wasn't thrilled to be signing any agreement, but given his limited alternatives, he consented because as a Controller, this deal met his interests reasonably well: he could determine his own destiny; he got his wife and kids to stay; the restrictions on his drinking and other habits were far from extreme and ultimately in his best interests, as was therapy; and Susan also had to comply, satisfying some of Ken's concerns about her. The deal met Susan's interests by giving her family a chance to remain intact, with an escape plan if things took a turn for the worse. *As a result of this approach, Ken would be less likely to breach the deal because he couldn't realistically comply or it clearly didn't meet his interests to comply.*

- **Create compliance mechanisms with monitoring and meaningful penalties.** The escrow account controlled by the arbitrator gave Susan an out, without having to convince Ken that she'd been wronged again. Penalties for excessive drinking, acts of indecency or verbal attacks would have allowed her to draw on some cash, but outright cheating gave her half a million dollars, an important percentage of Ken's wealth, and therefore a reasonable deterrent he wouldn't easily forget. Susan involved a network of family and good friends—including Jack who pushed Ken to confess his second violation—as informal Coercers to monitor Ken's commitments. *As a result of this approach, it was more difficult for Ken to forget, misunderstand, over-promise or break his word on purpose.*

In many relationships, Ken and Susan's agreement wouldn't make sense. This deal got done because: Ken cheated, so Susan had a good case for protecting herself; their prenuptial deal set a precedent for formal contracts within their marriage; Susan was prepared to walk away if a deal couldn't be reached while Ken's readiness to do so was less obvious; and Susan gently, yet firmly, pursued her husband's sign-off, making their deal reciprocal rather than trying to force Ken into one-way submission.

Susan did not get what she hoped for—a healthy marriage. But given her circumstances, she did a good job protecting herself against further violations, walking away with everything that still mattered to her after Ken cheated a second time.

Now, let's revisit the three compliance guidelines that Susan used, but see how each one on its own can be helpful to smaller players across a wide range of contexts.

CAPTURE DEALS EFFECTIVELY AND MAKE THEM MEMORABLE. An executive director, Lucie, is abruptly fired from her non-profit job over differences with her board chair, Helen.

Helen makes everything more difficult by constantly changing her mind. When she asks Lucie to meet her and another board member for lunch to discuss why she was fired, a severance package and other terms related to her departure, Lucie faces a dilemma. She wants to meet amicably but thinks Helen might distort their conversation or renege on what they agree to. On Sunday, the day before her meeting, as Lucie kneels down to pray at church, she looks up and finds the answer to her dilemma: he's standing at the altar.[32]

After the service, Reverend Tom agrees to attend the meeting with Helen. The next day, dressed in blue jeans and an open collar, and introduced by Lucie only as a friend, Tom goes to lunch, never saying more than "hello" and "goodbye." Back at his church, he jots down notes to capture the conversation, including the terms of the simple deal that was reached. Tom confirms to Lucie he'll appear in court on her behalf as needed, this time dressed in his minister's garb. Before that happens though, he's willing to phone Helen, a church-goer herself, if she dares to alter the agreement she shook hands on over lunch.

Sure enough, two days later, Helen phones Lucie, wanting to change their deal to "save money." Lucie stands firm, knowing she has invisible support from a power higher than Helen's. After several calls back and forth, their deal is confirmed as first agreed. Reverend Tom never has to utter a word. But Lucie says his presence at lunch made all the difference to her approach and confidence in dealing with the board chair.

Like Lucie, you may want to involve helpers during your negotiations with giants, not because they're critical to getting a deal, but because they'll broaden your "compliance net" afterward. An informal Coercer such as Reverend Tom is an illustration of this: someone your specific giant would find persuasive, who helps confirm the nature of a deal, while being able to take effective action should your giant break its word.

Tom's role is important here given that Lucie's agreement is based on spoken words. Oral agreements are legally binding in most nations. After all, there are many more oral deals than written ones, and societies would have trouble functioning if everyone were breaking their word all the time. The challenge, however, especially if helpers are not present, is remembering the scope and detail of an oral deal, and proving that a deal was actually reached and acknowledged by those involved.

Writing down brief, highlighted notes (in your agenda book, for example) can give you greater self-confidence, greater credibility and a potential source of evidence with both informal and formal Coercers. You can always follow up conversations with letters or emails, outlining the deal as you understand it, so your agreement is recognized and remembered. If your giant sees things differently, request immediate feedback.

Even remembering written deals can prove challenging once they've been filed away. To help forgetful giants recall existing agreements, the Size Wizards use simple deals, and simple, striking language to detail deals, making them more memorable. They shun dense legal wording, avoiding clutter that can lead to conflicts over what was intended. They put in writing the interests being served by significant clauses so interpretations remain consistent over time.

The Size Wizards also use vivid reminders of existing deals to encourage compliance. Screen savers, trophies commemorating a deal, and celebrations of a deal closing or its anniversaries help to keep a deal top of mind. One of my clients received a huge model of a building he'd agreed to finance when the project's developers suspected he was being distracted by other priorities. Indeed, it would be hard for him to forget his commitment to them with that model taking up an entire corner of his office.

At the extreme, to make sure a deal is remembered, you can etch it in stone, like King Hammurabi did 4,000 years ago in ancient Babylon (now part of Iraq). On a piece of black basalt, Hammurabi captured an agreement with his people and his gods over how their society would be ruled, placing the rock in a temple for all to see. The original copy of that eight-foot-tall deal survives to this day.

As smaller players, we can take big steps toward warding off any deal violations by crafting giant deals that are easy to understand—and tough to forget.

MAKE DEALS REALISTIC, MEETING THE INTERESTS OF KEY PLAYERS AT LEAST ADEQUATELY. If a deal doesn't meet your giant's interests, it's unlikely they'll continue to honor it.

So, as a smaller player, why would you ever craft an agreement if your giant can never comply with it in a meaningful way?

This is the fate of the Kyoto Protocol.

Cobbled together in Kyoto, Japan, by a small group of UN officials in 1997, this well-intentioned agreement aims to reduce the emission of gases that cause global warming and well-documented problems such as the melting of our polar ice.

Controllers from more than 170 countries have signed this accord, even China, soon to be the world's biggest polluter.[33] The problem is that China and others said they would only sign the deal as developing nations *if* they were exempted from its emission caps. Understandably, they don't want their hands tied as they grow their burgeoning economies. They point to the giant developed nations who created the problem and ask them to solve it first. But most developed nations are addicted to burning carbon-based fuels, with America currently being the number one addict.

Kyoto's UN crafters apparently moved forward *without* asking whether their solution could realistically tackle their problem (a 5% gas reduction does not). *Without* asking if the handful of giant nations needed to form its winning coalition could ever realistically say *yes* to their solution, monitor it, comply with it and undergo significant consequences for any violations (highly unlikely on all fronts). *Without* asking if a long-term, incremental approach makes sense when the problem is urgent and early supporters could be voted out of office (many were). And *without* fully exploring a less ambitious, shorter-term alternative with better prospects for implementation and the ability to expand on any successes (possibly a series of regional deals among similar-minded partners).

As they worked to gain acceptance from so many nations, UN officials diluted the Kyoto agreement and made it complex enough that the average person lost track of its terms. If people like you and me don't understand the accord, we'll be less inclined to pressure our politicians to implement it, nor will we do our part as 6.5 billion individuals to reduce our own emissions—crucial to any positive outcome. I believe that complying with Kyoto is too easy or too hard, but unrealistic either way. The wrong nations sign on, and the right nations stay away. To its credit, however, Kyoto is a rallying point for change, but a smarter deal might have launched real change a decade ago.

Perhaps if the right giant nations had been consulted in the right way, they would have been more inclined to say *yes* to a very different version of Kyoto. Letting your giant influence a deal can obviously raise the odds they'll comply with it. Not only might their input improve the deal and better satisfy their interests, but quite simply, as human beings we naturally feel more inclined to support and comply with outcomes we've helped create.

In putting together realistic deals to increase giant compliance, we have to account for our own compliance as well. In the world of consumerism, there is a great example of smaller players leaving money on the table with giants because we agree to a deal that most of us won't follow through on. What kind of deal am I talking about? Rebates. As consumers, all we have to do is fill in a form, mail it to a giant manufacturer, and we should get a check back, sometimes for hundreds of dollars. Do we do it? One store manager at a large retail chain told me that only 6% of us do. In that case, 94% of us sit on our hands, having been attracted to a deal because of a rebate that, realistically, we'll never take the time to claim—while our giant basks in its growing profits.[34]

In any giant deal-making, whether we're buying a big-screen TV with a rebate from Sony or selling an environmental deal from Kyoto, as smaller players we have to make sure our deals can realistically be implemented by our giants, and by us.

CREATE COMPLIANCE MECHANISMS WITH MONITORING AND MEANINGFUL PENALTIES. If your giant doesn't have a lot of cash—*un*like Susan's husband Ken—and has nothing else to place in escrow as a potential penalty, you can always give them something to lose, often acting on events that leave them vulnerable. In the international realm, the US could have tried this approach after coalition forces defeated Saddam Hussein in 1991's Gulf War, which ended Saddam's attempts to expand into Kuwait.

As we know, post-war sanctions were imposed, killing thousands of Iraqis, shutting down most of Iraq's oil capacity, establishing Saddam as a worldwide pariah and leaving him with little money to rebuild or pocket. Suddenly, the Iraqi leader had nothing more to lose. So Saddam began to take risks, bribing international representatives and breaking the UN agreement dictating that he could only export a fraction of his oil in return for humanitarian aid. No one stopped him: he kept getting stronger, crushing internal resistance, building up his personal bank accounts, and looking like an anti-US hero across the Middle East.

The US fretted. Iraq, its defeated oil-rich foe, rose again, regaining special giant status this time with its perceived threat of terrorism and weapons of mass destruction. President George W. Bush faced the stark choice of invading or not invading, with no middle ground. In 2003, he finally invaded, arresting Saddam and further destabilizing the region, at a cost of thousands of additional lives, hundreds of billions of dollars and a drastic drop in Bush's poll numbers.

Let's briefly go back to 1991, and look at a possible alternative to the flawed sanctions that gave Saddam nothing to lose, ultimately leading to a new war in 2003. Instead of using sanctions, we'll keep Iraq's oil production flowing at 100% capacity, but we'll control its massive oil revenues and put them in an escrowed bank account overseen by a neutral party. Based on defined good behaviors, an increasing percentage of all this new oil money will vest annually like a corporate share plan, becoming available to Saddam over time, so long as any freed-up funds are used peacefully to assist his country.

If Iraq doesn't comply with our agreement, or compliance is not verifiable, various amounts of money will be withdrawn from Iraq's billions of dollars of unclaimed escrow funds depending on the magnitude of the violation—large *or* small. These financial penalties, measured in both millions and billions of dollars, become inaccessible for a longer period of time, or come out of the escrow account permanently as warranted. Any money removed permanently from Iraq's clutches can help pay for UN programs around the world, or go straight into the pockets of Iraq's worried neighbors.

What are the benefits of this type of deal? Saddam would have been more likely to keep his promises if he'd had something to lose that was significant to him—money; innocent civilians wouldn't have suffered as much; Iraqis could have held their leader more accountable rather than blaming the UN and US for their plight; the world wouldn't have suffered uncertainty over oil price spikes because of Iraqi supplies being cut off (under sanctions, the country's oil infrastructure withered with a good part of it shut down, taking years to recover); and finally, the Iraqi war and occupation in 2003 might have been avoided.

No matter what the context—personal, business or international relationships—our giants must have something to lose for violating deals, even if we have to give it to them first.

 *Fend off broken promises—by capturing deals memorably, making deals realistic, and including smart compliance mechanisms with monitoring and meaningful penalties.*

Shelter Your Time

The most common hidden cost in giant deal-making is the time we spend negotiating deals, and implementing deals *after* they've been reached.

As smaller players, time is one of our most precious resources since we're forced to juggle so many responsibilities, yet time is rarely factored into our assessment of deals in any methodical manner. Giants happily take advantage of this fact, often moving at their own slow pace to get things done, wasting our time deliberately.

The defensive choices we make with respect to our time—how we spend it and factor it into our decision-making—can prove to be the difference between success and failure.

Story: Time to Act

"Show me the money, baby, just show me the money!" Steve jokes over a glass of wine, after their young children have been put to bed. "It's a damn good deal, and I think you should take it," the lawyer says to his wife, Jill Turney, as she stretches her legs out to relax on their couch.[35]

Earlier in the day, Jill received a signed offer, known as a "term sheet," from a venture capital firm she'd met six months before at an entrepreneur conference.

Portum Partners says it will value her small health-management software company at $10 million "pre-money" and invest $5 million to bring the total "post-money" valuation to $15 million, with Portum's resulting ownership stake being 33% ($5 million / $15 million). This offer is "generous and firm," the venture capitalists say to Jill, the CEO of Turney Software. They also say, "Take it, or leave it."

Jill confirms with reliable sources that Portum has only $5 million left in its current fund to invest in new deals after rapidly growing its portfolio over the past two years. The firm is committed to investing this remaining $5 million by year-end, just three months away.[36]

Despite her husband's enthusiasm, Jill isn't sure what to do. This offer comes as a surprise after several informal meetings. Terms had never been discussed, nor did Portum ever mention its intent to make a formal offer so soon. The usually unflappable CEO feels nervous negotiating with financiers who have the money she needs and experience closing hundreds of similar deals. This would be her first major financing, ever.

Jill knows she can say *yes* to Portum's offer and feel confident that she's done okay. On the other hand, she could interpret its offer as a sign that other giant investors might be interested, possibly offering better terms. But looking for one more investor and then negotiating with them as well would consume all her time during a critical quarter when she and her tiny team have a unique opportunity to generate some big sales increases.

A computer scientist by training, Jill is systematic in making decisions, especially as they relate to time. The following day, Jill buys lunch for another software entrepreneur, discovering that Turney Software could be valued at more than the $15 million offered by Portum, but only if she can attract another bidder to drive the price up. Otherwise, $15 million is likely what any single bidder would bid, at most. After a few phone calls and some more digging, Jill concludes that if she aggressively pursues a competitive bidder, she could land an offer in the range of $18 million post-money. This is a nice hike in value for her and other shareholders, and as a result, they'd give away less of their company ($5 million / $18 million = 28%, versus the 33% stake proposed by Portum). On this basis, Jill decides it probably makes sense to go after another offer.

But first, she has one burning question as she sits at the office contemplating her choices, while Steve puts the kids to bed at home: *What if I forget about any financing for now and just stick to growing new sales?*

To answer this question, Jill needs to calculate the benefits of spending all her time building the company's value through new sales during the next three months, only raising the $5 million afterward, early in the new year.

Sales have the potential to rise sharply before New Year's resolutions because Turney Software helps companies keep their employees healthy and productive through online tools that manage personal diets and fitness. Companies pay an annual fee for Jill's system, which has proven so popular with employees that no company has ever canceled its subscription. This means that sales grow every year from the base established in the previous year.

After going over a list of prospective clients in her head, Jill jots some numbers on a napkin, figuring out she'll generate estimated new sales of $375,000 in the last quarter of the year if that's all she and her team focus on.[37]

The past 12 months of sales are key in valuing health software companies right now. To value Jill's company, venture capitalists will simply multiply her preceding 12 months of sales by four or five times, typically using a multiple of four like Portum did. A bidder might go above four—to four and a half times, for example—if it felt Turney Software's fast growth justified a higher multiple *and* if it were being pushed by a competing bid.

Should she wait until January to raise $5 million, Jill knows Portum will be forced elsewhere, and she'll have to rely on one bidder, at best, since she'll need money immediately and won't have time to generate multiple bids. Her probable gain of $375,000 in new sales, multiplied by four, would boost her company's value in the new year by $1.5 million over the $15 million she'd get from any single bid, for a total of $16.5 million.

"Not bad," Jill says out loud about this higher valuation as she sips a hot tea and scans her numbers. "But the best way to spend my time seems obvious now."

An expected gain of $1.5 million in value through new sales in the months ahead pales in comparison to the projected windfall of $3 million in new shareholder value if she involves two bidders in her financing.

She picks up her cell phone, calling a friend who can connect her to a top venture capital firm. That firm won't be interested, but it will introduce her to another financier, Impact Partners, which expresses immediate interest after learning that one of its unnamed competitors has already made an offer. Jill heightens Impact's interest by getting a large Boston newspaper to write a glowing article about Turney Software and its services.

After several more meetings with both Impact and Portum, Jill believes that she'd be happy working with either one. Sticking to her self-imposed deadline so she can get back to growing her company, she asks for final bids, neither firm certain of the other's identity.

Portum wins, bidding $20 million post-money, a whopping increase over its first solo bid.

SHELTER YOUR TIME

Our CEO's projections were off somewhat, under-estimating the value of another bidder by $2 million. But Jill's rough calculations of how much new value she could generate in her limited time through negotiation activities, instead of through Turney Software's core selling activities, clearly propelled her in the right direction.

Sometimes the simplest calculations of how our time is best spent will drive us to consider different approaches in our negotiations with giants. Our time can be absorbed evaluating potential deals, defending ourselves, leveling the playing field, crafting deals, talking at the table, or as deals are being implemented and we're trying to fully exploit their value.

In preparing the defense of our time, we can be as calculated as Jill Turney, or not. What's most important about Jill's approach is that as a Size Wizard, she remains vitally aware of time, factoring it into all her decision-making:

- **Value time.** Jill always identifies the value of spending time on one set of activities over another, whether these activities relate to negotiations, core operations or both. She calculates how much time something will take, the likely value of a successful outcome and the odds of achieving that outcome, comparing choices. If two competing deals require different amounts of time, she assigns a reasonable hourly rate to her time and her team's time, subtracting the cost from the expected value of each deal. The Size Wizards believe everyone's time can be quantified in dollars as a common denominator.

- **Track time estimates.** Jill keeps tabs on herself and her team, comparing estimates to actual times. She adjusts estimates on new projects to reflect past realities, and offers incentives and disincentives for hitting or missing deadlines as part of internal negotiations over time. She knows that relevant individual and organizational experience can make a big difference in generating reliable estimates. As an example, Jill has heard that at one technology giant, your own estimated time to finish a programming task may be multiplied by *seven* in your first year, by *six* in your second year, and so on—all the way down to a multiple of *one* in your seventh year, at which point your estimates are judged to be accurate. The Size Wizards realize that their team's ability to produce timely results directly affects external talks with giant clients, giant financiers and others.

- **Think post-deal, too.** In comparing different alternatives, Jill doesn't just include her team's time pursuing and reaching giant agreements. She factors in the time likely required to implement and oversee deals after they've been reached, which can vary widely depending on the counterpart and the deal. Negotiations with Portum boded well for the future in terms of time: the deal was straightforward, the venture capital firm's role was clearly defined, and its partners had been reliable and respectful of her time throughout.

- **Pursue time deals.** Jill's deal with Portum required the venture capital firm to complete the deal, or make a big deposit, after just 30 days of detailed due diligence. The Size Wizards use "time clauses" like this to keep all sides honest in meeting deadlines on the way to a final deal. Assuming they're confident of meeting their own time commitments, they include mutual penalties and exit provisions for missed deadlines so they can pursue their alternatives.

- **Develop alternatives.** Jill used a friend as a Connector to hook up with her alternative, Impact Partners. A decent back-up plan to the

Portum deal helped Jill set firm deadlines with her giant, allowing her to walk away if needed.

- **Stay organized.** Jill knows that if she's well organized, it's much easier to impose deadlines on a giant. The CEO's efficient approach to gathering and funneling *all* information through her executive assistant meant she couldn't be blamed for delaying progress on the Portum deal. Eighty percent of the information Portum needed to close the deal and transfer its $5 million was placed at the firm's fingertips within three days of Jill signing Portum's term sheet.

- **Create time rules.** Jill sets realistic deadlines for herself and sticks to them, subject to change only if objectively justified. She knows that her giant will tend to be more responsive, sticking to its time commitments, if she models good behavior, returning its calls or emails within 24 hours, being at meetings on time and respecting deadlines. Most importantly, Jill knows that if she has firm rules for managing her time, it will be harder for any giant to steal much time from her.

Time crooks inside a giant's castle undermine us, sometimes on purpose, more often not. They can be devastating on time-sensitive projects, leaving us to rely on much weaker alternatives, or them alone. When we contact them, these specialized crooks take their time, which is really *our* time, for one or more of these reasons:

✗ They're managing their affairs poorly.

✗ They're distracted by events in their personal or professional lives.

✗ They need to consult others before getting back to us.

✗ They're indifferent because of their incentives and priorities.

✗ They're waiting for us to show them how serious we are.

✗ They won't respond unless a Connector is used.

✗ They're simply not sure if they're interested in what we have to offer.

✗ They have alternatives to us that appear to meet their interests better.

✗ They're signaling we're not important, possibly as a tactic.

✗ They want to worsen our alternatives, improve their own or see us fail.

Reminding ourselves of this checklist for time delays can help us manage our paranoia as smaller players, keep us on our toes or send us into action. Each of these potential reasons for a delay hints at either staying patient awhile longer, or pursuing any number of steps to move things forward, with or without our giant's blessing. Certainly, the more helpers we have lined up inside or outside our giant's castle, the better positioned we are to find out what's really going on, exerting our influence accordingly.

 *Shelter your time—by valuing it, staying organized, creating time rules, modeling timeliness and being ready to walk away from a giant deal if it's taking too long.*

HAZARDS TO AVOID

As you build up your defenses, here are some traps to sidestep:

Paralyzing or hurting yourself as you protect information. You can only manage the risks of stolen information, not eliminate them, unless you keep your interests and ideas locked away. Sometimes, having your idea stolen isn't such a bad thing if it means it will be used. Britain's Tim Berners-Lee, a founding father of the Internet, chose not to protect his idea because his goal was to change the world. Tim shared his web browser and server with everyone, letting them use his idea for free, instead of making money through patents and royalties which would have slowed the Internet's development. In terms of your own interests, hiding important goals, needs and concerns can be a smart move at times, but realize that your giant will be hard pressed to satisfy any interests it doesn't know about.

Becoming a public figure—unwittingly. As a smaller player in the United States, you can become a "limited purpose" public figure under the law if you raise your profile significantly in the media on a particular issue. This means that within the scope of the public role you've adopted, you may be as vulnerable as full-time public figures such as politicians and celebrities, and subject to similar searing criticisms without recourse to defamation charges, unless you can prove malice.

Hiring questionable players. If you hire an employee from a giant, you need to confirm that they're not violating any confidentiality or non-competition agreements with their former employer. Otherwise, your core activities can be attacked—legitimately.

Saying *yes* to any clause before looking at the entire deal. Giants may ask, "Are we in agreement on this clause then?" Often, our response is "sure," because saying otherwise can feel awkward, especially if our giant has worked collaboratively on an issue. The better answer for smaller players: "I can agree *tentatively* on this clause. I'll confirm with you after I've looked at our deal as a whole to see how well it meets my overall interests." To protect our deals from giants, it's unwise to firmly commit on one issue before knowing how well we've done on others.

Defending against potential broken promises in a way that undermines trust. If you have no history of mistrust with your giant, raising issues about compliance and penalties can cause mistrust, if done the wrong way. To ease tensions, mull over these approaches: frame mutual protections as satisfying both your giant's interests and yours; introduce desired protections as standard policy; explain that other players on your team, such as board members, request these protections; point out that the goal is to remove trust as an issue altogether so you can jointly and openly create as much value as possible; or let other players deal with these issues, such as legal teams from both sides.

Letting emotions rule your use of time. We can become so caught up in negotiations and conflicts that we lose track of how we're spending our time. Giant deals that take more time than expected because of a competitive bidding process, or one hassle after another, need to be re-evaluated. As a discipline, ignore time already spent on a deal and look ahead, comparing the benefit of spending more time on a questionable deal instead of spending new time on other deals or projects. If, in all likelihood, your time is better spent elsewhere, walk away. Sometimes, your best deals will be the ones you don't do.

FINAL THOUGHTS

To defend your information, remember how Michael Schiller guarded his floating fridge secret while changing the Vietnam bidding process, or at the other extreme, how the guys who pitched Disney were completely open about "Sports Island." If your reputation might be attacked, clean it up and focus on the truth like former Texas District Attorney Vic Feazell. If your core activities are a potential target, clean them up too, building defenses into them consistent with Sheldon Breiner's approach toward Apple. Think about A&M's Herb Alpert and Jerry Moss as you protect your deals, clause by clause. Discourage violations by planning for them, just as Susan Marx did with her husband, and the US should have done with Saddam Hussein after Iraq was defeated in 1991. And to shelter your time, follow CEO Jill Turney's lead, putting a concrete value on it.

Prepare for success. Before, or early in your negotiations, you should run through the six potential vulnerabilities we've highlighted, focusing on those defenses most relevant to your circumstances, shifting your focus over time to include other defenses as needed. Undertaking the preparations we've explored in *Defend Yourself from the Start* will deter or blunt attacks on your information, reputation, core activities and time, place you on the offensive afterward, and secure protections against bad deals or broken promises.

Follow these broad steps to dull attacks. Stay energized by focusing on positive steps forward until it makes sense to switch mental "compartments" and respond to any attacks. Some Size Wizards set up teams dedicated to pre-empting or countering attacks. An experienced "swat team" can coordinate, prioritize and monitor all your defenses, allowing you to promote your interests positively, without distraction. A swat team formed by Arkansas Governor Bill Clinton proved highly effective when the relatively unknown politician risked being undermined by ongoing attacks on his character and policies as he first took aim at the White House in 1992. James Carville served as the charming, savvy and saber-rattling spokesperson for Clinton's rapid response team, hitting back hard against critics or innuendo, helping Clinton claim the presidency.

Manage your paranoia. In business, Intel's Andy Grove is famous for his conviction that "only the paranoid survive." For all of us smaller players dealing with giants like Intel, the chip-making corporation Grove co-founded, paranoia is a critical part of everyday thinking and planning, from the very beginning of our influence efforts. But our paranoia only serves us well if it's used to defend our six key vulnerabilities while we continue to take calculated risks that move us toward our goals.

3

LEVEL THE PLAYING FIELD: MAKE THEM SMALLER AND WEAKER

Even things up by focusing on your giant's vulnerabilities.

THE GOLIATH MANY OF US LEARNED ABOUT IN SUNDAY SCHOOL was minuscule compared to the giants we've grown accustomed to over the past 25 years.

As young David stared up at Goliath, at best he was looking at someone twice his size. Today, if we translate the size of our biggest modern-day Goliaths into height differences, the vast majority of us are staring up at a huge foot, the top of which rises well above the clouds. As for our giant's face, we'll need a powerful telescope to see it, because it's at least 100 miles high, somewhere in outer space.

When you view our size divide this way, it becomes that much clearer why we have to work so hard *away* from the negotiation table to level the playing field, before we get too close to our giants or pursue any serious talks. In the next chapter, we'll look at how we can even things up by making ourselves bigger and stronger. But right now, we're going to level the playing field by making our giants smaller and weaker.

Out on the playing field, the Size Wizards use four approaches to deflate size and clout, bringing their giants back down to earth:

- They find a rulebook to undermine extreme positions.

- They change how the game is played so size and clout don't matter as much.

- They put on their giant's jersey to influence change as an insider.

- They make it difficult for their giant to play without them.

In applying these approaches, we'll exploit giant vulnerabilities—every giant has them. A Goliath's physical structures are not to be ignored as targets, including parking lots as we'll soon learn. But our main focus should be on the non-physical assets that underlie a giant's influence, enabling everything else that our eyes *can* see.

This Hidden Infrastructure, introduced earlier, encompasses the invisible political webs that giants weave; the decision-making structures they control behind the scenes; the wide-ranging rules they quietly create or change; the veiled connections that grant them access to key decision-makers and the media; the multi-pronged information, sales and marketing networks that stealthily access our priorities and pocketbooks; the concealed army of high-priced lawyers that lies in wait; and the secret moats around their castles that keep out the unwanted. Any or all parts of this Hidden Infrastructure can support a giant's need to grow, and protect them from anyone who threatens their growth as giant individuals, groups or organizations.

We'll watch as our Size Wizards often surface, upset or co-opt parts of a giant's Hidden Infrastructure to meet their interests as smaller players, drawing on assistance from one or more helpers.

The approaches we're discussing here are different than any collaborative efforts we might pursue in other circumstances and are only to be used when our giants aren't cooperating or clearly won't in the future. We need to tread carefully now, using what we've just learned from our first size and strength strategy, *Defend Yourself from the Start*, as we become more aggressive away from the negotiation table.

As we delve into how we can throw our giants off balance to get what we want, we'll travel around the world and through time, encountering an ancient king, models with eating disorders, a peeved arm-wrestler, parents concerned about their kids' schooling, a gutsy whistleblower, and an entrepreneur who doubles as a detective.

GET OUT THE RULEBOOK

Sometimes, rules that are being ignored can be used to great effect by smaller players.

STORY: ACCOUNTING FOR YOUR ACTIONS

"Bad news comes in small envelopes," Linda Cramer's father always used to say.

Well, he couldn't have been more right in this case. Linda stares down at a nasty letter from one of the executives at Kempt Paper Products. The letter says that the small marina she plans to build on Moonshine Lake would sit squarely on shoreline owned by the corporation. It insists she contact Kempt to discuss lease terms.

For the 36-year-old boating enthusiast, this letter represents a major hurdle. In her recent filings with local officials, Linda had assumed the shoreline for her dream project belonged to the state government, like most other lake shorelines. An international corporation such as Kempt, not known for doing anyone favors, would likely charge a hefty and possibly unaffordable premium over what she had expected to pay the state.[1]

A week later, Linda sits across from Dan Maven, the Kempt vice president responsible for growing the company's sales. He chastises her for not realizing sooner that her marina would be built on private property. Maven says he's not sure whether any lease will be agreed to, but he asks for her best offer. Linda suggests the standard rate paid for similar government-owned shoreline. Her suggestion is rebuffed. "Worth a lot more than that, young lady," the white-haired Maven laughs. "You'd better sharpen your pencil and come back to us with a *much* higher offer."

Linda leaves, discouraged. Her financial projections are at risk, and so is the project itself. She kicks herself for making a flawed assumption about ownership rights on the lake. Sure, she had only recently moved to this region after selling a small restaurant in the city, but Maven was right, she had not done her homework.

Better later than never, she thinks to herself. Linda drives to the regional Land Title Office to find out more about the area's real estate history. If need be, there might be another lake nearby where she can develop her marina more cheaply, though she cannot imagine a more beautiful setting than Moonshine Lake.

After several hours shuffling through dusty documents at the land registry, and a couple more hours at the local library, Linda is still putting the puzzle together.

She learns that in the late 1800s, a logging corporation agreed to build railroad access to Moonshine Lake so the area's rising population, and a senior state official named Billy Bunk, could get to their homes easily. In return, Blitzner Logging Incorporated received a big chunk of land around the lake— including the lake itself, apparently—allowing it to move logs into the water and across the bay to a connecting waterway that leads to another lake and a large pulp and paper mill. At the time, the land was valued at $5,000.

Linda discovers that ten years before, when she was still an accountant working at Ernst and Young, Blitzner sold its operations and land in the region to Kempt Paper Products. All this explains why Kempt claims ownership of the shoreline and wants to hit her marina with a big monthly fee. But a couple of puzzle pieces are missing.

Linda can't find anything in the original land title transferred a century ago confirming the lake was formally part of the land-for-railroad deal. Maybe, just maybe, she speculates, Kempt doesn't have any clear right to the lake today if the corporation that supposedly sold them that lake didn't own it either. Linda does more digging. She calls an old acquaintance at Ernst and Young. She wants to refresh her memory of federal tax law when land like this is sold by one corporation to another.

Three days later, Linda is back in front of an impatient Maven. She looks him in the eye and says she's willing to pay market prices for the shoreline she wants. She has his full attention.

Linda adds, "Mr. Maven, I'll only need two things from you before we confirm the details of our deal. First, if you can show me some kind of accounting that indicates how you value this strip of shoreline, we can quickly establish appropriate monthly lease payments. Second, and this is really just a technicality, before signing the agreement, I'll obviously need verification from your lawyers of a deed showing you own the land."

"That's it?" Maven says, smiling. He gets up and shakes Linda's hand, promising to call her once he's spoken with his accounting and legal departments. "Shouldn't be long before you hear back from me," he says confidently.

A week goes by. No word. Then a month. Linda emails Maven. Then phones him. And finally writes a letter. How ironic. Suddenly, the giant paper corporation is ignoring her—exactly what she was expecting.

Linda thinks that Kempt's accounting group has come back to Maven and said, "The last thing we want to do is put a price tag on any local land holdings." Why? Because, Linda believes, all their land is probably still valued at $5,000. Leasing even a small parcel of it could trigger an assessment of the entire property based on current market prices, generating a tax bill in the tens of millions of dollars. The federal government has the right to levy capital gains taxes on land, particularly if this land is sold after being held for generations.

Linda guesses that Kempt's legal group has told Maven: "The last thing we want to do is raise the issue of who owns the shoreline." They would have learned, if they didn't know it already, that it's not clear who owns the lake. It definitely works to Kempt's advantage in continuing to operate on the lake if everyone assumes it is the lake's owner.

So here's how the unspoken deal works: Linda boldly builds a larger marina than initially planned, and turns its docks, facilities and restaurant into a success-story worthy of her dream. Kempt never lifts a finger, never says another word to Linda.

The new marina gets free use of the shoreline, paying nothing for the long stretch of dazzling property on which it sits. As for Kempt, it also gets a free pass, avoiding exorbitant tax payments while still using "its" shoreline at will.

GET OUT THE RULEBOOK

Linda Cramer's detective work away from the negotiation table allowed her to subtly introduce existing tax and land ownership rules into direct discussions, weakening her Goliath and ultimately undermining its ability to demand any payments at all.

Linda learned that if she were charged rent based on the shoreline's market value today, current laws could push her giant to recognize a huge asset gain, attracting a whopping tax bill. As for who actually owned this land, Linda already knew the rules: if you own land legally, a simple deed should prove this.

The entrepreneur's surfacing of these rules and requests for information related to complying with them ensured that different parts of her giant would voice their concerns. The legal and accounting groups at Kempt may well have acted as informal Coercers to dissuade Dan Maven from taking further steps toward a lease agreement with Linda, over-riding his natural tendency to spawn more revenues as the vice president of sales.

In "getting out the rulebook," we draw on, or dig up if need be, accepted standards of play including specific rules created by governments or professional bodies—rules that can serve as a catalyst for smaller players looking to weaken their giants.

These standards of play set boundaries in the game of influence, helping guide our giants toward appropriate behaviors and outcomes. Relevant rules can relate to laws, regulations, policies, codes of conduct, organizational charters or constitutions. Other important standards involve established practices, precedents, expert opinions, market values, principles or logic.

While most compelling standards are independent of the parties to a giant negotiation, this is not always the case. I've seen many situations where a giant's own "standard" policies—discovered by a search through precedents *they've* set or within documents *they've* written—can help smaller players. Insurance companies offer one example, where declined claims are later accepted because claimants surface favorable fine print in policies drafted by their giant insurers.

Looking back at Linda's story, we can put together some guidelines for uncovering and applying existing standards:

- **Research relevant standards.** Use solid online and offline resources to identify persuasive standards for your situation, talking to your helpers—including expert Counselors such as lawyers if necessary—to weaken a giant's position. Look at other situations like yours, and see what standards were applied there. Linda built on her understanding of accounting rules by calling a former colleague to update her knowledge of federal tax law and land transfers.

- **Follow the silence.** If something isn't discussed or widely known, a giant may be trying to keep it that way because of rules that run contrary to its interests. Dozens of locals consulted by Linda didn't know that Kempt owned the shoreline she planned to build on. Either Kempt was keeping the ownership issue quiet on purpose, or Linda's giant didn't itself know the facts.

- **Question assumptions about your giant and the rules**. Make sure your giant is who it claims to be, owns what it says it owns, and has the right to do what it's doing, with no history of rule violations. Survey others who've dealt with them, check out online resources such as the Better Business Bureau, and consult your helpers to verify giant facts. Linda went to the regional title office and a local library as two helpful resources. If you're like Linda and your financial projections involve important assumptions (she assumed the shoreline belonged to the state), question *all* your assumptions early on, confirming the most basic pieces of information so you don't find yourself up against a giant you can't yet see.

We'll finish looking at how to "get out the rulebook" through detailed examples of three different sets of standards being used to weaken giants so smaller players can prevail—in a classroom, a mall and a corrupted corporation.

CLASS ACTION. Mary Romano is not a complainer, but she does talk regularly to her daughter's public school teacher about what the children in her third grade classroom *don't* appear to be learning. Mrs. Harper remains indifferent.[2]

Then Mary goes to the school's principal, who nods politely and does nothing on three separate occasions, explaining this is Mrs. Harper's final year before retirement. "This is my daughter's final year in third grade," Mary shoots back.

Mary wonders how to prove that Mrs. Harper is underperforming. A friend suggests she go online to see if the state publishes formal learning objectives for third grade. Indeed, Mary finds objectives with clear timelines laid out on a government website. It's now obvious that Mrs. Harper is completely off-track and way behind schedule.

Mary gathers schedules, class assignments, work samples and a print-out of the state's objectives. She arranges to see her giant again, this time with independent standards and measurements in hand. The principal, expecting another rant, is surprised and persuaded as a Controller by Mary's detailed discussion of standards along with evidence of how they're not being met. In January, Mrs. Harper is quietly replaced by a new teacher.

A LOT OF RULES. Phil Richardson is worried. A giant grocer located in the same mall as his tiny convenience store plans to expand. This will put him at an even greater disadvantage on pricing and selection, threatening his store's future.[3]

As Phil stares out at the mall's busy parking lot, he suddenly realizes that parking may be his savior. He speaks to one of his wealthier customers, Monica Dawson, who will act as a Connector, introducing Phil to a powerful member of City Council. The complaint: expansion by his giant will likely breach municipal by-laws with respect to the number of parking spots available per square foot of retail space.

Too many cars with too few spaces causes overflow into surrounding neighborhoods. Citizens living nearby are already complaining about the parking situation in their streets.

The City, as a formal Coercer here, notifies the giant grocer that to be legal, any expansion must include new parking facilities. The giant grocer is hemmed in. The cost of building new parking would outweigh the benefits of expanding.

Phil gets what he wants.

WHISTLING IN THE DARK. After being tipped off by an informant, a Crack inside her own organization, Cynthia Cooper suspects that her employer is inflating its financial results. Her highly respected superior, WorldCom's Chief Financial Officer Scott Sullivan, angrily tells her to drop the issue.

As the head of WorldCom's internal audit team, Cynthia isn't about to drop anything. "When someone's hostile, my instinct is to find out why," she says of Scott Sullivan's reaction.[4] One of her jobs is to ensure financials are reported accurately to shareholders. Another of her jobs is to keep senior executives happy. She'll have to move cautiously.

She quietly calls together members of her team. They work late, night after night, redoing some of the financials already handled by Arthur Andersen. In late May of 2002, they discover a major problem: someone has reported significant current expenses as capital expenditures, wrongly spreading these costs out over many years. If recognized accounting standards were to be applied, the previous year's $2.4 billion in profits would turn into $662 million in losses.

Cynthia puts herself in her giant employer's shoes to fathom a possible justification for its approach, but she can't come up with anything. Sullivan, who is one of her mentors, asks her not tell anyone yet. She says she can't wait. Another senior official privately confirms that the accounting is flawed. On June 20, 2002, Cynthia meets with both the board's audit committee and Sullivan— who can't provide any plausible explanations. Audit committee members, acting as Convincers, then influence the board as a whole to fire Sullivan.

WorldCom's stock plummets when the huge change in its results is announced. The giant telecom soon declares bankruptcy and restructures itself. Cynthia sticks around to clean up the mess while Scott Sullivan goes to jail with WorldCom CEO Bernard Ebbers.

Cynthia's story reminds us once again that giant organizations are made up of unique individuals who hold different knowledge of a giant's activities, different perspectives on these activities, as well as distinct personal interests and morals.

Now 42 years old, Cynthia says her mother was the best Counselor during her ordeal as a whistleblower holding up the rulebook to her giant. Her mom would constantly say to her, "Never allow yourself to be intimidated; always think about the consequences of your actions."[5]

Cynthia's actions, and corruption unveiled at several other American corporations, would lead to the Sarbanes-Oxley law. This law makes corporations more accountable and supports smaller players who want to report violations of established standards at public corporations operating in the United States. Many nations have since adopted similar laws.

Get out the rulebook—research relevant standards, follow the silence, and question your most basic assumptions about your giant and the rules at hand.

CHANGE HOW THE GAME IS PLAYED

One of my clients, a businessman named Michael Frick, isn't happy. A big local executive search firm insists he owes it thousands of dollars in fees, even though it has never found his company one suitable candidate to fill a senior marketing position.

Michael takes the search firm's managing partner to lunch and proposes a straight-forward, old-fashioned way to settle things. "I'm sorry, Michael," says the managing partner, Sam Stevens, "I must have misheard you. Did you say *arm wrestle?*"

"That's right, Sam. It's winner take all. If you win, I cut you a check," he says holding up his checkbook. "If I win, your firm never sends me another bill."

Sam sits in disbelief. Michael is serious. Sam sizes up his much smaller counterpart and figures he'll win easily. People sitting nearby assume the two men are friends having some fun as they remove their suit jackets, clear aside their place-settings and lock hands.

In fewer than 15 seconds, it's the back of Sam's hand that smacks the table first. Michael smiles triumphantly. Sam sighs, managing a smile of respect. His lunch partner has caught him off-guard, changing the traditional fee-paying game in a radical way, with new rules that clearly favored Michael's strengths and interests, not Sam's.[6]

Michael, and a Brazilian housewife you're about to meet, are both master rule-changers.

Story: Women Rule

Lucia Pacifico's monthly budget has always been tight, but now she wants to pull her hair out as she moves frantically through the aisles at her local supermarket. She cannot find *any* meat that's affordable. The prices this month are ten times what they were last month and her husband's salary has only gone up slightly.

How am I ever going to feed my family, she mumbles, looking for something for supper.

It's the mid-1980s. Inflation is pounding Brazil and despite Lucia's best laid plans, prices of basic supplies like bread, butter, milk, meat and toilet paper continue to spiral out of control, up 4,000% from the year before.

What's frustrating is that none of this is her fault as "dona de casa"—a Portuguese phrase used to describe a highly respected "housewife"—but Lucia *feels* responsible since it's her job to oversee her family's budget and put meals on the table.

She doesn't know exactly who to blame. Everyone is suffering. Like her, millions of Brazilian housewives are hunkered down, waiting for an end to this economic misery, while trying to make ends meet every day.

Lucia Pacifico decides that she's had enough. If no one else is doing anything to make things better, why can't she at least try?

The school teacher and mother is no longer willing to let the whims of the price-setters at the major supermarket chains upset her family's daily existence. She wants to change the rules of the game so there's greater certainty. She'll start by gathering together a small group of other concerned women.

Lucia Pacifico's last name means *peaceful.* "Despite my surname," she says, "I am a real fighter."[7] This will become obvious as more housewives unite behind her.

With her outgoing personality, Lucia begins lobbying the politicians drafting Brazil's new constitution, laws and regulations following two decades of military rule. She corners legislators to talk about the interests of housewives, promising them that women voters will look favorably on any politician helping to create rules that promote these interests. She uses a mixture of charm and aggressive tactics to be heard, sometimes slipping past security and barging uninvited into high-level meetings. The media love her fearless challenges to the chaotic status quo.

Lucia quickly becomes a national figure in Brazil. Her growing influence leads to unique laws and regulations being approved, reflecting the concerns and needs she has voiced to government representatives. Among other innovations, Brazil's new consumer-protection code will allow for pricing agreements between retailers and citizen groups.

On behalf of housewives everywhere, Lucia Pacifico now takes the reins in negotiations with giant retailers, haggling over prices.

No retailer can be forced to enter into any agreement, but once an agreement is reached, it is binding by law. When a large group of supermarkets agrees to fixed prices for 30 to 60 days, other retailers follow suit so they won't be punished by consumers. Participating retailers put up signs trumpeting their compliance with the latest agreement.

The new rules, where none existed before, clearly weaken the power of giant retailers. No longer can they change prices on a daily basis to meet their own interests, maintaining profit margins at the expense of shoppers.

Over time, Lucia's efforts become highly organized, with members of a national housewives' association paying annual dues to support price surveys, lectures on household budgets and simple operations located in offices donated by a municipality. These women don't fundamentally change the turbulent Brazilian economy, but they do reduce the impact of huge price swings.

On occasion, some retailers try to lower the quality or quantity of a product while sticking to an agreed price, but this maneuver is covered by the nation's regulations. Lucia and her team uncover such a scheme in 2001. Those giants who don't immediately adjust their ways are hit with hefty fines by the government.

In December 2002, as Lucia negotiates with Adilson Rodrigues, the head of a big supermarket group, Rodrigues asks for a "force majeure" clause which will allow his group to break from agreed prices under extreme circumstances. "Forget it," Lucia tells Rodrigues, because this type of clause will undermine the very purpose of their agreement. He can only shake his head and relent, knowing Lucia—a grandmother now—has helped forge the rules for how business is to be conducted in their country.

CHANGE HOW THE GAME IS PLAYED

Create new standards of play that better meet your interests, weakening your giant so you can get what you want.

Lucia Pacifico successfully took on major retailers operating in Brazil, including Wal-Mart and France's Carrefour Group, by influencing legislative authorities—formal Coercers with different interests than her giants—to develop new laws and regulations.

My client Michael, the arm-wrestler, didn't have to go to a higher legal authority for permission to introduce new rules into his fee negotiations. He just had to convince his giant Controller, Sam, that changing the rules was a good idea, all things considered.

In changing the way the game is played, you can change specific rules, or referees, and sometimes ignore the rules altogether:

- **Change the game by changing the rules.** As we've seen, you can create new rules yourself or influence new rules being developed by others. One cable entrepreneur I worked with, Richard Contardi, went to a US senator's sister he'd met a few times socially to see if she could help him. As a Connector, she lands Richard a meeting with the senator so he can make his case for a minor but critical revision to cable industry regulations. The meeting is a success, with the senator later spearheading broad industry changes. These changes include a new regulation that will enable Richard to bring more giant bidders to the table as he auctions off his cable business, weakening the grip of one giant buyer who would have been the only bidder had the changes not been made.[8] In other situations, you may have to break old rules first to draw attention to the need for new rules that will rein in your giant, though as we'll see shortly, this approach can exact a personal toll.

- **Change the game by changing referees.** While the specific rules of the game may be fine, the people overseeing them or applying them might not be. A graphic artist, Anand R. Mani, had the clothier Giorgio Armani abruptly demand that he hand over his personal domain—ARMani.com—because his first two initials and last name overlap with Armani's brand name. The dispute goes to WIPO, the World Intellectual Property Organization. After a little digging, Anand is shocked to discover the arbitrator selected by WIPO to hear his case is Milan-based, with strong ties to Armani. He hires a lawyer as a Counselor, who urges WIPO to appoint a new referee, wisely arguing any perception of bias could hurt WIPO's credibility, instead of arguing the arbitrator *is* biased, which would be interpreted as an attack and be less persuasive. He gets another arbitrator—and wins his case. Vindicated, he tells me he then sold his domain to Armani for an undisclosed amount that made changing referees worthwhile. If a judge, arbitrator or mediator does not meet your interests, get another formal Coercer who does.

- **Change the game by ignoring the rules.** If you cannot penetrate a giant's castle and access giants like you're supposed to, consider ignoring the rules. One small Internet phone service provider can't get into a giant's head office where corporate policy dictates they go for a *yes* or *no* on any service offerings. Instead, salesperson Stephanie Noll decides she'll start quietly at a division where a college friend can act as a Connector, introducing her to the division head, Pieter Stike. Pieter likes Stephanie's Internet service, pilots it, and then as a Convincer, gently recommends it to his head office for corporate-wide implementation. Head office, as the Controller, doesn't appreciate being bypassed, but it respects Pieter and realizes Stephanie's solution makes sense. Her well-targeted, outside-inside approach works, making her giant smaller and easier to influence.[9]

As vulnerable smaller players, *how* we go about trying to change the game matters. *How* we ignore rules, *how* we break rules, *how* we introduce new rules or *how* we bring in different referees can be critical.

We'll conclude with two more examples of Size Wizards using new standards of play to weaken their giants, just as Lucia Pacifico and Richard Contardi did. In the first case, notice *how* Carmen Gonzalez doesn't try to change the rules of the giant modeling industry by going directly to her giant. In our second short story, see *how* Rosa Parks acts—even when she's breaking the law.

MODELING CHANGE. Carmen Gonzalez battles eating disorders in Spain, but her group's impact could soon extend around the world.

Working for Spain's Anorexia and Bulimia Association in 2006, Carmen and her colleagues convince Madrid's regional government to pursue a weight rule for models at a major fashion show there. The government, acting as a Coercer, uses its influence as a sponsor of *Madrid's Fashion Week*. Under pressure, show organizers agree. Their models will now need to meet weight requirements relative to their height.

The goal is to encourage young women watching the show or seeing pictures of it afterward to take away a positive and realistic image of what a healthy body looks like, rather than imitating waif-like models who may suffer from anorexia or bulimia.

Thirty percent of the models who apply to the Madrid show are turned away because they're too thin. Despite being the first show to screen its models this way, *Madrid's Fashion Week* is warned to stay vigilant and not give into pressures from giant modeling agencies seeking to undermine the new rule in the future: "If they don't go along with it, the next step is to seek legislation, just like with tobacco," maintains Carmen.[10] Other cities say they may follow Madrid's lead.

THE BUS. It's 1955 in Montgomery, Alabama. Blacks sit at the back of the bus, whites at the front, and if there's any doubt as to who should go where, a white driver decides.

Rosa Parks is heading home from work after a long day. She sits down on the bus to rest. The driver orders her to move so a white person can take her place. The 42-year-old African American department store worker is a savvy, active member of the National Association for the Advancement of Colored People—the NAACP. She decides it's finally time to challenge the rules. Rosa calmly refuses to move from her seat. She is arrested.

The NAACP jumps on her case as a rallying cry. Blacks unite, saying they won't use public buses in Montgomery until things change. With Rosa as a well-spoken, peaceful rule-breaker, and with the help of a then unknown pastor named Martin Luther King Jr., the movement gains momentum. Her lawyer takes the issue of racial segregation all the way to the Supreme Court of the United States, the ultimate formal Coercer. A little more than a year after Rosa's arrest, her nation's highest court outlaws public bus segregation in the state of Alabama—and across the rest of the country.

Rosa is free to sit wherever she wants. The world is aware of how poorly American blacks are treated. And the previously unknown pastor is heading a national civil rights movement that will one day see every state promise equality for all.

Finding work suddenly becomes harder for Rosa, given her high profile as a rule-breaker. But it could be worse. Other protestors such as King have their homes bombed.

Decades later, Rosa had no regrets about her decision to break the rules. "I didn't hesitate to do so because I felt we had endured that too long," she said. "The more we gave in, the more we complied with that kind of treatment, the more oppressive it became." [11]

Change the way the game is played—change rules or referees, or just ignore the rules.

WEAR THEIR TEAM JERSEY

Sometimes, it makes sense to put on your giant's team uniform if you can't get what you want any other way.

This doesn't mean you defect to the other side and become a full-fledged supporter of your giant. You just have to join your giant long enough to influence things from the inside, later removing your jersey if, or when, it no longer fits.

STORY: AN INVESTOR'S BEEF

If you've ever been frustrated by a poor performing investment in a public corporation, feeling powerless to do anything but sell or hang in until you've lost even more money, you'll like Guy Adams and his moxie.

It's 2001. Guy is a tiny shareholder in Lone Star Steak & Saloon Inc., a publicly listed chain based in Wichita, Kansas, owner of hundreds of restaurants nationwide. The middle-aged, recently divorced investor and businessman holds just 1,100 shares out of millions issued, but the size of his shareholdings doesn't matter to him. This is about the principle of accountability. Guy is mad. He wants changes made at Lone Star.

The corporation's CEO and his executive team keep granting themselves big raises and stock options, even though the restaurant chain's profits and share price have been in freefall for years. If you'd put $100 into Lone Star stock back in 1995, your investment was worth only $22 at the end of 2000. On average, that same investment would be worth $150 if you'd put your money into similar chains.

Rather than fight for change as an outsider, Guy decides to try joining the corporation's board. The person who is coming up for re-election next, and who Guy will be aiming to replace, is none other than Lone Star's CEO and board chair—James Coulter. Coulter also happens to be one of the company's founders and its largest shareholder.

Guy is a savvy investor of reasonable means, but he's never done anything like this. He formally notifies the company of his intent to run, which then allows him to contact other Lone Star investors—expressing his concerns about management's performance, proposing solutions and asking them to support his election at their annual meeting.[12] Most shareholders won't attend this meeting, so Guy asks people to send in a signed proxy, confirming his authority to act on their behalf. He can then vote for himself.

His giant isn't impressed. Lone Star argues that Guy has no experience on boards or in the restaurant industry, saying he "would disrupt, if not destroy" the corporation's progress.[13] It launches a suit against Guy.

The board claims Guy is making false and misleading disclosures in his proxy battle and that he is being inappropriately funded by an unnamed outside source. The court dismisses the suit, ruling that Guy is acting within his rights and that there is no proof of any outside funding source. However, it instructs Guy to correct some of the past statements he has made to shareholders, which he does.

A big shareholder lines up behind Guy. CALPERS—the California Public Employees' Retirement System—supports his candidacy, a major coup. Ted White from CALPERS describes the board's efforts to entrench itself and undermine Guy as "shameful." [14]

Guy wins his board seat, removing stunned board chair James Coulter from his. Coulter gets to stay on as CEO though. The other board members give Guy the cold shoulder, excluding him from some of their committees and informal meetings. The pint-sized shareholder describes board meetings as "tense" because he asks a lot of questions and challenges the board, but Guy soldiers on.

Now that he's on the *inside* of his giant, with a mandate from shareholders outside, Guy exerts his influence. Unmerited hikes in management's compensation are no longer sought or approved. The board announces several governance changes that will directly affect how much money Lone Star's executives can earn. One change boosts the number of board seats from five to eight, with the addition of three outside members who are not part of management. Another change ensures the CEO's role is permanently separated from that of the board chair, who can then provide true oversight. The board also agrees to hire an independent advisor to guide Lone Star in its overall strategic planning. [15]

With his main campaign pledges met, Guy agrees to resign from the board just a year after his election. Sticking around probably wouldn't be much fun anyway, given his frosty relations with board members and the corporation's CEO.

By becoming part of his giant, Guy makes his giant more accountable— and more valuable. Lone Star's stock price rises 140% during the time he is involved, meaning his 1,100 shares are now worth roughly $15,000 more than they were before he got mad.

"I'm proud of what I did at Lone Star," Guy says. "I think I showed what can happen when shareholders stand up and insist on better performance from the executives managing the companies they've invested in." [16]

Wear Their Team Jersey

One or more benefits drive Size Wizards to join their giants rather than stay on the outside looking in:

- **Gain insider influence.** You can favorably change your giant's perspectives and actions once on the inside by better influencing Controllers as a Convincer, and by becoming a Controller yourself, actually making decisions or casting votes. This was Guy Adams' reasoning in becoming a board member at Lone Star.

- **Access giant resources and insights.** You gain access to some of your giant's resources and insights to help get what you want. A far-sighted entrepreneur may decide he or she is better off learning an industry while receiving a steady paycheck from a giant—before leaving to start up a niche venture to partner or compete with this giant.

- **Tip their boat.** You can hurt your giant's chances of getting what it wants by the very fact you join their team. In Canada, where bank mergers are frowned on, the announced merging of two big banks into one Goliath in the late 1990s looked like it might be ignored by the government as an exception. A third bank, TD, wasn't convinced mergers met its interests. It preferred to grow organically, but worried the new Goliath would hurt it competitively. What to do? Rather than oppose the merger with a small voice, TD loudly proclaimed that it, too, had plans to merge with another bank. The government reacted, protecting consumers from a growing trend: it declared *no* mergers would be approved. TD got what it first wanted—no mergers—by briefly throwing on the same jersey as its Goliath.[17]

Here are two final short stories to show us how Size Wizards in totally different contexts can move inside their giants and get better results.

NUCLEAR POWER. Frustrated with New Zealand's government, a woman in her early twenties runs for national office, hoping to influence her giant from the inside.

At the age of 23, Marilyn Waring wins her seat in 1975, becoming New Zealand's youngest parliamentarian ever. Plans for a career as a classical musician are set aside as she prepares to shake up New Zealand's political establishment, especially on issues that matter most to women.

Marilyn isn't different just because of her age. She's only the fifteenth woman in her nation's history to be elected nationally. Sitting in parliament for the first time, looking around at dozens of much older, highly experienced male politicians is daunting. But in addition to her age and gender, Marilyn can be pretty sure she is the only lesbian in the chamber. On top of this, her politics are left-leaning, even though she has just won a seat as a member of the governing, right-leaning National Party.[18]

In this atmosphere, Marilyn maintains her balance by remembering what matters to her. On her wall, she places an inspiring quote, which reads: "Risk—risk anything. Care no more for the opinions of others, for those voices. Do the thing hardest on earth for you to do. Act for yourself. Face the truth." [19]

Marilyn's honesty, eloquence and irreverence will get her through. In the chamber, when others talk nonsense, she sits knitting. Predictably, she butts heads with her party's main Controller, Prime Minister Robert Muldoon. Yet this doesn't stop her from taking on high-profile roles in the years ahead, influencing important decisions as she chairs committees and leverages government resources to pursue her interests in areas such as disarmament.

In 1984, Muldoon insists that American nuclear-armed or powered ships be allowed into New Zealand's harbors. Marilyn is passionately opposed to the world's nuclear build-up and this intrusion into her nation's waters. She makes it clear that she will not support her government's position. Her defection on the issue leads a visibly upset Muldoon to go on television and call a snap election, which the opposition Labour Party will win.

The new government declares the country a nuclear-free zone, which it remains today.

After influencing her giant as an insider, then toppling it, Marilyn Waring leaves politics to negotiate with giants globally—over human rights for women.

NOT OUR SCHOOL. Pam MacKenzie and Joel Haslam love Elmdale, their daughter Sydney's public primary school. It has a strong curriculum, excellent sports, great art programs, caring teachers, large grounds and it's minutes from their home in Ottawa, Canada.

In June 2000, the local school board announces that Elmdale is slated for closure.

Four other urban schools across the city are also targeted because of outdated facilities, declining enrollment trends and the need for more schools in fast-growing suburban areas. The 12 board trustees say they'll make their final closure decisions in the fall.

Pam MacKenzie swings into action, coordinating with other Elmdale parents who are outraged. As television producers, Pam and her husband make a 15-minute video, showcasing Elmdale for trustees. Another parent is an engineer; he analyzes Elmdale's facilities, presenting a professional, positive assessment. A parent in real estate values the school board's unused land holdings at $24 million, enough money to keep all the schools open. A parent who's a lobbyist gets involved. SOS signs (Save Our Schools) go up across Ottawa. Rallies take place. A letter-writing campaign floods trustee offices.

Finally, it's October. The board votes. A simple majority of the 12 trustees will determine the fate of Elmdale. In a 7 to 5 vote, all five closings are *approved*.

"We were shocked by that vote," says Pam. "We'd worked so hard and so effectively. The chair of our parent committee, Bill Pristanski, told us not to get down. He said we were going to fight another fight." [20]

That next fight involves school board elections. All trustees, one in each of the 12 school zones, are up for re-election in late November. The parents' goal is not just to get the right trustee for Elmdale's zone. To shift the balance of power, Elmdale's parents need two more anti-closure trustees inside their giant. They offer financial and organizational support to candidates anywhere in Ottawa who will oppose the closings. Pam and others raise money to fund their efforts through auctions and donations. They campaign door-to-door for several candidates citywide, licking stamps for them, passing out pamphlets and planning media coverage.

It's Election Day: November 28, 2000. Citizens go to the polls. The result: seven of the newly elected trustees, the majority, are now against any closings. In December, the giant formally reverses its previous decision by a 7-5 vote. Elmdale remains open. Pam and Joel's two younger children,

Madi and Tait, will soon join their sister Sydney at the school, all benefiting from the terrific education their parents negotiated for them.

Wear their team jersey—gain insider influence as a Controller and Convincer, access giant resources and insights, or tip your giant's boat over.

WORSEN THEIR ABILITY TO PLAY WITHOUT YOU

I am 21. I move into a house with an acquaintance. Lumpy, as he's nicknamed, seems like a great guy—until I get my phone bill. I owe $1,200 for calls *he's* made on my line while I was away. I ask him to pay up, but he won't. After I move out, Lumpy ignores me.[21]

Since $1,200 is greater than my net worth at the time, Lumpy becomes my giant. One winter night, I go to his house. He isn't home but his new roommate, Brad, lets me in. As I ponder whether to wait for Lumpy, a terrible thing happens: I become the Grinch who stole Christmas, or more precisely, the Grinch who stole Lumpy's floral sofa ensemble.

Mesmerized by the TV, Brad slips onto the floor as a friend and I nervously take the couch from beneath him. With two couches and a big chair, I head home, smiling crookedly in my youthful exuberance—thinking it won't be long before I get my $1,200. After all, who can ignore a missing living room?

The answer, unfortunately, is Lumpy and Brad.

Lumpy calls me a few weeks later, wondering, "What happened to my stuff?" He doesn't seem too bothered though; apparently, he and Brad enjoy sitting on the rug.

I end up selling the furniture at a garage sale in the spring, recouping maybe $700.

Legalities aside, I'd had the right idea in claiming something from my giant. As smaller players, we can indeed increase our odds of success by making our giant's status quo less comfortable so they'll be more open to compromise in their weakened state.

I just forgot to make sure my giant's rug wasn't as comfortable as his floral couch.

The barons will avoid making the same kind of mistake in their dealings with the King.

STORY: NEGOTIATING MAGNA CARTA

Clouds gather ominously overhead as the King of England leans forward, affixing his green and black wax seal to the parchment.

The tall monarch rises slowly from his chair, smiling as he takes in the dozens of onlookers surrounding him at Runnymede, England. They've gathered in a marshy meadow running along the Thames River, some 20 miles west of London, to witness what they believe is a historic event. *They will be wrong*, King John thinks slyly.

The year is 1215—the day June 15th. The sealed parchment looks a little like the weather: dull and gray. Its meticulous, tiny words and 63 clauses detail an agreement between King John and the nation's barons— an agreement to be known as Magna Carta.[22] This pact guarantees basic rights for British subjects, including rights related to religion, fair trials and traveling freely. It also assures the barons of their rights as significant landowners and taxpayers. If doubts ever arise as to whether the King is administering these rights properly, a committee of 25 barons can now overturn many of his decisions.

Nothing quite like Magna Carta has ever existed before this moment. The deal the King just sealed amounts to Europe's first written constitution, laying out a core set of principles and rules for how the state is to be governed.[23]

Never would I have consented to this if not placed in such a weak position, King John reflects, forcing another smile onto his lips for the benefit of those in attendance. None of them can know his true intentions—not yet. *These lowly barons will pay for this with their lives*, the King re-affirms to himself, politely shaking the hand of another baron.[24]

So how did these barons get exactly what they wanted from their giant, King John, when just a month earlier, in mid-May, such an outcome seemed all but impossible?

Before May 17, 1215, the King's alternative to negotiating with the barons was simply to maintain the status quo, continuing to deny his subjects the rights they had been clamoring for. People viewed King John as a tyrant who had clearly overstretched himself outside England. To drum up the money he needs to win back the lands he's lost through failed wars in western France, the King has become ruthless in his approach to English taxation, tax evaders and other governance matters.

The land-owning barons have borne the brunt of the monarch's fundraising efforts and heavy-handed rule. They plead with King John, asking him to lighten their tax load, stop being such a brute and grant his people reasonable rights. But he won't concede much. He doesn't need to. The King's power base across the country is not impregnable, but it's strong enough that he's vowed never to give in to the barons and their demands.

The barons are led by Robert FitzWalter, a man who resents the King's policies and hates him for a long-standing personal affront. *This so-called King of royal blood is nothing but a common criminal! He tried to rape our daughter, and for that, he'll pay dearly,* Robert swears to his wife.

What Robert does next will tip the balance of power dramatically in negotiations with the King. On May 17th, he takes something so valuable from King John that the monarch can no longer ignore the barons. The King's nemesis pockets one of the world's oldest and most precious jewels: the City of London.

In 1215, the walled city, with its 75,000 inhabitants, is already one of northwestern Europe's two greatest cities—Paris being the other. London is alive with economic activity, goods from around the world, and theater. Where previous kings have often had their courts and treasury operations based far from London, King John depends on the city and its surrounding area as a platform for reigning over his empire as a whole.

But Robert FitzWalter is Lord of Baynard Castle, one of the city's most prestigious bastions, located along the western edge of London's walled perimeter. Being an insider helps Robert persuade London's leaders and citizens that he holds their interests close to his heart. When the city finally agrees to open its gates and let Robert's followers take over its streets and defenses, Magna Carta suddenly looks like a bold possibility.

King John is furious when he discovers his urban jewel has been stolen from underneath his nose. What the barons have done is preposterous— but smart. Rather than try to defeat the King's forces nationwide, they've focused their efforts in the one area they believe they can take and hold, gaining the most leverage possible in a short amount of time.

After London's fall, negotiators shuttle back and forth between the barons and the monarch, eventually reaching agreement on the articles contained in Magna Carta. Two of these articles, 12 and 13, refer specifically to London, promising it certain liberties and protections—a reward for allowing the barons to claim it and keep it from the King.

At Runnymede on June 15th, as the barons shake hands with their King in celebration of Magna Carta, they suspect, correctly, that he's already plotting how to tear up their agreement, despite his feigned acceptance of its terms. As a precaution, the barons will hang onto London, until they can be absolutely sure their giant remains true to his word.

In the summer months of 1215, the King does keep many of his promises—but only as he waits for his opportunity to strike. When the time is right, he asks the Pope to annul Magna Carta, and he seeks his revenge. He goes on to win a number of impressive military victories against the barons during the following year, but not in London. The barons continue to control the city.

King John never gets the chance to reclaim his jewel. The monarch dies of dysentery in October 1216, over-indulged in food and wine.

Those in the King's royal circle quickly proclaim his young son to be the nation's new monarch. Among the first things nine-year-old King Henry III will do: re-affirm and re-issue Magna Carta in a slightly modified version, one his advisors can live with.

The barons decide that it is now safe to hand back London. They have what they were after—Magna Carta—which will guide their nation for the foreseeable future.

Different versions of King John's acknowledgement of his people's fundamental rights and freedoms are posted in taverns and churches across England, and will be for centuries to come.[25] A number of these kingly commitments are translated into formal laws. New nations such as America will even draft their own constitutions based on the agreement's main tenets.

WORSEN THEIR ABILITY TO PLAY WITHOUT YOU

Magna Carta serves as a lasting reminder that countless famous documents are not just statements drawn up out of thin air by strong leaders who suddenly come to see what's right.

Often, these hallowed documents, including constitutions, charters, laws and declarations, are the most visible and enduring result of negotiations between giants and smaller players. Robert FitzWalter and many other Size Wizards like him had to take something from their giants in order to gain their full attention at the negotiation table.

By taking London, the barons not only got their hands on something the King wanted back, they also seized a command and control center from King John that made it harder for the monarch to seek his revenge.

There are two main ways the Size Wizards worsen their giant's ability to play without them, helping to level the playing field:

- **Claim one of your giant's important assets**. Occupying a giant's physical infrastructure is against the law, but in the case of the barons, breaking the law was justified given the context. Other ways to claim giant assets include going after: their reputation; their most coveted information; their money through well-timed lawsuits; or their time by tying them up in a deal for so long that walking away isn't attractive.

- **Remove valuable players from their team.** Taking players off a giant's core team, or extended team, can weaken a giant's performance and get you what you want. Before winning Congress in 2006, Democrats drew attention to the extreme tactics used by President Bush's main strategist, Karl Rove, as he undermined Republican adversaries—rendering Rove less effective and ultimately leading to his departure. At times, giant defectors may join you: a small company hires an expert away from its giant, quickly landing an outsourcing contract because its giant can no longer perform on its own. Defectors can also act as Cracks, supplying vital information: when Mississippi successfully went after the tobacco industry for health damages in the 1990s, it started by getting Liggett—the most financially vulnerable company—to turn on other companies inside the giant industry, revealing how they'd all hidden or misrepresented the dangers of smoking.[26] Finally, you can remove someone from a giant's alternatives: a banker discovers a male colleague could be offered the job she's after at a giant employer, so she tells her colleague about another job better suited to his strengths, which he gets, leaving her as her giant's best—and only—choice.

Here are two more short stories that show how giants can be weakened by losing assets from their physical infrastructure and people from their Hidden Infrastructure.

GAINING A PLATFORM. Four determined climbers pull themselves toward the top of a hulking metal structure located in the middle of deadly cold and choppy waters. Their sneak attack is executed with military precision, catching one of the world's largest corporations completely off-guard.

It's April 1995. The structure being invaded is the Brent Spar oil platform in the North Sea near Scotland. A recent deal between the British government and Shell Oil gives the company permission to sink the abandoned platform and its dirty containers, which were once used to store drilled oil from the sea before tankers came to collect it.[27]

Shell hopes to sink the structure hastily. Europe's environment ministers are meeting in early June to discuss limiting the discharge of hazardous materials into the North Atlantic waters between Britain and the continent. The giant corporation has dozens of platforms to discard in the decades ahead and wants to set the right precedent, avoiding costly procedures that it says aren't justified by the environmental risks. Shell also insists that dismantling the platforms, instead of sinking them, would be dangerous work.

The climbers now aboard the Brent Spar belong to the Greenpeace environmental group. Their message is simple: the seas should not be used as a dumping ground for waste just because an oil platform no longer serves Shell's financial interests.

Occupying the isolated platform proves effective for many reasons. The act targets the object of the protestors' concerns, no one is there to protect the platform, and the visual contrast of tiny climbers scaling the huge structure is too good for the media to pass up.

Journalists board the Brent Spar to experience the takeover first-hand. Greenpeace supplies them and others with a constant stream of information, even setting up a website with images and diaries from the occupiers. The organization releases a report detailing the ecological cost of platform disposals while proposing other options it says are safe, cost-efficient and environmentally friendly.[28]

Shell struggles to respond. The Dutch-Anglo giant splits its decision-making between Holland and Britain. Slowing it further, it has a lot to think about: next steps; potential precedents for its interests around the globe; how consumers and shareholders will view its reaction; the impact of the events on its more than $100 billion in annual sales; and what any decision might do to its share price.

Meanwhile, Greenpeace responds nimbly to the early success of its takeover by pouring more money, people, publicity, lobbying and legal efforts into the Brent Spar project. Its sea vessel, the *Moby Dick*, hovers around the oil platform, capturing video and letting the world know whenever Shell tries to dislodge the protestors or begins making moves to sink the platform. With the high-profile takeover triggering widespread awareness of the Brent Spar situation, many European consumers begin to express their concerns about Shell's plans by staying away from its gas stations.[29]

At the North Sea Conference in June, Greenpeace releases a confidential Shell-sponsored report, presumably leaked to it by a sympathetic Crack inside its giant. The report says the Brent Spar can be disposed on land at a much lower cost than Shell has indicated publicly. The corporation maintains the report isn't complete in its cost assessment.

On June 20, 1995, Shell announces it will not sink the Brent Spar. The giant acknowledges too many consumers and nations have voiced concerns about dumping the platform.

In due course, the Brent Spar will be torn apart, recycled and used to build the foundations of a new ferry terminal. Shell estimates the cost of this re-usage at close to 45 million pounds, about ten times the cost of sinking the platform.[30]

In 1998, the governments of the north east Atlantic region—including Britain, Germany, Norway and Sweden—come together as formal Coercers to ban the dumping of steel-built oil installations. Greenpeace oil and gas expert Jan Rispens is delighted with the final outcome: "It protects the ocean, it creates jobs, and it reuses the material." [31]

PAPER LION. Kevin Thomas is stunned by what lies around him.

When the 20-year-old medical volunteer agreed to help fight an outbreak of tuberculosis in a remote northern Canadian Native community in 1988, he didn't expect such squalor. No running water, no plumbing, and the homes look broken, with cold air rushing through them. It's obvious to Kevin that the health of Lubicon Cree band members has deteriorated with their surroundings.

Life changed when oil and gas were discovered here a decade earlier. As roads arrived, oil pumps sprouted up and wildlife left, ruining traditional hunting grounds. Welfare rates jumped from 5% to 85% among the Lubicon band's 500 members.

Kevin learns the situation is going to worsen. Daishowa, a giant Japanese pulp and paper corporation, has paid the provincial government for the right to harvest logs in this 6,000-square-mile area. The Lubicon have asked Daishowa not to log until their land claims are settled with the provincial and federal governments. Band members say that losing their trees would wipe them out. The Japanese Goliath listens, but begins to cut wood anyway. Band protests accomplish nothing.

Through an aboriginal rights group, Kevin Thomas meets two young men, Stephen Kenda and Ed Bianchi, who've also experienced the poverty of the Lubicon first-hand. They establish Friends of the Lubicon in Toronto, Ontario—thousands of miles east of where the Lubicon live—but smack in the heartland of Canadian consumerism.

The Friends don't have the means to run costly media campaigns, so they raise money through baking and garage sales while keeping their influence strategies just as simple. They write letters to Daishowa's main buyers— companies such as Pizza Pizza, Woolworth's, Country Style Donuts and Roots—explaining their concerns and urging them to stop buying. These buyers aren't formally part of Daishowa, but they're important members of its extended team, since they contribute millions of dollars annually to its coffers by purchasing the giant's paper bags and cardboard boxes.

For some buyers, the first letter is all it takes. They leave the giant's team. Other buyers receive follow-up letters threatening to picket their stores, which causes them to defect. "I found the letters intimidating and the risk was not acceptable for our franchise holders," says an executive vice-president from Country Style Donuts.[32]

The protestors widen their influence net, launching a public boycott in Ontario. They focus their limited resources by organizing concerned citizens to picket only two of the higher profile companies, Pizza Pizza and Woolworth's. This is called a secondary picket because it's not aimed at the pulp and paper mills of the giant manufacturer, it's pointed at the busy retail stores of Daishowa's buyers.

Pizza Pizza's own buyers are the masses, consumers more easily reached and open to influence in this situation than a difficult-to-access giant in Japan. These consumers are also members of the giant's extended team. If they stop buying products from corporations using the controversial paper products, Daishowa will feel the pressure on its bottom line—and may give in.

Consumers react as hoped, pressuring those selling to them. Pizza Pizza and Woolworth's change their paper suppliers. In the end, the Friends are so effective in removing players from their giant's team, more than 40 companies in all, that Daishowa lashes out at them. It goes after Kevin, Ed and Stephen, suing them personally, saying it has lost $14 million in sales because of what it claims is an illegal pressure tactic: a secondary picket. The Japanese giant gets a court to issue a temporary injunction against the retail picketing.

The Friends turn to the Sierra Legal Defense Fund, a non-profit Counselor providing free legal services to environmental groups. With its support, the three men battle their giant in court. They argue picketing at the retail level is one of the only ways smaller, disadvantaged players can be heard when mass media campaigns are unaffordable.

An Ontario judge rules their secondary picketing is legal.[33] He says the situation involves "speech concerning public affairs" and deserves "respect, protection and a forum." But he prohibits the Friends from saying things he deems to be grossly unfair and defamatory, such as describing Daishowa's activities as "genocide." [34]

The Friends can continue their campaign if they play by the judge's rules. But Daishowa knows the game is already over. It can't afford to keep losing valuable buyers from its side. The giant relents, agreeing not to log on the land claimed by the Lubicon Cree.[35] It drops its suit against Kevin, Ed and Stephen. They in turn agree to end their boycott.

"What really made a difference was our stubborn persistence, as well as the times we'd get a letter from a company saying it was joining the boycott," says Ed Bianchi. "But there was no thunderous moment, just a lot of hard work." [36]

Worsen their ability to play without you—claim one of your giant's significant assets or remove valuable players from their team.

HAZARDS TO AVOID

As you make your giant smaller and weaker, here are some traps to sidestep:

Assuming *you* must bring out the rulebook. Sometimes, if anyone is going to do the right thing and blow the whistle on your giant, it has to be you. Other times, to protect against counterattacks, or to be more credible and influential, think about sending information confidentially or anonymously to one of your helpers. You'll probably want to choose people outside your direct chain of command, and only those likely to share your interest in seeing certain rules followed. Mark Felt of the FBI, "Deep Throat," chose *The Washington Post*'s Bob Woodward—who worked closely with Carl Bernstein—to blow the whistle on President Nixon and his team. As an insider, Felt trusted Woodward and knew the journalist would share his interest in slowly and credibly unveiling misdeeds in Nixon's Administration, without jeopardizing Felt's reputation or safety.

Resorting to violence to change the game. Violent acts limit the breadth of your support, often alienating essential helpers. Rosa Parks and Martin Luther King Jr. validated the approaches of India's Mahatma Gandhi who helped his nation to independence through non-violent non-cooperation. When British troops used violence against the masses in India, British voters became increasingly uncomfortable with their giant nation's tactics in the colony, ultimately giving Gandhi what he wanted. In rare situations, violence may be appropriate for defensive purposes. Even Gandhi ruefully admitted that stopping aggression by someone like Hitler might not be possible without force.[37]

Acting inappropriately as an insider. If you put on a giant's jersey, you can't share confidential information gained as an insider with others outside your giant organization; breaking ranks is always an option, but you risk undermining yourself and your cause. Similarly, once inside, you'll want to focus on your main targets for change rather than risking your credibility and influence by standing firm on less important matters, including how you dress: New Zealand's Marilyn Waring didn't revel in compromises, but as a young woman, she wore more conservative clothes once in government and did not dye her hair three different colors—until she'd left public life.

Being naïve when you take assets or people from your giant. The Friends of the Lubicon story ended with the Friends getting what they wanted for the Lubicon Cree. Before this success, however, came mind-numbing stress when their giant caught them totally off-guard with its lawsuit. The more you think about giant influence as you would a chessboard, the more you'll anticipate your giant's next moves, preparing to counter them or choosing safer moves. Right after the barons angered King John by taking his capital city, it wasn't a coincidence they found themselves safely on the other side of London's massive walls. When Greenpeace claimed the Brent Spar, it always had cameras nearby to capture giant moves or counter-attacks, holding Shell accountable to a world audience.

FINAL THOUGHTS

To make your giant smaller and weaker, become a detective like marina developer Linda Cramer, figuring out what can throw your giant off balance. If the existing rulebook isn't helpful, remember how Lucia Pacifico changed pricing rules in Brazil. If you're frustrated as an outsider, follow the lead of investor Guy Adams, going inside your giant to weaken its resistance. Or seek inspiration from Baron Robert FitzWalter, making it hard for your giant to ignore you by claiming something they value.

Prepare for success. If you're feeling things are beyond your control and there's no room for negotiation, that's probably how your giant wants you to feel—and may be the signal that it's time to reduce their size and strength. In these situations, ask yourself: 1) Are any relevant rules being ignored? Where can you research standards and a giant's compliance with them? Which of your helpers might lend a hand? 2) As you consider ignoring certain rules, changing a game's rules, or changing referees, which of these approaches, if any, makes the most sense? And again, who might help out? 3) If you were to join your giant, how would you do so, or is someone else on your team a better candidate to become an insider? 4) Which players can you remove from your giant's team, or which assets—including their time, money, reputation and information?

Follow these broad steps to make them smaller and weaker. If you can credibly threaten to undermine your giant's size and strength without having to act, and without tipping off your giant so they can defend themselves, all the better. You'll save yourself time, effort, risk and hassles. If you do have to act, no one can advise you to violate the law as part of your strategy. As we've seen, however, smaller players who break the law raise their odds of success by ensuring that the broader context favors them, no one is hurt, nothing is damaged and standards beyond the law support their efforts. As Rosa Parks battled segregation, one of the fundamental standards that worked in her favor came from America's own Declaration of Independence: *All men are created equal.*

Find weakness in strength. Putting yourself in your giant's shoes is incredibly useful for understanding their interests, especially their biggest concerns and related vulnerabilities. In scanning a Goliath's mental make-up, physical assets or Hidden Infrastructure, it's worth noting that their greatest vulnerabilities often lie on the flip-side of their greatest strengths. One of Microsoft's big strengths: its monopoly on operating systems. One of its big weaknesses: this same monopoly, exposing it to justice officials and inhibiting its growth in other areas. One of Martha Stewart's big strengths: uncompromising attention to detail in the pursuit of perfection. One of her big weaknesses: an inability to overlook minor imperfections—in her stock portfolio, for example.

4

LEVEL THE PLAYING FIELD: MAKE YOURSELF BIGGER AND STRONGER

Even things up by maximizing your size and clout in unique ways.

JESSE RASCH'S CREDIT CARDS ARE MAXED OUT and the start-up he's funding could disintegrate any moment. Rather than negotiate with a giant to sell his distressed company at the worst possible time, the young entrepreneur decides to get bigger, just as a skinny-framed kid might decide to bulk up through weight lifting.

Instead of weights, Jesse uses a series of deals to bulk up. In the last chapter, we leveled the playing field by making our giants smaller and weaker. Now, we'll pursue more even-handed negotiations by increasing our size, strength and influence as smaller players. To do this, the Size Wizards apply these approaches:

- They complete a series of smaller deals before getting to their main giant deal.
- They expand their team through coalitions.
- They prepare to walk away to back-up plans.
- They create their own media or hit the mass media to spread their message.
- They take advantage of *their weaknesses* and *their giant's strengths*.

We'll learn the magic of coalition-building as we follow Nelson Mandela's steps to a podium, a prison, and a presidency. We'll see a homeowner dissatisfied with his Internet service take on a big phone company by setting up his own communications venture—in a barn. We'll look over the shoulder of a housewife in the 1850s as she rushes her kids to bed so she can get back to helping end slavery in the United States. We'll feel a consumer's pain when his credit card is taken away by a big bank, and watch him get it back in a startling way.

But first, we'll go to Russia for a quick sniff of vodka, before returning to Jesse Rasch, who is about to string together a stunning sequence of deals that will leave one of America's biggest corporations gasping for air—not once, not twice, but three times.

SEQUENCE YOUR DEALS INSIDE-OUT

In the 1800s, a highly confident, resourceful matchmaker named Olga bets her friend Natasha a bottle of vodka she can get the daughter of oil tycoon John D. Rockefeller to marry Natasha's son, Igor—a strapping young Russian farmer.

"You're on!" says Natasha.

Olga talks to Igor: "How would you like an American wife?" Igor is not interested. "What if she were the daughter of the world's richest man?" Igor is very interested.

The matchmaker heads to Zurich, somehow wrangling her way in to see the chairman of the world's biggest bank. "How would you like a handsome young Russian farmer on your board?" The banker is not interested. "What if he were the son-in-law of Rockefeller?" The banker is very interested.

Olga now crosses the ocean to see Rockefeller. "How would you like a handsome young Russian farmer to marry your daughter Edith?" The businessman is not interested. "What if he sat on the board of the world's biggest bank?" The businessman is very interested.

Finally, Olga rides out to see Edith. "How would you like to marry a man who sits on the board of the world's biggest bank?" Edith is not interested. "What if he were a handsome young Russian farmer?" Edith looks up, a smile spreading across her face.

Olga confirms the marital arrangements, returning to Russia to collect a bottle of vodka from her incredulous friend. Or so the folktale goes.[1]

Our mythical matchmaker knows how to unveil and satisfy important interests. Olga also knows how to begin with the end in mind and organize her deals from start to finish.

That's exactly what Jesse Rasch will do.

STORY: A GOOD CONNECTION

The stress of building a business on the back of his personal credit cards has been brutal, but this is worse.

Some well-funded start-up in New Jersey says it is suing Jesse, claiming he stole their name. *Come on, you've got to be kidding,* Jesse Rasch thinks. Over the past year, the 22-year-old Canadian has put a good part of his meager resources into promoting the brand name "DynamicWeb" to distinguish his website hosting service from others. Now, in early 1998, Jesse faces an agonizing choice: fight to keep this valued brand name, a battle he's sure he can win, or come up with some other name.[2]

In his quest to constantly grow bigger so he can either sell his venture to a giant or take it public, Jesse makes a monumental decision. He'll avoid a costly, time-consuming legal conflict and look into his next best choice for a name: Webhosting.com. The domain has already been claimed. *Rats!* Jesse contacts the owner—who is also based in Toronto, Canada—tells him about his start-up, and asks if he can buy the domain for a reasonable price. They reach a verbal deal. The domain's owner calls back, saying he has another offer. Jesse guarantees he'll hand over $20,000 within a few hours if the domain goes to him. The deal is back on. Jesse scrambles, delivering a certified check just in time.

The domain is his. The sandy-haired, university drop-out smiles broadly, hoping this is the right move, his fingers crossed that the switch from DynamicWeb won't hurt his business too badly. He'll soon have his answer. As people worldwide look for a service to host their small websites and give them simple tools for managing these sites, they search on what they obviously believe is the perfect name for a web hosting service. Within three days of Jesse activating Webhosting.com, it pays for itself through new sales.

Jesse continues to fund his business on his credit cards, often going well past his due dates for making payments. It's a shock then, when a month after launching his new domain, the cash-strapped entrepreneur is offered $1 million for it.

Wow! He pinches himself. Taking this offer would make his mother happier. She's been mad at him ever since he quit McGill University's commerce program: the year before, when his student apartment overflowed with computers storing websites for clients, Jesse figured he and his roommate Michael Apted were on to something (Michael is a minority shareholder in their company, InQuent Inc.). Despite the disappointment he knew he'd be causing his mom, Jesse decided commerce studies could wait—but commerce could not.

As much as he would love to make amends with his mom by accepting this $1 million offer just a year after leaving school, Jesse believes the domain Webhosting.com is worth keeping. Hanging on to it will help his company grow faster, making InQuent Inc. more valuable when he sells all or part of it some day. Jesse turns down the $1 million. The California-based group making the offer can't believe his nerve.

Next, Jesse buys a collection of smaller clients from a giant American player, Frontier Telecommunications. Frontier is not as well placed to service and care for these smaller accounts. The deal reached: Jesse pays smaller amounts upfront for these accounts from his steadily mounting cash flow, and commits to making additional payments to Frontier contingent on how profitable his new clients prove to be.

A year later, in 1999, with InQuent Inc. considerably bigger and more credible in the hosting industry, Jesse is approached by various giant telephone, cable and Internet providers. They want to use InQuent Inc.'s technologies but label and brand them as their own when they service their smaller clients directly, with InQuent Inc. taking a slice of the revenues in return. Jesse won't be able to increase the profile of his brand this way or make as much money off each smaller client. However, if he resists, he believes these Goliaths—companies such as KPN Telecom, Bell Canada, and Comcast—will use one of his competitors as an alternative to him.

They might even put him out of business. So he says *yes* to these client deals, further boosting the size and strength of InQuent Inc.

To fold these giant deals into his existing operations, he breaks his company into two distinct brands and divisions under the InQuent Inc. umbrella: the *InQuent* division will do the hidden work, known as private labeling, for Goliaths; the *Webhosting.com* division will continue to sell directly to smaller players through the Webhosting.com domain, with no mention of InQuent Inc. or *InQuent* (I'll always refer to the divisions in italics).

Sales spiral upward. Positive word-of-mouth continues to spread about both divisions. Indirect sales through giants and the *InQuent* division soon surpass direct sales at *Webhosting.com*. As Jesse looks around him, he can't believe that his once struggling start-up isn't only viable, it's exploding, with sales in the millions of dollars.

To keep up, he stays up, working 18-hour days, gulping coffee, and running air conditioners in the company's Toronto offices—mid-winter—to make sure he and his fast-growing team stay focused. "When I shower, I think about the company," Jesse says. "When I eat breakfast, I think about the company. When I eat lunch, I think about the company. I really enjoy doing this—it's not work to me."[3]

In the summer months, during a rare break from work, Jesse catches some people sneaking into a private barbeque where he's hanging out with his staff. It turns out they are venture capitalists, and rather than apologize for their actions, they offer to put $20 million in his bank account the next day for a stake in his business. This extra money might help him grow faster, but InQuent Inc. is becoming self-sufficient. Besides, Jesse doesn't need the expertise or contacts from these venture capitalists, or the headaches that might come with their involvement as demanding shareholders.

Jesse says *no* this time—and on every other occasion that he is offered venture capital.

Along comes SBC Communications. The Texas-based giant decides that like other Goliaths, it could also use *InQuent*'s services on a private label basis. SBC is one of the so-called "Baby Bells" spun off in the 1980s after the US government broke AT&T Corporation into different regional phone players and a separate long distance carrier that retained the AT&T name.[4] Like Rockefeller's Standard Oil, the old AT&T was viewed as too big, dominant and anti-competitive. With deregulation in 1996, SBC began extending its own reach from local phone service into higher growth areas such as long distance, wireless communications and the Internet.

As SBC starts sniffing around, Jesse's partner, Michael Apted—an important contributor—tires of the impact of work on his personal life. He sells most of his shares to Jesse, staying on as a regular employee. With this internal deal completed, Jesse now owns almost all of his company's shares.

In early 2000, SBC has a change of heart. Rather than just become a client, the giant believes that Jesse's company might make a smart strategic investment. It pursues a large ownership stake in the InQuent Inc. umbrella company that holds both the *InQuent* and *Webhosting.com* divisions. SBC's apparently been frustrated in the past by holding an ownership stake below 51% in another web hosting company, which was eventually sold to an SBC competitor despite the Texas giant's opposition. This time, SBC wants control.

Jesse thinks SBC could meet his interests in ways that venture capitalists simply cannot. SBC's role as an institutional Connector, through its investments in more than 20 telecommunications companies around the globe, would give Jesse easy access to new clients. SBC's knowledge and large cash coffers would allow InQuent Inc. to continue growing its operations. Finally, a good part of SBC's investment would go into Jesse's pocket, which does not generally happen in deals with venture capitalists.

Before entering formal negotiations with SBC, Jesse reaches another deal. This one brings an experienced lawyer onto his core team to lead discussions with the giant. Wayne Bigby leaves the Toronto law firm that supports Jesse's company and becomes his lead negotiator and Counselor on a full-time basis. Wayne once worked at Kodak so he is familiar with how Goliaths like SBC think. With him aboard, Jesse stays focused on building his business. In addition, by staying away from the negotiation table himself, Jesse can also be more objective and avoid saying *yes* to anything in the heat of the moment that he might later regret.

If SBC doesn't give him what he wants, Jesse believes his best back-up plan is to sell shares to the public. By early July of 2000, however, he's getting antsy. After six months of talking, the deal with SBC still has not been confirmed. Meanwhile, there's been tumultuous trading in the stock markets with the NASDAQ index losing 25% of its value in one week alone. This threatens Jesse's alternative of a public offering. He wants his deal with SBC to move forward—now.

Despite the turmoil in the markets and Jesse's weakened alternative, SBC's negotiators won't revisit the terms of the deal that has been under discussion for months. They either don't want to bother senior Controllers at SBC who have given them their marching orders, or they don't want to risk undermining an agreement that has eaten up so much of their time and will likely account for a good part of their year-end bonuses.

SBC finally seals the deal. It agrees to pay $118 million cash for a 51% stake, valuing InQuent Inc. at almost a quarter of a billion dollars. As part of the deal, SBC gets to name the company's new CEO and CFO. Jesse will be chairman of the board and appoint the chief operating officer (COO), responsible for running the company on a daily basis. Although Jesse is thrilled to see his "baby" valued so highly, he is not thrilled about giving up control. As a minority shareholder though, he gains certain negotiated rights and vetoes over major issues affecting the company's future—which will prove critical.

Some of the $118 million goes into InQuent Inc.'s operations in return for new shares issued by the company. The difference goes mainly to Jesse himself as payment for a portion of his own shares which he sells to SBC as part of the deal.

Less than a year later, in 2001, the stock markets go into a freefall, the global economy enters a serious decline and growth in the web hosting industry slows dramatically. In spite of all this, SBC continues to hire new people and expand InQuent Inc. The company's costs leap. Revenues stand still. By 2002, InQuent Inc. is losing money. Because SBC successfully demanded 51% of the venture, under accounting rules it must now record the venture's losses in its financial reports to SBC shareholders.

The giant telecom decides to shift oversight of InQuent Inc. from its profitable data-broadband group that made the investment, to a new e-commerce company in the SBC fold, Sterling Commerce, which is losing money. SBC likely does this to dump most of its bad news into one weak group so it can show stock analysts that its *core* operations remain strong and profitable. Also, Sterling has expertise to help turn things around.

But Sterling executives have no loyalty to the deal with Jesse, who says he wants out if nothing is done to improve results at InQuent Inc. Sterling just wants to stop the bleeding from its own profit and loss statements. This distinct goal is about to work against SBC's long-term interests as a whole, while meeting Jesse's interests in an extraordinary way.

A Sterling representative acting for SBC contacts Jesse and tells him that InQuent Inc. needs to be shut down. Sterling intends to write the deal off as a one-time investment loss that won't reflect on its ongoing activities and financials. Jesse urges Sterling not to panic, maintaining InQuent Inc.'s underlying business is still sound. When Sterling insists on a shutdown, Jesse invokes his right to veto actions like this under the terms of his deal, supported by his legal rights in Canada as a minority shareholder. But the entrepreneur says he won't be unreasonable. If SBC's Sterling Commerce unit really wants to kill his company, he'll give it a chance to buy out his remaining 49% stake.

You might argue the first half of the company cost $118 million not even two years before, so the second half should cost somewhere close to that. This would be aggressive given declining results and the poor operating environment. Instead, Jesse offers a discount, which is accepted. Even though Sterling Commerce sees no remaining value in SBC's existing investment, it agrees to pay roughly $75 million dollars to Jesse so giant SBC can finally own 100% of InQuent Inc.—and shut its doors.

The deal is completed and Jesse's company, the one he co-founded in university and nurtured for years, is gone.

Any feelings of emptiness won't last long.

After the entrepreneur has been paid everything due to him, and as SBC prepares to wind down InQuent Inc. in mid-2002, SBC's executives in Texas receive a surprising phone call: it's Jesse, saying he thinks he can save them a lot of money.

Rather than incur all the costs and time involved in overseeing the shutdown of InQuent Inc. from Texas, Jesse asks if his giant would consider selling the whole company back to him so he can deal with it.

SBC executives snort, hesitate, then grudgingly say *yes*.

Jesse pays them a nominal, confidential amount—maybe as little as $1—and assumes the company's liabilities and commitments.

SBC has learned plenty from InQuent Inc. about the hosting industry and its technologies. However, the only truly tangible thing it gets to keep from its dealings with Jesse Rasch is the domain Webhosting.com. At an effective cost in the range of $200 million, it might just be the most expensive domain name in the history of the Internet.

SBC walks away from a company with sales at least two thousand times smaller than its own, despite Jesse's best intentions and pleadings not to give up.

Anyone who was a shareholder of the giant telecom at the time might well wish this story were over, but there's a final deal to be done. This one won't involve SBC.

In late 2002 and early 2003, Jesse nurtures his reclaimed company, reduces some of the bloated costs introduced by SBC, tightens InQuent Inc.'s focus, and starts to rebuild revenues and earnings. By mid-2003, InQuent Inc. returns to health, doing business under the domain name InQuent.com.

As the last step in orchestrating his deftly-sequenced founding, building, selling and repurchasing of InQuent Inc., 27-year-old Jesse Rasch decides the time is right—to sell once more. The exact terms of his 2003 deal with Mallory Ventures in Massachusetts are confidential, but it's safe to assume Jesse makes tens of millions of dollars—again.

SEQUENCE YOUR DEALS INSIDE-OUT

SBC was no doubt aghast over young Jesse growing wealthier and wealthier as the Goliath's seasoned veterans and hordes of MBAs watched the sequencing of their deals go awry.

SBC suffered, as did many corporations who raced into the buying frenzy at the turn of the new millennium. But what may seem like a massive amount of money to smaller players is often pocket change to a giant. The $200 million debacle involving InQuent Inc. represented only 3% of SBC's annual net profits at the time, or approximately the same amount the corporation paid its CEO between 2000 and 2005.[5]

Being a Goliath clearly has its benefits.

So does being a smaller player—if you get your sequencing right.

Had Jesse Rasch re-ordered, re-timed, redone, or *not* done any single deal as negotiated, his financial results would have been much less impressive, and possibly disastrous. His decisions to reject certain deals at critical junctures also made a big difference.

Jesse's carefully sequenced deals over seven years hold important insights for all of us:

- **Start with the end in mind.** Once you have a destination roughed out, you can map backward from there, or forward from where you are now to sequence the growth of your size, strength and influence. Jesse thought ahead strategically to selling all or part of his business, but stayed flexible on his exact plans, quickly adjusting for unforeseen opportunities or hazards in his deal-making. As for our fabled matchmaker Olga, she began by envisioning her ultimate deal with Edith Rockefeller, using tentative "if-then" commitments to favorably link and attract the participation of three key players beforehand, finally confirming her entire string of deals simultaneously. You don't always need to know all your deals in advance, but you should have an idea of what any final deals might look like, while knowing today what your next few deals will bring. Each new deal ought to take advantage of insights from past deals, helping move you toward the end you have in mind.

- **Negotiate inside-out.** Before entering into giant deals, the Size Wizards take care of significant internal negotiations to strengthen themselves. Jesse and his co-founder negotiated a solid working relationship early on, clarifying individual responsibilities, risks, and ownership levels. Michael Apted later cut back in all three of these areas, giving Jesse absolute control over the SBC deals and their proceeds. In other situations, many successful entrepreneurs distribute more ownership to their internal team to raise motivation and performance in the lead-up to a big deal. Either way, lasting success usually comes from negotiating inside-out. In the fundraising world, experts often first raise money for a non-profit organization from its board, employees and even its volunteers, showing strong internal support and sacrifice for a cause, before moving on to make their strengthened case to external donors.

- **Think small.** If you're an entrepreneur, bulking up at the outset through deals with smaller clients can make sense. These deals are often less attractive for bigger players because of the scale of their revenues and operations. Jesse's focus on smaller website clients targeted an untapped market, while also requiring less capital, since one server can supply hundreds of these clients. In contrast, hosting a single large corporation or government can require dozens of expensive servers for just one client. These big clients need more intensive servicing, and often try to use their size and clout to ratchet down monthly fees.

- **Just say *no* to some deals.** The Size Wizards say *no* to those deals that may meet their short-term interests but risk undermining their long-term goals. Before saying *no* to any deal, they return to the basics: does it meet my overall interests now *and* in the future? And is it better than my alternatives? One of SBC's alternatives was another web hosting company whose founder wanted to sell, only to be overruled by his venture capitalists who insisted they needed higher returns. This competitor of Jesse's later collapsed. By saying *no* to venture capital early on, Jesse could later say *yes* to the lucrative SBC deal.

- **Avoid some conflicts, sequence others.** If they have a choice, the Size Wizards say *no* to conflicts that risk disrupting their sequencing and growth, like when Jesse decided to drop the battle over DynamicWeb. If multiple conflicts are unavoidable, the Size Wizards do their best to at least sequence them so they can keep moving forward. A young company once asked me to negotiate a $3 million valuation being offered by a venture capitalist. I encouraged it to decline the offer, which it did. Instead, we tackled—one-by-one—conflicts between the CEO and his co-founders over roles, ownership and pay levels. These conflicts were holding back their ability to create value together. We then spring-boarded into a series of deals, bringing in: a chief operating officer who had worked at McKinsey; a high net-worth individual investor; and a bank to finance receivables. The new COO and money spurred new service offerings and rapid growth. In ten months, the company's value rose from $3 million to $20 million.

- **Say *yes* to a deal, then figure out how to deliver.** Jesse did this when he agreed to execute private labeling for Goliaths. Likewise, Bill Gates owes much of his wealth to promising IBM something he didn't have, but he'd take a bigger risk than Jesse. In 1980, Gates tells IBM he'll deliver a unique operating system for its revolutionary personal computer. Tiny Microsoft develops computer languages, not systems that manage a computer's hardware and software. An anxious Gates must get his hands on the right system, if one exists, because it's critical to IBM's soon-to-be-launched PC. He gets a break: Seattle Computer calls, confiding it's just created a new operating system, the precise system IBM needs. Gates says nothing about IBM, buys the operating system as part of a separate deal, turns around, licenses it to his giant—and captures the world.[6]

- **Plan to get lucky or unlucky.** Size Wizards like Bill Gates and Jesse Rasch, who keep their destinations in mind as they sequence their deals, are more determined and resilient in coping with bad luck and are more likely to know what to do with any good luck they experience along the way. Knowing he wanted to dominate the computer world, not just IBM, Gates didn't just license Seattle Computer's operating system when he discovered it by chance, he bought it outright. Then, he didn't just hand it over for a one-time fee. Instead, he licensed it to IBM on a *non-exclusive*, ongoing royalty fee basis—meaning Microsoft could license it to other PC-makers, making Gates a dominant force.

Sequence your deals inside-out—starting with the end in mind, avoiding disruptive conflicts and saying no to deals that risk undermining your long-term interests.

GROW THE SIZE OF YOUR TEAM

I grew up daydreaming about David Livingstone, a doctor, missionary, explorer and one of my ancestors. As an adult, I retraced some of Livingstone's travels in Africa, discovering the modern nations that now lie in his famous but distant footsteps.

Millions of people in these nations had been, or soon would be, overwhelmed by violence and wars—including one in Zaire where I'd later co-chair talks among those affected.[7]

As I made my way down to the relative peace in South Africa, my respect only grew for this country, its accomplishments and its leaders. Livingstone's footsteps died out here and I picked up the trail of Nelson Mandela.

STORY: NEGOTIATING WITH A WHITE GIANT

At birth, he was named Rolihlahla, meaning "Troublemaker."

Now, as a tall, handsome man, he strides confidently toward the podium, taking long, urgent steps. His target: an Indian speaker urging the crowd in this Johannesburg suburb to defy the white government's brutal apartheid system in South Africa.

Anger propels his legs, though his body displays the same grace you could see when he runs cross-country races, kicks a soccer ball or sidesteps a punch in the boxing ring. He propels himself onto the stage, his hands taking over, grabbing the surprised speaker and pulling him off the stage as the audience stares.[8]

Nelson Mandela silences Indian leader Yusuf Cachalia—honoring the Troublemaker name bestowed upon him by his father.

It's 1950, and the 32-year-old Mandela, a lawyer by training, cannot bear to have any group, including Indians, communists or Coloreds vie for the anti-apartheid spotlight with him and his trusted colleague, Oliver Tambo. Mandela believes that their group, the African National Congress, or ANC, should *not* join forces with any other that has not experienced the challenges of South Africa's black majority. Publicly confident, Mandela is privately insecure, worrying that new partners might dictate the beliefs and direction of an unsteady ANC organization as it attempts to regain its footing after the National Party's shocking election victory two years earlier. In 1948, an extreme bloc of Afrikaners— South African whites of Dutch origin—had claimed power, putting the interests of Afrikaners ahead of all others, even the descendants of white British colonists who had also settled here centuries ago.[9]

The leader of the National Party, Dr. Daniel Malan, a man who supported the Nazis during World War II, has quickly imported some of Hitler's tactics to South Africa. Where non-whites have always been treated as inferior, they've never been systematically segregated by race—until now. Malan oversees a radical change. To ensure the 15% white minority further asserts its dominance, the government cordons off non-whites into distinct living areas, divides public places by race, outlaws cross-race sexual relationships and requires passes for non-whites going from one area to another.

With Malan busy constructing apartheid (meaning "apartness" in Afrikaans), and the ANC seemingly incapable of drumming up opposition from the nation's 75% black population, Mandela finally sees the light. As a growing leadership force within the ANC, he overcomes his own stubbornness and defiance (traits he says undermined his father as a tribal chief) and in 1952, agrees the ANC must join forces with Indians, Communist Party members, many of whom are white, and Coloreds, those of mixed race.[10] Yes, they have different backgrounds and beliefs, but Mandela realizes that what separates these groups from blacks is less important than what binds them together: they share the same giant—the white population that helps sustain apartheid in South Africa.[11]

The ANC's new partners contribute much more than numbers alone. They bring organizational skills, sophistication and connections to other allies. The pay-off is immediate. The ANC, with Mandela playing an instrumental role, runs its first successful mass disobedience campaign in June 1952, empowering blacks and making it a badge of honor to be arrested.

As the new coalition flourishes, Mandela's insecurities melt away. He learns that partners in strong alliances do not need to fear differences if they're united on key fronts.[12]

Mandela moves across the country in the mid-1950s, spreading word of a new Freedom Charter. Crafted by the ANC and its coalition partners, this charter champions a multi-racial, democratic society, where everyone will be treated as equals.[13]

In 1960, things worsen—again.

Police fire on a rally of 10,000 protestors at Sharpeville in the Transvaal province, killing 69 people. The ANC and other protest groups are banned. They can't even be mentioned in conversations. In response, the ANC makes a pivotal decision. It will use violence to promote its goals and keep the impatient black masses onside.

In the past, the ANC has pursued non-violent disobedience only. Where Gandhi believed in non-violence as a principle, Nelson Mandela sees it as just one tactic to counter his giant's overwhelming military strength. It's time to shift tactics. He goes underground to head up the ANC's new military arm, Umkhonto we Sizwe—"Spear of the Nation"—which will be referred to simply as MK. The unit's agents won't carry weapons on their missions and will target government and military infrastructure, not people.

"Because it did not involve the loss of life it offered the best hope for reconciliation among the races afterward. We did not want to start a blood feud between white and black," Mandela would later say.[14] He knows that sabotage on its own will lead many governments and groups to withhold their support, but he and his ANC colleagues believe this trade-off is acceptable. And if sabotage does not get them the freedoms they seek, MK will escalate things, resorting to guerilla warfare and terrorism as required.

While MK recruits members, Mandela slips out of his country for the first time, to attract more players to the ANC team. He gets financing and other forms of assistance from newly independent African nations including Tunisia, Sierra Leone and Guinea.[15] Later, Zambia and Tanzania will provide bases for the ANC to coordinate its international efforts, train guerillas and broadcast news to the masses in South Africa.

In his travels, Mandela is caught off guard by strong criticisms of his coalition with non-blacks and communists. He explains his logic, stating that the ANC doesn't support communism, nor is it being co-opted by whites from the Communist Party. Making things tougher for Mandela, a splinter group that has broken away from the ANC—the Pan-Africanist Congress, or the PAC—excludes non-blacks, broadening its appeal among those black nations that have recently gained their freedom from white colonial powers.

Mandela returns to South Africa in 1962, ready to do battle. To ramp up MK, he disguises himself as a chauffeur so he can move from one meeting place to another without detection by authorities.

Someone betrays him. A police motorcade pulls his car over. He is arrested.

Mandela is found guilty of leaving the country illegally and inciting workers to strike, and is sentenced to five years in prison. A year later, a number of his senior MK colleagues are captured, and as MK's leader, Mandela finds himself back in court, this time on a more serious charge: sabotage. He mesmerizes the court, and the world, by sharing his story and explaining why the ANC's actions are necessary. Though he has never formally headed the ANC, Mandela's riveting oratory confirms that he is his organization's most influential leader.[16]

Mandela and eight other co-conspirators are sent to prison for life on Robbens Island, the South African equivalent of America's infamous Alcatraz. Mandela refuses to appeal. He wants the extreme punishment to resonate inside and outside South Africa.

Many among South Africa's black masses are attracted to the bold, inclusive ANC vision Mandela paints, and they love his gentle manner and wide smile, which he flashes even under duress. In the decades to come, as his absence from public view adds to his mystique, these supporters will lie in wait, ready when called upon—or not—to go on strike, boycott, violate laws or risk their lives by demonstrating.

During his confinement, Mandela's long-time confidante Oliver Tambo runs the ANC. With Tambo living in exile in nearby Zambia, he and Mandela communicate through prison visitors—Mandela's wife Winnie, lawyers and other trusted couriers—sometimes sneaking messages back and forth in books, other times speaking in code. These infrequent exchanges manage to keep Tambo and Mandela united in their thinking.

Tambo tours the globe on behalf of the ANC, building on existing coalitions and creating new ones. He solicits support from leaders of nations,

Non-Governmental Organizations (NGOs) and major corporations, asking them to impose sanctions aimed at change. India, Holland, Norway and Sweden join the ANC's efforts early on.

Encouraged by the local communists and their coalition with the ANC, the Soviet Union enters into its own coalition with the ANC, providing it with financial support, military training and arms. Eastern Bloc countries and Cuba also help out, offering aid that proves vital. Mandela insists that none of this assistance requires a commitment to communism.

At times, Mandela experiences serious doubts about the potential for success, especially in the late 1960s when the ANC is having little impact while government Controllers based in the capital city, Pretoria, maintain their rule with powerful white fists. These officials won't even let Mandela attend the funeral of his eldest son, who dies in a car accident in 1969, leaving Mandela to lie in misery in his jail cell—inconsolable.

Seven years later, there's a flicker of hope for Mandela and the ANC as black students in the Soweto Township protest plans to teach them half their classes in Afrikaans, the language of their giant oppressor. This hope is snuffed out, however, when one of the leaders who inspired the Soweto uprising, Steve Biko, is tortured to death by police.

Margaret Thatcher takes power in Great Britain in 1979, another blow for the ANC. Influenced by Afrikaner friends, including author Laurens van der Post, whom she'd later grant a knighthood, Thatcher labels Mandela a "communist terrorist." She supports the "non-communist" Zulus, headed by Chief Buthelezi, who is touted as a reasonable leader by South Africa's government. Buthelezi wants power for himself, with his own territory carved out. He opposes all sanctions, saying they'll only hurt blacks. Thatcher gives Buthelezi profile and credibility. To make things worse for the ANC, when President Ronald Reagan wins office in 1980, Britain's Prime Minister persuades America's new leader to adopt her views—not difficult given Reagan's hostility toward communists.

But the tide will turn, astonishingly.

The ANC's carefully planned strategies to support old and new coalitions are about to make a big difference as events unfold. The 1960s and 1970s may have favored its white giant, but the next two decades will belong to the ANC—and Nelson Mandela.

In the early 1980s, Mandela's contact with outsiders is loosened slightly. He writes letters to church leaders, urging them to support the ANC's goals, consistent with their own religious teachings. He greets visitors from any nation allowed to meet with him.

Inside South Africa, the masses demonstrate more frequently as coordinated efforts mount. The sabotage of government targets is on the rise through MK's operatives. Winnie Mandela's strident words and actions are controversial, but help boost the ANC's profile on her husband's behalf.[17]

On the religious front, the Roman Catholics speak out. The Anglicans will soon appoint the charismatic Desmond Tutu as Archbishop of Cape Town, a first for black Africans. Even the Dutch Reformed Church, the Afrikaners' main place of worship and one of the early sources of apartheid thinking, starts to come around. It denounces racial oppression, giving the ANC some inroads into white voters and government officials.

Influenced by Reverend Leon Sullivan, the first African American board member at General Motors, US corporations apply pressure. Many sell or wind down operations in South Africa when the white government chooses to ignore them.

The United Nations raises the ANC's profile, but its resolutions lack teeth because any mandatory sanctions would run into vetoes from the US and the UK, both of which have significant economic interests in South Africa and continue to worry about ANC links to communism. The European Community and British Commonwealth are similarly constrained, by the UK alone. The Commonwealth, however, does bar South Africa from competing against its sports teams.

In the mid-1980s, with Soviet leader Mikhail Gorbachev calling for an end to the Cold War, the ANC suffers and gains: it loses support from the Soviet Union, which cuts back on its financing of foreign allies, but it benefits since its critics can no longer credibly use arguments against it related to threats posed by the organization's links to communism. This will open the door for others to come onside, including the US.

As promised, MK ratchets up its tactics in response to ongoing state-sponsored violence. Civilian buildings are now targeted—malls, restaurants and bars—with inevitable casualties, leading to international condemnation of these acts.

In 1985, blacks, who account for half of retail sales in South Africa, launch a successful boycott on white-owned businesses; the country's major business groups call on the government to answer the nation's growing economic crisis with political change.[18]

Later in 1985, a state of national emergency is declared because of uprisings among the black masses. Television coverage of police and military brutality spurs international protests. The US masses demand their financial institutions withdraw their capital from South Africa: Chase Manhattan Bank in New York isn't necessarily empathetic about apartheid or the ANC's plight, but it listens to shareholders and clients who want out.[19]

Chase stops rolling over $500 million in short-term loans to the South African government. This is a problem for the government since it's been relying on short-term foreign financings. Chase is big and influential, and soon, other financial groups follow suit, pulling their lines of credit or jacking up interest rates to reflect increased risk. The rand—South Africa's currency—tumbles, hiking the cost of imports, fueling inflation and shaking investor confidence. In 1986, the pressure from America builds. The US Congress overrides Reagan, launching its own sanctions, with bans on new investments, loans, airport landing rights and oil exports.[20]

Mandela's release from jail becomes the focal point for change, so the government tries to get him out, its way. It plans for someone to help Mandela escape. He refuses. If he'd gone along, the government intended to kill him. On other occasions, Mandela is offered his freedom if he denounces the ANC, remains out of sight or makes other concessions. Again, he refuses, saying there will be no conditions on his release.

President P. W. Botha suffers a stroke, and is replaced by F. W. de Klerk. The new President speeds up talks with Mandela. Worse than dealing with Mandela, de Klerk fears, would be trying to negotiate with the PAC or other extreme splinter groups if the ANC can't show real progress to its supporters.

With the ANC still banned, new protest groups step up as surrogates to represent its interests. In 1989, the United Democratic Front (UDF) joins with the Congress of South African Trade Unions (COSATU) to form the Mass Democratic Movement (MDM), which will coordinate nationwide civil disobedience.

In late 1989, South Africa's central bank adds its voice to the growing calls for change, saying the nation must pursue political reforms to reverse economic stagnation. New sanctions keep popping up. More governments push for change. More corporations pull out, taking jobs with them. More ANC bombs explode. Metal detectors dominate entrances to white malls. Arrests, strikes and protests spiral upward. The giant's loss of wealth accelerates: its stocks, currency, minerals, diamonds and gold mines are hit hard. South African morale drops nationwide. Divisions grow within the white giant, as whites no longer uniformly support their government's extreme behaviors.

South Africa has become a pariah, and increasingly, so has each white person living in it.

The government must move faster. Important prisoners are released, including Mandela's old friend and ANC colleague, Walter Sisulu. White-only laws are repealed, the death penalty is suspended, and banned groups such as the ANC and the Communist Party are *un*-banned.[21] For the first time in decades, people can say "ANC" without fearing arrest.

As these changes occur, Nelson Mandela remains in prison. Just into his seventies now, he has not been photographed in decades. The broad thirst that's building up for his involvement in South Africa's future can be quenched by only one thing—his release.

The pressure on all fronts is so intense that President de Klerk believes he is better off freeing the aging icon. At least this way, de Klerk won't be easily blamed if anything happens to Mandela. Besides, he and other Controllers are convinced that "Mandela the myth" will not live up to public expectations.

But 27 years in prison have only polished Mandela's rougher edges: allowing him to improve through self-reflection, reading and discussions about history, politics and philosophy; allowing him to further build the relationships and coalitions he and the ANC will continue to rely upon; and allowing him and his colleagues to hone their vision for a new country.

On February 11, 1990, Mandela is released without conditions.

Blacks are euphoric, celebrating in the streets. Whites are nervous, many hunkering down in their homes. Will Mandela prove to be a terrorist after all? Will he ignite a civil war? Will he and his followers go on a killing spree to avenge his time in jail?

Instead, Mandela goes on tour, first inside South Africa and then worldwide, reinforcing the ANC's coalitions and thanking people for their support. He urges partners to maintain their sanctions until negotiations are complete, countering Britain's Thatcher who is already pushing the European Community to lift its voluntary sanctions. Most leaders will listen to Mandela, not Thatcher.

In August 1990, the ANC decides de Klerk must have something to show his followers in return for the freedoms he has granted, so the group agrees to *suspend* its use of violence in the lead-up to negotiations with the government over South Africa's future.

Mandela will soon doubt this decision.

Hundreds of ANC supporters and Zulus die as fighting breaks out between blacks in the eastern part of the country. The ANC suspects that the government is working with Chief Buthelezi and his Zulus to spur the unrest: if the Zulus stir up riots and killings among the black masses, the government can argue to the world that blacks are incapable of self-governance, undermining the ANC's credibility.

The violence carries into 1991. Although both sides keep talking about the structure for formal talks, progress is slow. The ANC's mistrust grows, overflowing in July 1991 when the Guardian newspaper breaks a blockbuster story: it reveals documents that prove the government has supported and funded Zulu attacks on the ANC. De Klerk claims ignorance, shuffles his cabinet and apologizes, his own credibility undermined.

As formal negotiations finally get underway in late 1991, Mandela becomes directly involved at critical junctures, but for the most part, it's the ANC's Cyril Ramaphosa—a smart, experienced union leader—who sits at the negotiation table.[22] He handles detailed discussions on a daily basis while Mandela and other senior ANC members guide progress from the sidelines, staying objective and plotting strategy.

On June 17, 1992, in the township of Boipatong, 46 blacks are slaughtered, mostly women and children, the fourth mass killing of ANC people that week. The police do nothing, nor does de Klerk. Despite releasing Mandela, unwinding apartheid laws and saying the right things, the government is still trying to cling to power.

The ANC walks away from the negotiation table. It hopes to establish once and for all how that table should be set, and who holds the real power in South Africa in the 1990s. Mandela threatens to revert to violent means of influence, but for now, the ANC will move aggressively in other ways.

Mandela tells his followers that the government is playing deadly games and needs to be reminded of its limited choices. He calls for a series of escalating protests. The masses deliver, their efforts peaking in August 1992 with a general strike involving four million people, the largest political strike in South Africa's history. During a march the following month, however, 29 protestors die at a city called Bisho after troops open fire.

The nation is mired in crisis.

De Klerk concedes, again, saying he'll release all political prisoners and impose strict restrictions on Zulu activities. As well, he commits to a multi-racial constitution and free elections, without any of the white vetoes he has been pushing for.

Intense talks nail down the details in late 1992 and 1993, with more upsets along the way as extremists on both sides—conservative white right-wingers and black Zulus—become more violent, trying to derail talks that don't favor their interests.

At last, agreement is reached on all fronts, and a date is set for everyone to vote for the first time as a nation of equals—communists, blacks, whites, Indians and those of mixed race. At Mandela's urging, international and domestic coalitions begin to relax their pressures to reward the white giant for its move toward real change.

On May 2, 1994, F. W. de Klerk announces that his government has lost the election. It will immediately turn over the reins of power to the ANC and Nelson Mandela, the new President of South Africa.

GROW THE SIZE OF YOUR TEAM

Without building size and strength through others over the course of five decades, Nelson Mandela and the ANC would never have negotiated their way to the table, achieved what they wanted once there, or been able to hang onto power after claiming it from their white giant. Without his broad array of coalitions, as incredible as it may seem, Mandela would probably still be in prison, the ANC outlawed and apartheid still a reality.

Smaller players form coalitions any time they join with one or more independent parties to work toward the same basic result in a giant negotiation, regardless of whether they coordinate their efforts or whether they're motivated by the same interests.

Some of Mandela's coalitions required open coordination, while others evolved with partners who quietly aligned themselves in pursuit of the same outcome. It doesn't always matter if we plan a coalition or it just takes root—unless we believe that being associated with another party could hurt us, in which case we may want to distance ourselves from them. What matters most is that, like Mandela, we remain aware of how all of our decisions might affect arrangements with existing or potential Coalitionists.

I've identified five major types of coalitions the Size Wizards draw upon to bulk up, four of which are defined by the size of our coalition partners. Depending on circumstances, as smaller players we can call on one or more of these coalitions: All-Small Coalitions, Big-Player Coalitions, Giant Coalitions, Mass Coalitions or Trojan-Horse Coalitions.

Nelson Mandela—a master coalition builder—used and orchestrated all five types, with one coalition often leading to another, or reinforcing others.

The ANC's coalitions came together to put an end to apartheid for a range of underlying reasons, creating a super-coalition that got Mandela what he wanted for South Africa.

All-Small Coalitions. In this type of coalition, we align ourselves with other smaller players roughly our size. These partners are generally easier to access, easier to find common ground with, and less likely to hurt us than larger coalition partners.

The ANC's All-Small Coalition with Indians, Coloreds and the Communist Party proved crucial. This coalition was based on: similar goals around reform; its different followers totaling 85% of the nation's population; better combined resources and organizational skills; solid personal relationships between the diverse leaders, once Mandela overcame his concerns; and a justified joint fear of their increasingly malicious giant. Where Mandela's early pursuits emphasized empowering blacks exclusively, this coalition signaled an important acceptance of his revised goal—a multi-racial democracy. The government tried to divide and conquer the ANC's All-Small Coalition in the 1980s by granting Indians and Coloreds greater rights than blacks, but everyone saw through the maneuver and the strong bonds among members only tightened.

Before entering the ANC's multi-racial coalition, Mandela's first All-Small Coalition was a simple one, bonding him together with Oliver Tambo, his beloved college friend and most trusted colleague, without whom the ANC might have vanished during Mandela's imprisonment. While some coalitions document their working agreements in writing, the Mandela-Tambo coalition relied on the trust that comes from mutual respect, understanding one another's goals and aspirations, and endless hours shared together.

Big-Player Coalitions. We partner with a bigger player than us, who adds to our size and clout. Some of these larger players might be Giant Coalition partners in other settings but not the one we're currently in. These partners are often involved in the background and less intensely on the frontlines with our giant. They're usually willing to help us out because of their broader interests in a successful outcome to our negotiations.

Mandela called on more than a dozen Big-Player Coalitions to join him in pressuring South Africa's government for change, either through lobbying, sanctions, funding, or other resources including operational bases outside South Africa. These coalition partners encompassed Christian groups, African nations, non-African nations such as Holland, multinational corporations and international organizations, the UN being one example. Those taking action were driven by principle, protests by their constituents or because their constituents were directly affected, as in the case of India. It was certainly easier for countries to act if their economic ties with South Africa were not significant. With all these players, the ANC was clear about what it needed, and on occasion, it publicly called out existing or potential coalition members who weren't doing enough.

Giant Coalitions. We come together with a secondary giant we're not negotiating with as our main objective. Working with giant partners can be dangerous because of their size and clout, particularly if they want to misuse our information, or move against us at some point. The benefits, however, can be significant. These giant partners tend to get actively involved on the frontlines because they have considerable interests in play, one of which may well be undermining the giant we're trying to get something from.

One of Mandela's three giant Coalitionists was the Soviet Union, as it divided countries worldwide into either its camp or America's, betting on the ANC when no one else was. Following on its heels much later was the US Congress, feeling pressure from voters who were taking to the streets. Finally, who would have thought in the 1960s that the giant global finance community would ever find itself aligned with the "communist-infiltrated" ANC, helping to hand Nelson Mandela the presidency? That's exactly what happened when the major banks finally judged their financial interests were no longer served by a white government, signaling their need for change by moving money out of South Africa—causing a run on the rand and a crisis that left whites reeling. Chase Manhattan Bank wanted the same thing as the ANC in the end, but for very different reasons.

Mass Coalitions. Here, we gain the support of the masses surrounding our giant—hundreds, thousands or millions of people. Being likeable on a personal level as a smaller player can be important to all types of coalitions, but it can be particularly helpful when trying to appeal broadly to individuals whose obvious alternative is to stay home and let others raise a fuss.

For the ANC, its domestic Mass Coalition was formed by blacks drawn together over common concerns about their economic and political plight. Blacks respected and liked Nelson Mandela. They knew how much he had sacrificed for their cause. They applied pressure through boycotts, rallies and strikes, sometimes on their own initiative, more often at the urging of the ANC or ANC allies such as the Mass Democratic Movement. Even early ANC rivals, including Steve Biko's Black Consciousness Movement, helped to keep this Mass Coalition activated at key points by sparking anti-government protests.

When television relayed images of the black masses being assaulted by white police or soldiers, outrage erupted, leading to international Mass Coalitions that pressured individual governments to act against the white giant in South Africa. Funding from the Giant Coalition with the Soviet Union helped pay for a number of the ANC's ongoing efforts to keep its Mass Coalition intact, while the ANC's Big-Player Coalitions with Tanzania and Zambia allowed it to broadcast radio messages to this Mass Coalition.

Trojan-Horse Coalitions. We reach across the divide to hold hands with people inside our giant who have the ability to influence internal thinking and actions. Our ability to do this is helped by staying away from unjustified extremes in our giant dealings, while proposing solutions that fall within accepted standards.

As pressures mounted on the white giant from other ANC coalitions, a growing number of whites inside the apartheid system felt the need to speak out. Included in this Trojan-Horse Coalition were many South African businesses hurt by boycotts, the nation's central bank, as well as dissenting white politicians, academics and members of the British community. By 1992, when President de Klerk held a white referendum to decide if ANC talks should continue, 69% of whites voted *yes*, completing the evolution of Trojan-Horse support from something less than 1% decades earlier.

As the ANC prepared to take power, Mandela made sure he'd be helped by white government officials with knowledge and expertise: he supported a transitional government with cabinet members from any party earning five percent of the vote in the 1994 election, while also protecting the jobs of white civil servants for a period. There were many in the ANC who saw this multi-racial cabinet transition as a sell-out, but once again, Mandela understood the importance of working with diverse coalition members.

Mandela targeted one other white group that had to work with the ANC—not against it.

The ANC needed white Afrikaner military leaders to keep the peace during elections and during the transition to a multi-racial democracy. Mandela used his people-skills, never shying away from flattery as he met with influential white generals, telling them he required their support and wanted them to stay on.

No set of partners was more vital to a peaceful transition than these Trojan-Horse Coalitions that bridged the gap between the ANC and its white giant. Without these partners, blacks would have been isolated, less influential nationally and internationally, and undermined at every turn by South African whites prepared to fight to the end.

Over the decades, Mandela consciously fostered the potential for this white support as he set his goals and pursued them: he and the ANC embraced all races; he endorsed violence only as a last resort, directed it at infrastructure and kept the armed struggle on hold even when he knew the government and Zulus were coordinating attacks; he trusted until he learned otherwise, which allowed him to take constructive risks in relationship building; he acted forgivingly toward whites, even those who imprisoned him, attacking racist behaviors and the apartheid system, but not whites as a race; he learned the Afrikaners' history and language, giving him a greater understanding of his giant; and in his dealings with whites, despite what they'd done, he was invariably polite and respectful, though never afraid to voice his interests, sometimes through heated exchanges.

Although Mandela had his flaws—suffering from stubbornness, defiance and a quick temper—he was successful because he learned from his early experiences and mistakes, focused on his broadened goal of a multi-racial society, did whatever was needed to make this dream a reality, and did nothing to undermine it. His reasoned, consistent approaches played well domestically with whites when it most mattered to him. These approaches also enhanced his coalition-building worldwide, lifting the ANC above its more extreme black rivals, and making it a supportable organization.

You, too, can achieve the completely unexpected by remembering Nelson Mandela's story and following some simple guidelines as you put together your own coalitions:

- **Pick the right glue for coalition-building.** In teaming up with others, you can gain: access to more contacts, support, information, expertise and resources; more ways into your giant's castle; a louder voice; greater sources of pressure; and enhanced protection. Judge your coalition's potential by how well each partner will likely satisfy your interests in one or more of these ways as you pursue a common outcome. The odds of an explicit coalition being successful in the long run go up the more partners share a common culture, values, positive past experiences, strong two-way communication, and mutual respect.

- **Pick the right coalition for your situation.** When choosing between All-Small, Big-Player, Giant, Mass or Trojan-Horse Coalitions to extend the size and might of your core team, you'll want to consider the benefits of each type, the risks, and the potential for using one coalition to help build or reinforce others. Like Mandela, your aim is to assemble a winning coalition, one that includes enough key people on your side to overcome any efforts to block you, while compelling your giant to say *yes* to what you want. You'll coordinate actively with some partners, and other times you'll simply find Coalitionists uniting in your favor. In either case, you need to remind yourself of the beliefs, behaviors and actions that will attract appropriate outside support without compromising your interests.

- **Use Coalitionists to get *and keep* whatever you're after.** If you were with the ANC, and you managed to somehow grab power without coalition-building, you'd then face the challenge of remaining in office without widespread domestic and international support. This challenge proved too great for many who seized power in other African nations where governments have since come and gone through coup after coup. The United States slammed into this barrier in 2003 following its unilateral military successes in Iraq. And countless leaders inside organizations of all descriptions fail for the same reason when they're parachuted into new roles.

- **Add a Coalition of Losers to your repertoire.** This coalition can prove useful if you and others of any size are jointly experiencing losses, or are threatened with losses. The ANC's All-Small Coalition was bound together more tightly because its partners not only shared a common goal, they were also all losers under apartheid. In America, the decimated city of New Orleans needed to better negotiate timely support from its giant, the federal government. If the city had spearheaded a Coalition of Losers years before Hurricane Katrina hit in 2005, it would have significantly raised its odds of persuading federal officials to act in advance of an inevitable catastrophe. Who might have been identified as powerful potential losers, even in the 1990s? Start with certain insurance companies, neighboring states that would be forced to handle refugees, oil companies whose refineries would be wiped out, environmentalists, the city's inhabitants, well-known personalities who call New Orleans home, and African American groups.

Here are examples of each major type of coalition across a range of situations:

AN ALL-SMALL COALITION. Two elite hockey players in the NHL, Paul Kariya and Teemu Selanne, package themselves together as free agents in 2003. They sign with the Colorado Avalanche so their combined talents can help their giant excel—which it will—advancing to the quarter-finals of the Stanley Cup playoffs. Less talented athletes in many sports could form coalitions of two to three players, bringing complementary skills to a club, earning more and winning more.[23]

A BIG-PLAYER COALITION. Martin Cora develops new software he thinks will be of interest to one giant software company in particular. Rather than go directly to the giant on his own, he teams up with a bigger company already servicing the giant, cuts them in, and they successfully approach their Goliath together. Martin joins another Big-Player Coalition by becoming a member in an entrepreneur association that gets him a 20% to 40% discount from giant suppliers.[24]

A GIANT COALITION. In the 1970s, workers and intellectuals struggle inside Poland to free it from the Soviet Union's iron grip. Protestors draw on the giant resources of the Roman Catholic Church inside and outside Poland for help, in a nation where the majority are Catholic. When one of their fellow countrymen, Karol Wojtyla, becomes Pope John Paul II in 1978, assistance from Rome intensifies through donations, a papal visit raising confidence and morale, churches being used to organize dissenters, and high-profile advocacy worldwide. Led by union leader Lech Walesa and his Solidarity movement, Poland gains its freedom in 1989.[25]

A MASS COALITION. Legal assistant Erin Brockovich goes door-to-door in Hinkley, California to get 600 residents to file a class-action suit against the local utility company. She claims that Pacific Gas & Electric's use of a chemical called "Chromium 6" has led to more than half-a-dozen serious illnesses, including cancer. She wins a settlement worth $333 million for residents, with the lawyers taking a 40% cut since they worked on a contingency basis. The size, profile and emotional impact of Brochovich's coalition pushes the giant utility to settle, even though some experts doubt that Chromium 6 could ever cause such broad health problems.[26]

A TROJAN-HORSE COALITION. In 2000, George W. Bush is elected President with 40% of his votes coming from white evangelical denominations who believe the Bible is truth and Jesus is the only way to salvation.[27] Evangelical representatives reach into the giant US government to influence its policies, knowing they can link arms with a powerful Christian group inside that includes Bush, many of his advisors, and at least one of his main speechwriters. Similarly, Israel benefits from a religious Trojan-Horse Coalition inside the US as a whole; more Jewish people live in America than Israel, and many are highly influential in government circles. This helps ensure the US will keep adding to the $100 billion in aid it has already delivered to its strategic Middle-Eastern partner over the past 60 years.[28]

Three short stories will complete our exploration of coalitions, showcasing in greater detail two All-Small Coalitions, and the Giant Coalition that won America its freedom.

FOREVER FRIENDS. As the six main actors from the *Friends* television series enter their third season in the mid-1990s, each faces a giant negotiation challenge: their show is a hit and they want big raises, despite the fact they all have three years left on their original contracts.

They decide to bond together in an unprecedented way, negotiating the same terms for each actor, rather than letting Warner Brothers dictate the negotiation process. In forming this All-Small Coalition, they blunt the studio's ability to threaten any single actor with a firing, they make it much harder to play one actor's value against another's, and they maintain their great off-screen relationships, not allowing salary issues to divide them.

Their joint leverage gets them a four-fold increase in salary to $100,000 per episode. This spurs them to continue negotiating as one in the years ahead, with escalating results. By the time the show ends in 2004, after a decade on the air, each actor is earning $1 million an episode.

The idea for this successful coalition came from actors David Schwimmer (Ross) and Courtney Cox (Monica). Although they were the two better-known actors among the ensemble when the show started, they realized that their long-term interests would be best served by negotiating together as a group of six. Matthew Perry (Chandler) says Cox set a collaborative tone from the start, telling them, "There's no star of this show. Let's all look out for one another." [29] If a non-star had said this and suggested a coalition, it's less likely the others would have listened.

This solidarity among the *Friends* actors was supported by their common culture, values, general interests, acting talents and financial profiles. In spite of inevitable efforts by Warner to upset their shared position on higher pay, the coalition remained strong.

CRUDE COMPANIONS. In September 1960, oil sits at around $2 a barrel, priced that way by Western oil players such as Shell, BP and Standard Oil of New Jersey (now part of Exxon Mobil). These giant corporations source much of their oil from financially struggling nations in the Middle East that provide access to reserves lying within their borders.

Iraq calls its competitors together in Baghdad—a meeting that will change the world. An All-Small Coalition is formed between Iraq, Saudi Arabia, Iran, Kuwait and Venezuela, a group that comes to be known as the Organization of Petroleum Exporting Countries, or OPEC. Soon, Qatar, Libya and Indonesia also join. [30]

By coordinating their production and pricing, these coalition members stabilize oil prices in the 1960s and begin to reclaim their reserves rather than letting giant Westerners control them. With its early successes, OPEC adds more members, including Algeria and Nigeria. As the All-Small

Coalition's share of the global market rises, oil prices rise as well—to $11 in 1973, $36 in 1979 and more than $90 in 2007.[31]

There are big pricing fluctuations along the way, reflecting supply, demand and different interests among suppliers: if prices are too high, big reserve owners such as Saudi Arabia want to bring them down so Westerners won't start looking too seriously at alternative energy sources, potentially undermining Saudi's long-term financial prospects. Meanwhile, poorer, vastly populated nations such as Nigeria, with much smaller reserves, are less concerned about the viability of oil in the future. They need each dollar they can earn now and tend to want oil priced as high as possible.

Due to their different profiles and interests in general, over time some OPEC members invariably cheat on their agreed quotas, producing more than they're supposed to, earning more money individually in the short-term, but often dragging the price of oil down with their excess supplies.[32] This, perhaps not surprisingly, is different behavior than what we saw from our six actors in *Friends*, whose bonds ran so deep on so many fronts that they never cheated each other.

Like OPEC, coalitions that come together over just one main position, interest or trait—but with little else in common—are more prone to cheating and shorter lifespans. OPEC members, however, have little to worry about so long as demand for oil remains high, they keep control of the majority of the world's exports and reserves, and members continue to share a dependence on oil for generating wealth.

A REVOLUTIONARY NEGOTIATION. In 1777, just a year after America unilaterally declares its independence from Great Britain over taxation and trade issues, the fledgling nation's military finds itself in dire straights. It's out of money, supplies are low and America can't afford the ships it needs to counter its angry giant's superiority on the water.

Inventor, publisher and diplomat Benjamin Franklin heads to Paris. There, he suggests a coalition: France can provide desperately needed money and ships, and in return, when America wins its war and Great Britain's trade monopoly is broken, the French will secure access to the fast-growing American market.[33] Franklin points out one other obvious benefit for France—it will deal its global arch-enemy a devastating blow.

King Louis XVI offers limited support at first, through debt relief and some cash, but ramps up assistance as Franklin informs him of progress being made. In 1778, 16 French warships head to New York, immediately putting the British on the defensive. In the following years, thousands of French ground troops and dozens of French ships will fight alongside Americans, shifting the tide of the Revolutionary War in the new nation's favor.[34]

From this position of strength, Ben Franklin turns to negotiate a peace agreement with Great Britain in 1782, confirming America's independence. General George Washington is later elected his country's first President in recognition of his battlefield exploits. He and his troops were clearly indispensable, but without Franklin forging a timely Giant Coalition with France, Washington wouldn't have had the means to keep fighting.

Grow the size of your team—through an All-Small Coalition, a Big-Player Coalition, a Giant Coalition, a Mass Coalition or a Trojan-Horse Coalition.

PLAN TO WALK AWAY

In the 1730s, some 50 years before he'd help negotiate America's independence, young publisher Ben Franklin finds himself struggling with an ethical dilemma: an important customer has asked Franklin to print an article in his upstart newspaper, *The Gazette*, but Franklin views the material as "scurrilous and defamatory." So why would he consider printing the article? Because Franklin is broke and needs the money.

There are two criteria that will guide Franklin's decision on whether he should walk away from this customer. The first criterion: does running a piece like this violate his principles? The answer is *yes*. The second criterion: can Franklin afford to live by his principles? This must be put to a test. Here's an excerpt from Franklin's diary:

To determine whether I should publish it or not, I went home in the evening, purchased a twopenny loaf at the baker's, and with the water from the pump made my supper; I then wrapped myself up in my great-coat, and laid down on the floor and slept until morning, when, on another loaf and a mug of water, I made my breakfast. From this regimen I feel no inconvenience whatever. Finding I can live in this manner, I have formed a determination never to prostitute my press to the purposes of corruption and abuse of this kind for the sake of gaining a more comfortable subsistence.[35]

Being able to walk away from a giant can make us much stronger than we would be otherwise. Any credible back-up plan that meets at least our basic interests gives us more confidence and greater clout with our giant so we can either get what we want from them or walk away—even from mighty Wal-Mart.

STORY: SEEDS OF STRENGTH

Tom and Emmy Droog sell brilliantly flavored sunflower seeds you can snack on.

The Dutch-born couple had started out by targeting their seeds at birds, but when an employee suggested adding different flavors to make the seeds tastier for humans, their small business based in Alberta, Canada really took flight.

Their Smokey Barbeque, Chili Lime, Dill Pickle and Salted seeds are poured into small designer bags with re-sealable tops before being distributed to retailers for sale. "Spitz" is what the Droogs call their company, and after building it from nothing, they get a phone call late in 2002 that entrepreneurs dream about. A buyer from Wal-Mart says the retail chain wants to sell their tasty treats in some of its stores, turning Spitz into a highly visible brand. The head of sales at Spitz—Jack Higgins—is ecstatic, quickly saying *yes* to a deal.[36]

Tom Droog is not as euphoric. He feels his company has priced its product too low for the Goliath. He doesn't want to discourage Jack and his sales team though, so he agrees to see how things go, knowing that Arkansas-based Wal-Mart is infamous for grinding down supplier prices over time. The giant plays suppliers against each other, forcing prices lower, encouraging efficiencies, sometimes wreaking havoc on how businesses are run. Many suppliers move jobs overseas to compete. Others, such as Vlasic pickles, lowered prices so much through Wal-Mart's stores that they cannibalized their sales elsewhere and undermined the value of their brands. Vlasic and a number of other Wal-Mart suppliers have ended up in bankruptcy, at least in part due to the giant retailer.[37]

By early 2004, just over a year into their new relationship, Spitz's sunflower seed sales to Wal-Mart hit $1 million annually.

But Tom was right. Wal-Mart is paying too little for each package it buys, meaning that only a small piece of this $1 million in sales ends up on his bottom line as profit. The co-founder of Spitz arranges a meeting at Wal-Mart with a senior buyer and his superior. Tom has heard Wal-Mart likes to intimidate people with its size and history, often putting visitors in uncomfortable seats and making them wait a long time. To avoid this fate, he writes an email in advance, saying that he and Jack Higgins plan to wait a maximum of 15 minutes at the giant's offices, and they'll leave if no one sees him by then. When they arrive, they are immediately ushered into their meeting.

Tom tells Wal-Mart's representatives he isn't making enough money on their account. As Jack begins to sweat, concerned at losing a big client and a big annual commission, Tom gives Wal-Mart two weeks to raise his company's take by 15%—or he'll walk away.

"What? You can't walk away. No one says that to Wal-Mart," Tom is told.

A few minutes later, the president of Spitz is offered an eight percent increase. His head of sales is visibly shocked at the giant's significant concession, and more than a little relieved—until his boss speaks again: "Let me know when you find the other seven percent," Tom responds, rising from his seat. "My offer's only good for two more weeks."

As they leave the Wal-Mart building, Jack turns to Tom in some pain, pointing out that he's just lost Spitz $1 million in sales. Tom says, "That's your problem, Jack, not mine. You'll have to find us more profitable sales somewhere else."

There is no change in Wal-Mart's position. So tiny Spitz, with its millions in total sales, walks away from a Goliath with hundreds of billions in sales and a huge market presence.

The decision isn't a hard one for Tom. If he can't make enough money from Wal-Mart, and he can make more money from other new customers, why wouldn't he walk away?

Six months go by.

Wal-Mart calls back.

The giant retailer says customers are asking to see Spitz back in its stores. Tom's told demand is strong enough that Wal-Mart thinks it can now raise its own prices and pay him the 15% increase he's looking for.

"Thank you," says Tom graciously in his booming Dutch-flavored voice. "We really appreciate your business."

PLAN TO WALK AWAY

Tom Droog genuinely loves Wal-Mart: its distribution clout through thousands of mega-stores, its relentless focus on consumer needs and the way it does business so shrewdly. He just doesn't want to become one of its victims.

To make it easier for Spitz to walk away from Wal-Mart, and to make it harder for Wal-Mart to walk away from Spitz, Tom's company does many things that we can all do—mainly away from the negotiation table—to maximize our strength and clout:

- **Know your strengths and build on them.** Tom Droog works tirelessly at his number-one priority and strength: offering a high-quality, unique product—setting his company apart from dozens of competitors. Spitz was the first to introduce flavored seeds and re-sealable bags. It will keep bringing out new flavors, new products and new packaging to distinguish itself from other wannabes. Lowering costs is a priority at Spitz, but not its first priority. The more valued you are for being different, the harder it is to be replaced on price alone if you threaten to walk away from giants, or they threaten to walk away from you.

- **Know your weaknesses and counter them.** Tom has two potential vulnerabilities with Wal-Mart. The first is the giant buyer's ability to informally collude with Tom's own sales force because of a shared interest in getting a deal done. Based on his experience with Wal-Mart, the president of Spitz now does his best to keep his team united as one in talking to any buyer, and he has adjusted compensation to ensure the financial incentives of his sales group are aligned with Spitz's interests in new *and* profitable business. Spitz's second vulnerability lies in its product secrets. When Wal-Mart wanted to be sent a detailed list of ingredients, saying consumers required it, Tom responded cagily: "1) Sunflower seeds. 2) Salt." He knows that if he shares more than this, Wal-Mart could send this information to another supplier and try to bid down his prices.

- **Apply decision-making criteria.** After his barely profitable dealings with Wal-Mart the first time around, Tom began applying these guiding rules prior to taking new business, or walking away from existing business: 1) All buyers are offered the same rates, with standard discounts based on volumes because selling more to the same buyer does save Spitz money on administration, transport and supplies. 2) Any sales arrangement must help the company's brand, positioning and reputation. 3) No single buyer can surpass 20% of the company's total sales, making it easier for Spitz to stick to its first two criteria. In all contexts, your decision-making criteria should take into account your interests and any relevant guiding standards, including precedents, laws, rules and principles—like Ben Franklin's personal principle that he'd walk away from client material he considered "scurrilous and defamatory."

- **Send signals through *how* you negotiate.** Tom knows that he needs Wal-Mart to believe he's serious about pricing and walking away. By sending an email before the meeting at Wal-Mart, he let his giant know it couldn't play around with him on the negotiation process itself, which implicitly sent a signal that it couldn't play around with him on pricing issues either. If he'd been kept waiting longer than 15 minutes, Tom would have left or risked his reputation for doing what he says, whether that's walking away or delivering a quality product. He later gave Wal-Mart two weeks to respond to his 15% fading offer, and walked away on cue. If we don't send clear, consistent signals about our intentions, giants may assume we're like everyone else and take advantage of us.

- **Generate back-up plans, choose your best one, then improve it and test it.** At $1 million in sales, Wal-Mart represented roughly 5% of Spitz's overall sales when Tom walked away in 2004. The one benefit of the Goliath's small initial contribution to profits is that Spitz could replace Wal-Mart's lost profits with new clients buying considerably less but at more reasonable prices. If Tom had been really concerned about the impact of losing Wal-Mart, he could have asked Jack to line up new clients or leads prior to walking away. Before saying *no* to any deal, we want to focus on our best alternative, improve it, and test it to make sure it truly meets our interests better than what we will be walking away from.

Tom Droog knows that if Wal-Mart can ever better meet its interests and those of its customers elsewhere, then the giant will walk away from his sunflower seeds. Likewise, he is constantly thinking ahead to the day he might need to walk away from Wal-Mart—again. When we're negotiating with giants, having an alternative in our back pocket is always helpful, if not essential.

The Size Wizards use distinct types of alternatives, often catching their giants off-guard. To maximize your leverage, you can tailor and improve a back-up plan from these choices: operate on your own, in the short term at least; hook up with a smaller player instead; say *yes* to your giant, even though you actually mean *no*; break your giant into parts and walk away from some parts but not others; find another giant to work with; walk away from one individual or group, escalating things inside your giant; or pursue a very different back-up plan that meets very different interests of yours.

In finishing up, I'll tell a quick story to highlight each of these approaches to walking away, or credibly threatening to. Once you have a feel for the entire range of alternatives at your disposal, you'll be able to brainstorm ideas under several different types of plans—choosing the one that best meets your interests:

OPERATE ON YOUR OWN. A lawyer named Carl Oppedahl decides to leave New York City and move far away from its stress, noise and irritations. He chooses a small, 40-home rural community in Colorado called Ruby Ranch, where he hopes to find serenity.

Then Carl talks with his new phone company. Qwest says he cannot have high-speed Internet at his house. The giant says he's too far away from major hubs, with too few homes around him. Carl does some research, talks to people in his neighborhood, and when Qwest once again turns him down, he triggers his back-up plan.

He and his neighbors chip in $5,000 for high-speed equipment including modems and a central hub. They'll use copper phone lines, not nearly as fast as coaxial cable, but convenient, since Qwest has already wired extra copper lines under their homes. Carl buys his equipment online through EBay at a fraction of retail prices and plans to run his system just as cheaply—out of a nearby horse barn.

Before the venture starts up, Qwest raises a fuss about its copper lines being used, but Colorado's public service commission gets involved, eventually granting Carl access. Qwest doesn't want to make this easy for him, worrying that others could follow in Ruby Ranch's footsteps, undermining one of the giant's fastest growing revenue sources.

In the spring of 2002, Ruby Ranch kicks off its high-speed services, becoming the first subscriber-owned cooperative of its kind in America. Qwest had told Carl that his start-up costs alone would sink the venture, but the wired innovator says it took only $12,000. The monthly payment for each household is set at $60, but it's expected to drop over time. "It's unfortunate it took so much effort to get this going," says Carl. "But hopefully we paved the way for others." [38]

FIND A SMALLER PLAYER INSTEAD. Jake Langley is such a good jazz guitarist that Universal snaps up his first CD, distributing and marketing it under the giant's Verve label.[39]

But after his CD launch, Jake's main contact at Verve is transferred, and his replacement seems to have other priorities. Jake watches as his CD sits unpromoted while all the rights remain with Universal Music.

When Jake has to decide where to go with his follow-up CDs, he no longer wants to hook up with a giant player. While he knows there's some cachet in signing with a Goliath, he instead chooses to work with a smaller player, where he can gain more influence over how his CDs are marketed. He signs with an independent label, Alma, where he is much happier, launching two additional CDs—each outselling his first at Universal.

"I like knowing that the guys at Alma wake up in the morning and worry that they may have trouble paying their bills if they're not doing a good job marketing my CD," says Jake, whose international profile continues to grow. "My smaller CD deals mean a lot more to a smaller label than they ever would to a giant like Universal."

SAY *YES* TO YOUR GIANT, EVEN THOUGH YOU ACTUALLY MEAN *NO*. Paris, August 1944. The German general responsible for the occupation of the French capital, Dietrich von Choltitz, feels sweat dripping from his brow. The Führer's Chief of Staff, Alfred Jodl, is shouting at von Choltitz on the phone. The tide has turned against Germany and Adolf Hitler wants to know if Paris is being blown up—before the Allies re-capture it.

Von Choltitz tells Jodl that despite some unforeseen delays, Paris will soon be wiped out, in keeping with Hitler's direct orders. During the days ahead, the general finally begins to oversee the placement of explosives at each of the city's historic sites, including its oldest bridges, palaces and monuments. Hitler's wrath won't show leniency for sentimental favorites: the Arc de Triomphe, the Eiffel Tower and the 600-year-old Notre-Dame Cathedral are all targeted for destruction.[40]

Hitler asks again, "Is Paris burning?" The general says he's working on it. The preparations continue. Hitler grows more impatient. "Is Paris burning?" he keeps asking. The Führer's man in Paris explains the job is almost complete, with detonation lines now snaking their way into most sites, ready for him to deliver his final command.

As the Allies descend on Paris, Dietrich von Choltitz never does issue this command. He refuses to go down in history as the person who destroyed the world's most beautiful city. Hitler turns apoplectic when he learns his general has walked away from his orders. The Führer dies before exacting his revenge on von Choltitz and his "yes, yes" stalling tactics.

In the decades to follow, millions of successful smaller players working for giant bosses and organizations will walk the same risky line as von Choltitz—the "Savior of Paris." These smaller players never say they *won't* do something, because that would get them in trouble. But they also never deliver, because they never intended to, it isn't a priority for them or they suspect that their giant's priorities will shift over time.

BREAK YOUR GIANT INTO PARTS AND WALK AWAY FROM SOME PARTS BUT NOT OTHERS. In early 2001, New England Patriots head coach Bill Belichick faces his own giant: a losing football team made up of 53 players, each with their own ego and agenda. His squad has just finished in last place in their division. According to Las Vegas bookies, things aren't going to get much better next season. They have the Patriots pegged as 70-1 long shots to win the 2002 Super Bowl.[41]

This will only be his second season with the team, but Belichick has seen enough.[42]

He goes to work, breaking his giant into 53 distinct parts, one player per part. He has three main criteria to determine who stays, who goes, and who will replace those who go. He asks: 1) Who desperately wants to win, and is willing to put everything else aside toward that single-minded goal, including their ego? 2) Is this player really good *and* versatile enough so we can use him creatively in game plans and shift him from one position to another to cover for injured teammates as needed? 3) Given the team's salary cap, and salary ranges we've set for each position, can we afford this player while avoiding bad precedents and not upsetting other players?

Belichick talks to players one by one, applies these criteria and builds a renewed giant by walking away from half of his old one. When he lets a player go, it's done respectfully, and the reasons are clear. If money is an issue, some players are amicably told to pursue better offers from other teams, knowing they can always re-sign with the Patriots—as many will. Remaining players are on their toes, knowing their fate if they don't live up to the three criteria. The late sports columnist, Will McDonough, told me at the time that Belichick's walk-away strategy and no-nonsense approach didn't necessarily make him popular with players, but that he was widely respected, and that's what really mattered.[43]

Belichick's systematic, consistent, criteria-driven restructuring is one of the most dramatic ever undertaken in football—and his results are just as dramatic. Against the odds, the Patriots go on to win the league championship in 2001-2002, and follow up this first success with two more Super Bowls, winning three in a span of four years.

In different situations, we can walk away from some parts of our giant while continuing to embrace others, relying on crisp criteria to guide our decisions and help ease relationship tensions. On the professional front, if you're a supplier, you may stop providing an unprofitable service to one division of a giant, while maintaining services to other parts. In your personal life, if you're divorcing a powerful spouse, you may not live in the same house, but you might keep running a jointly-owned business together.

FIND ANOTHER GIANT. Shari Heightner's "Bedtime Baskets" business is taking off as it delivers baskets of toys and books to kids as a special nighttime gift.

With growth comes a problem: Shari needs a line of credit to bridge the gap between when she owes money and when she receives it. A major domestic bank has said it will give her business a loan, but its interest rate is high, and worse, the giant wants her guarantee that if the loan's not repaid, she'll pay it back personally. Her giant assures her that every bank will require a personal guarantee despite the growth at Bedtime Baskets, because this is her first venture and it's such a young company. Shari is still in debt from school and hoping to do an MBA some day, so taking on this additional risk is either a deal-breaker, or a huge amount of stress in the months and years ahead. *But what choice do I have?* she asks herself. None—yet.

Shari lines up a meeting at a giant Asian bank that operates downtown. She has heard that it's "more lenient" since it is trying to establish itself in a new market. The entrepreneur discovers she can get a loan from this second giant at a lower interest rate and *without* any personal guarantee.

She breathes a sigh of relief, calls up her first giant—the domestic bank—and tells her contact there about this offer from "another major bank." [44]

Shari is about to benefit from the fact that as smaller players, we often look more valuable to a giant when another giant has already acknowledged our value.

Within 48 hours, the domestic bank Shari first approached tells her it will match the Asian bank's offer. Shari signs the papers with this domestic giant as she'd prefer to do business with an American financial institution that has more expert resources and local services than its foreign competitor. She calls the Asian giant back, thanking it anyway. It says to stay in touch; she will. Shari may need to walk away again from the bank she's just said *yes* to. As it turns out, she'll later end up using both banks, reducing her dependence on any single financing source.

Many giant representatives in consumer service organizations such as phone and cable companies have triggers, words *you* use, that can authorize them to give discounts or other concessions. For example, you might mention switching to a specific giant competitor, and only then, according to their rules, can they give you what you want.

WALK AWAY FROM ONE INDIVIDUAL OR GROUP BY ESCALATING AN ISSUE. I buy the sofa for our kids' playroom, agreeing with the salesperson at Sears that should I need to return it for any reason, I'll be out 25% of the price—but I'm confident we'll be keeping the couch.

When it arrives, the Sears guys delivering it can't get it past one of our inside doors. They leave with my couch, and I'm on the phone minutes later with the salesperson, Dan. I admit to him that I'm an idiot for not taking more precise measurements. He agrees: "I did explain the rules," he says. I ask to speak with his supervisor. "She's busy, but she'll only repeat what I've told you."

Dan's supervisor calls me after I again ask to hear from her. I tell Melissa the mistake was mine.[45] I add that the Sears movers told me not to feel badly—they regularly had the same sofa rejected at the homes of other buyers because of its unusual dimensions. I say this would have been helpful information had Dan mentioned it to me.

Melissa gets it. She waives the 25% penalty. Walking away from Dan and escalating my issue worked here because his interests in an immediate commission are different than Melissa's and her store's broader interests: long-term customer satisfaction and repeat sales. At most large consumer-based corporations I've worked with, frontline operators and salespeople have distinct limits placed on their authority, and with good reason. They're usually not offended if we ask for their superiors, as long as we're polite about it.

In non-consumer situations, the impact of walking away to someone higher up in an organization can be softened if you include the person you're trying to go above in your next steps, rather than being overly aggressive or making them look bad: "Kristin, maybe it makes sense for you, me and your boss to sit down and discuss this together because I realize your hands may be tied by your firm's policies."

PURSUE A VERY DIFFERENT GAME PLAN THAT MEETS VERY DIFFERENT INTERESTS OF YOURS. It's 1960. Carl Brewer, a defenseman for the Toronto Maple Leafs in the National Hockey League, is preparing for a face-off: the 21-year-old rising star is still owed $100 by the Maple Leafs for medical-related expenses from the previous season.

Since he doesn't have an agent, Carl raises the issue with his gruff general manager and coach, Punch Imlach, who ignores him, saying he's got better things to worry about, like training camp for the upcoming season.

Imlach must choke on his breakfast when he opens up his national newspaper at the start of training camp and sees a large photo of Carl Brewer—wearing a *football* uniform. In the article, Carl says he's quitting hockey and playing football. He's slated to play at McMaster, one of the area's university teams, because he likes the game and he's been hoping to go back to school for some time.[46]

Amid a growing uproar among Maple Leaf fans, Imlach sends his assistant, King Clancy, to talk some sense into Carl.

When Clancy realizes the hockey player is serious about quitting the Maple Leafs, he offers up apologies for the late $100 payment, saying it will be made immediately. Carl isn't impressed. Clancy keeps ratcheting up his offers as Carl continues to decline them. The final agreement reached: the club will pay their defenseman $200 in expenses, twice what he was owed. In return, he'll throw away his cleats and put his skates back on.[47]

It's a good thing Carl decided in favor of his skates, because the following year he would help lead the Maple Leafs to their first of three consecutive Stanley Cup championships.

Going to university and changing sports was a credible alternative for Carl given his known passion for learning and the fact he was a multi-sport athlete who had once turned down a pro baseball contract. He could have just threatened to sit out the season, or play for another hockey team, but in light of the circumstances, league protocols and Carl's personality, these walk-aways would have been seen as bluffs.

If you're unhappy at work and long overdue for a raise or promotion, and threatening to go to a competitor isn't reasonable, you might consider returning to school or changing fields. Sometimes, major changes will meet your interests better than your current giant ever can.

Plan to walk away—by applying clear criteria while improving and testing one of these alternatives: operate on your own; hook up with a smaller player or another giant; say yes to your giant when you mean no; walk away from some parts but not others; escalate things inside your giant; or pursue a plan that meets very different interests of yours.

MAGNIFY YOUR IMPACT THROUGH WORDS AND IMAGES

In the 1950s, Rachel Carson uncovers troubling links between bird deaths and pesticides. The scientist believes giant corporations that have made millions from the extensive use of chemicals such as DDT during war-time are continuing to grow through consumer sales that threaten the health of wildlife and human beings.

To make her argument in a detailed and compelling way that cannot easily be refuted by chemical Goliaths around the world, Rachel writes *Silent Spring*, a non-fiction book introduced through *The New Yorker* magazine. The first chapter describes the silence a small town would experience if it woke up one morning to find that all of its wildlife had died from pesticides. While this approach grabs the attention of readers, the book's vivid writing and well-researched facts are attacked by chemical giants and major media outlets, claiming Rachel Carson is either wrong or exaggerating.

On the heels of her book's growing readership, Rachel testifies before Congress in 1963. The following year, still in her mid-fifties, she dies of breast cancer, never knowing that the true extent of her influence will ultimately include the banning of DDT, the establishment of America's Environmental Protection Agency, and the early development of the environmental movement itself. As well, Rachel dies without knowing whether exposure to pesticides through her work contributed to her own premature death.[48]

A century before Rachel Carson, another woman looking to create change also used writing as her main means of influence—with an extraordinary outcome.

Story: Novel Approaches

It's January 1852. After putting her children to bed and cleaning up their Maine home, Harriet Beecher Stowe races to a desk in front of a roaring fireplace, pulls out a quill and begins to pen a pivotal scene in her unfolding story. Her main character, a black slave named Uncle Tom, is about to be sold for the last time.

"I could not control the story," she'd later say, "it wrote itself." [49]

So far, *Uncle Tom's Cabin* has been well received by abolitionists who follow Harriet's weekly installments in an anti-slavery newspaper. They are enraptured by Uncle Tom, a Christian, God-fearing man who does good for his friends, family and masters. What these readers don't know yet is that Tom will soon die a martyr, much like Christ. He'll be whipped to death by his final owner, Simon Legree. Tom's humble cabin, where he left his family years before, becomes a memorial to the destructiveness of slavery and the healing powers of Christianity.

Harriet draws on detailed information she has gleaned from books and first-hand accounts, mainly from African Americans, since she's never lived in a slave state herself. She describes slavery's living conditions, the beatings, the sexual assaults and the owners who split up families for profit. She portrays slaves as victims of an evil institution, and turns Tom into an unlikely hero—if you're a white reader.

Glancing up from her newest scene, the passionate 39-year-old stares into the fireplace. Silently, she thanks her sister-in-law for suggesting she support the fight against slavery with her writing skills, even as she looks after six children while her husband, a professor, completes a posting in Cincinnati.[50] Many white men and women who make up her giant in the North and South won't listen to a woman on this issue. Harriet hopes they'll at least heed one of her white male characters, George Shelby, who believes that slavery is inconsistent with Christian beliefs.

Before she can expect to have any broader impact, however, Harriet must find a publisher for her novel. This won't be easy with such controversial material. Whites in the South rely on slaves to work their plantations, and in the industrialized North, many simply don't see blacks as humans, nor do they believe that slaves like Tom are actually abused. As Harriet searches for a publisher, she hopes her profile as a part-time writer for magazines will prove useful, along with her broader family's profile in the anti-slavery movement. But still, she questions whether a simple housewife can attract a wider audience and make any difference in the affairs of state.[51]

In March 1852, a Boston publisher agrees to print the book based on the success of her serialized newspaper installments, despite the fact these installments only targeted a narrow audience of abolitionists.[52] Harriet cannot afford to pay any printing costs, so she'll receive just 10% of the proceeds from sales.

Publisher John P. Jewett moves quickly. Immediately after sealing Harriet's book contract, 5,000 copies are printed, weeks in advance of when her final newspaper installment is due to appear. To Harriet's utter amazement, readers paying 56 cents each snap up all 5,000 copies of *Uncle Tom's Cabin* in a matter of days.[53]

Her words spread like wildfire across her nation of 23 million inhabitants, and then over to Europe. Helping fuel this fire are high-profile attacks from defensive southerners. Within six months, printing presses run day and night on both sides of the Atlantic. One year after its release, *Uncle Tom's Cabin* hits 350,000 books sold, well on its way to becoming the world's best-selling novel.[54]

Harriet finds herself staring at royalty checks worth $10,000, more than her husband can earn in an entire decade, making her a wealthy woman. Overnight, she becomes a sought-after speaker worldwide on the topic of slavery, now an issue being widely debated in the northern American states and abroad.

Sales rise above one million, two million, then three million. By the late 1850s, it's said that almost everyone in the North has read her novel or had it read to them by their mothers. Those reading it in the South often do so at the risk of punishment: in one case, a man is sent to jail for ten years after being caught with a copy.

One observer concludes that President Abraham Lincoln's election victory in 1860 results from boys, influenced by Harriet's book, maturing into young voters and favoring the candidate most likely to rid their country of slavery. Another commentator maintains the new Republican Party that Lincoln represents would never have been founded if not for the acceptance of Harriet's message.

After Lincoln is elected, the southern states declare their secession from the Union over deep-rooted conflicts, many of which are linked to the North's pursuit of a manufacturing base while the South continues to focus on agriculture. Cheap labor in the form of slavery, however, soon becomes a catch-all issue that highlights the economic and political divide between the two sides.

The Civil War breaks out.

Harriet travels to see Lincoln in December 1862. He greets her with respect and a touch of humor, saying: "So this is the little lady who made this big war." [55] She urges Lincoln as her country's ultimate Controller on this issue to free slaves nationwide. Harriet believes she can convince government officials in Great Britain—still smarting from their loss in the Revolutionary War—not to support the South, but only if Lincoln takes a firm stand against slavery, which he has not yet done despite being morally against it. He has argued in the past that slavery is entrenched in the Constitution, even though it isn't referred to specifically, and that it's up to Congress to do away with it, not him.

Not long after his meeting with Harriet, President Lincoln makes a bold move. Using a military rationale, which allows him to act without congressional approval, Lincoln formally issues the Emancipation Proclamation on January 1, 1863, freeing slaves in the break-away states. These slaves are urged to flee their captors, and join the northern army. The Proclamation helps swing the Civil War in Lincoln's favor since the South not only loses hundreds of thousands of productive laborers, but now these former slaves are fighting against it. Influenced heavily by Harriet, Britain never does support the South.[56]

In 1865, the southern states surrender, ending America's bloodiest war ever, with some 600,000 troops dying in battle, more than ten times the number that will perish a century later in Vietnam. Following the North's victory, American lawmakers pass the 13th amendment to the nation's Constitution, doing away with slavery.

MAGNIFY YOUR IMPACT THROUGH WORDS AND IMAGES

By the time Harriet Beecher Stowe died in 1896, she knew that, at ten million copies sold, *Uncle Tom's Cabin* was second only to the Bible in world book sales spanning the 19th century.[57]

After her death, Harriet's ground-breaking novel became less relevant as Americans moved on to grapple with new racial issues, and the civil rights movement brushed aside her outdated characters, now viewed as racist creations by 20th century standards.[58]

What shouldn't be brushed aside, however, are the influence lessons from the author's phenomenal success, at a time when she couldn't appear on *Oprah* to talk up her book. Indeed, these lessons are even clearer because their origins remain unaffected by modern media that might confuse our understanding of what works when we're negotiating with giants through words. What works is word-of-mouth. Why? Because we're most likely to act on any kind of message when we learn it from, or have it reinforced by, people we know and respect. So while an ad for Harriet's book might intrigue us, having a friend recommend it will actually get us to go out and buy it. Harriet was a Size Wizard of the first order, and the more we apply her messaging approaches from the 1850s to sending our messages today, the greater the odds are that we'll get what we want:

- **Send a simple, actionable and positively controversial core message.** *Slavery goes against everything Christians believe in and should be abolished.* The simplicity of Harriet's message made it easy to understand and pass along. The controversy surrounding her call to action played a positive role in that it attracted widespread discussion and attention, without alienating the author's core audience. A review in the *The Independent* newspaper said, "Spread it round the world! is the feeling which comes first, the instant, urgent, inevitable impulse, as one arises from the perusal of this fascinating book." [59] The Size Wizards keep their core messages tight, memorable and positively controversial whenever fitting, knowing that fiery messages can spread like flames.

- **Target your message thoughtfully and not always at Controllers directly.** Harriet expected women, especially Christians, to buy her book, read it, and be most influenced by it. While unable to vote, these women could act as valuable Connectors, connecting her book and its message to other women as well as to their own husbands and sons who, as Convincers, would cast future votes towards ending slavery. Harriet also targeted a distinct set of Coalitionists. Imagine respected leaders standing at street corners throughout a city, proclaiming the author's message, urging others to read her book and act against slavery. Got the image? Now, simply add a collar to their clothing and put them in a church. These men of the cloth saw an opportunity to re-tell Christ's story, promote Christian values and attract new worshippers through Tom's riveting struggles. For Harriet, ministers who opposed slavery were natural allies in a nation where the majority believed in God and church attendance was growing fast. By first using a serialized format, she understood who would be drawn to her message and then repeat it, preparing her for a broader launch. If Controllers inside your own giant are tough to access, consider other well-placed targets who can spread your message, exerting their influence as Connectors, Convincers, Coalitionists, Coercers or Cracks.

- **Get the right person to send *this* message.** When Harriet wrote her novel, many excellent books, pamphlets, articles and speeches had already described slavery's atrocities from the perspective of African Americans (Frederick Douglass was a leading black advocate for change and he'd act as a valuable Counselor to Harriet on her book). In the end, however, America's white giant found itself most persuaded by those resembling it.[60] Hearing stories of oppression from blacks was more predictable and less credible for many whites at the time. Hearing these same stories from another white person was ear-opening. Yes, Harriet was a woman and this diluted her influence inside a giant dominated by males, but she overcame this limitation through her "novel" approach and by using a white male character to make some of her strongest arguments. If *you're* not the right person to send a message, get someone else who is.

- **Use persuasive standards directed at your audience's brains.** Harriet applied logic as one standard, arguing that not all slave owners were evil, but so long as slavery existed, a minority of mean-spirited whites would abuse blacks. This made whites less defensive and eased her burden of proof. In opposing slavery, she also used Christian standards like "the golden rule"—treating others as you'd wish to be treated. A new law requiring citizens to return escaped slaves to their owners had to be weighed against other standards, like those from the Bible. As one of Harriet's characters tells her husband: "Now, John, I don't know anything about politics, but I can read the Bible; and there I see that I must feed the hungry, clothe the naked, and comfort the desolate; and that Bible I mean to follow." [61] The author did *not* use racial equality as a standard—it wouldn't be persuasive in the 1850s. Nor was Harriet one-sided. The *Boston Morning Post* said she painted "the slaveholder as he lives and moves, with no touch of bigotry or fanaticism." [62] To win over converts, the Size Wizards take a thoroughly factual, balanced approach, using arm's-length standards that subtly favor their interests.

- **Strike and stick to your audience's hearts.** Uncle Tom's brutal experiences left people reeling. To reinforce the standards that opposed slavery, or bypass them, Harriet went after emotions, urging readers to do what they *felt* was right. The *London Times* described Harriet's technique this way: "With the instinct of her sex, the clever authoress takes the shortest road to her purpose, and strikes at the convictions of her readers by assailing their hearts. (…) *Euclid*, she well knows, is no child for effecting social revolutions, but an impassioned song may set a world in conflagration." [63] The review said Harriet showed a "mastery over human feeling," grabbing readers with her authentic characters and situations. Before sending your own message, ask yourself whether your giant is most likely going to be persuaded by what *feels* right, what *sounds* logical, or both.

- **Blend the right mix of seriousness and humor.** Negative and positive newspaper reviews in the 1850s talked about how Harriet deftly used humor to offset her book's tragic subject matter. This delicate mix accomplished three things: 1) By showing that even abused slaves had a sense of humor, the author humanized blacks and made them empathetic personalities. 2) By contrasting drama with scenes that got readers laughing aloud, Harriet heightened the undulating impact of her drama and humor, each complementing the other. 3) Harriet's humor showed she understood a range of emotions, making her less intense as an advocate, more believable and not as open to criticism from men for being an extremist. The Size Wizards use humor to enhance their messages, but if ever in doubt, they drop it.

- **Choose the best medium to deliver your message.** Harriet was a strong writer, and only a book could argue comprehensively against slavery while entertaining readers. Harriet might have sent her message through a non-fiction book but it would have lacked the emotional appeal of *Uncle Tom's Cabin*. Since she hadn't lived in the South, a work of fiction based on real stories was faster to write and more credible. Where Harriet's choices for media were limited, today smaller players can choose one or more far-ranging media formats to grab selected audiences, drive home messages and ignite word-of-mouth. Choices include: video clips, blogs, documentaries, text-messaging, websites, physical symbols, photos, speeches, PowerPoint presentations, television, satellite radio, and of course, electronic or printed books. Any time we use new or unexpected media, just as Harriet used the novel, our messages are bound to be more striking and stick longer with our audience. If you want to catch a giant's attention in the email era, think about sending a hand-written letter or phoning them directly.

Regardless of which media they choose, the Size Wizards model any behaviors they want their giants to adopt, making their messages more convincing and easily acted upon. If the abolitionist author of *Uncle Tom's Cabin* had used slaves in her own home, Harriet and her book would have been much less persuasive. Likewise, in the early 1950s, when Dr. Jonas Salk develops a promising polio vaccine that involves injecting people with a supposedly non-threatening version of the deadly polio virus, the brilliant researcher faces a huge challenge. How can he go on the radio and ask his giant, the American public, to try his unproven remedy? Salk's solution: he uses the vaccine on himself, his wife and his three children, helping spur the world to take the same risk, ultimately saving millions from the ravages of the disease.[64]

Harriet Beecher Stowe was the first of many authors to significantly influence America's government, with its elected leaders acting either as Controllers or Coercers.[65] In the early 1900s, Upton Sinclair penned *The Jungle*, a fictional but realistic profile of Chicago's sordid meat-packing industry, leading to changes in laws and regulations while generating the nation's first consumer movement. Later, in the 1960s, just after Rachel Carson's *Silent Spring* took on chemical giants and their pesticides, a young lawyer named Ralph Nader exposed safety issues in the auto industry. In *Unsafe at Any Speed*, Nader criticized political lobbying that opposed safety improvements such as seatbelts, singling out General Motors with detailed data claiming the Chevrolet Corvair rolled over too easily; new car safety laws were passed in 1966.

Authors or not, the Size Wizards execute at least two of the distinct messaging approaches used by Harriet, depending on their audience. Smaller players who fail in their messaging typically fall short on all fronts, but sometimes only mishandle one critical approach. Prior to the US elections in 2004, Michael Moore tried to shift opinion against Republican

President George W. Bush's war on terror through his film *Fahrenheit 9-11*. However, by emphasizing an emotional, striking message—instead of a balanced and well-supported message that might have converted moderate Republicans to vote for the Democrats—I believe Moore undermined his own daring efforts.

Here are examples across five different media of Size Wizards successfully magnifying their influence through words or images to get what they want:

DOCUMENTARY FILM. Morgan Spurlock is a glutton for punishment. The director hears about two obese teenagers suing McDonald's over their poor health, and decides to find out whether the fast food restaurant's menu can really be that bad. The result is a 2004 independent film called *Super Size Me*.[66] It begins by capturing Morgan on-camera as he receives a clean bill of health from doctors at the start of a cross-country odyssey. During his trip, he'll eat only McDonald's food—three meals a day—for a month.

Before long, Morgan undergoes physical trauma that includes vomiting, depression, heart problems and liver damage. He gains 25 pounds. He's urged by his doctors to stop the experiment, but completes it anyway. Watching him, we're led to the conclusion that we should be concerned about fast food.

Coinciding with the launch of *Super Size Me*, McDonald's announces it is doing away with its enormous "Super-Sized" servings while introducing new and healthier menu options. The giant denies its move is linked to Morgan's film.

STILL PHOTOS. Following America's Civil War, slavery gives way to child labor in the South, while an economic boom in the North sucks millions of children into factories. Instead of going to school, many youngsters toil in terrible working conditions for pennies an hour, suffering lung illnesses, accidents and emotional scars. A group of activists responds, setting up the National Child Labor Committee—the NCLC. But efforts go nowhere as giant employers deny what's going on behind closed doors.

In 1908, the NCLC hires photographer Lewis Hine to criss-cross the nation documenting child labor. Lewis enters factories either by posing as a fire inspector or a Bible salesman, other times waiting outside for children headed home. Some of his more dramatic black and white photos starkly capture the muddied, weary faces of the "breaker boys," children who endure 14- to 16-hour days breaking up rock and coal.

The passionate advocate behind the camera believes that if voters and politicians can see the impact of extreme labor on young bodies through selected magazines, books and exhibitions, they'll also see the need for new labor laws. He is right. New awareness and laws subsequently produced by state politicians, acting as formal Coercers, create pressure on employers, cutting child labor in half by the early 1920s—with national laws later setting minimum ages and working conditions. The head of the NCLC at the time, Owen Lovejoy, said the work of Lewis Hine "was more responsible than all other efforts for bringing the facts and conditions of child employment to public attention." [67]

EMAIL. Student protesters in Indonesia try to overthrow their president, not with tanks and weapons, but through emails. In an autocratic nation with thousands of islands, costly phone services and tightly-controlled media, organizers rallying against President Suharto's corrupt regime share updates, exchange tips for resisting troops, coordinate their efforts and inform media around the world about unfolding events—all electronically. Suharto is forced to step down in May 1998—the world's first successful revolution using email and the Internet, according to Tufts University Professor W. Scott Thompson, an expert in international politics.[68]

WEBSITES. In 2005, a website is criticized for giving convicted murderer Scott Peterson a platform to declare his innocence, argue his defense and post pictures of himself hugging his wife, Laci. The controversy arises because Peterson has just been sentenced to death in California for killing his wife and their unborn child.

The Canadian-based website's co-founder, Tracy Lamourie, explains that Peterson's material is consistent with her tiny group's mandate to provide a voice for any American prisoner due to be executed. The Canadian Coalition

Against the Death Penalty hosts free web pages for 500 death row inmates. More than a dozen prisoners have since seen their convictions overturned. In a number of cases, Tracy says lawyers have scanned CCADP.org, found questionable convictions, got themselves hired as Counselors to represent prisoners, then argued successfully to overturn convictions—often relying on new DNA evidence to persuade judicial Controllers.[69] "At what point can we say, that's it, they're done—they don't deserve to speak in their own defense? Not until the justice system is a whole lot better," says Tracy.[70] Her site receives up to 20,000 visits a day.

MAGAZINES. Ida Tarbell grows up hearing her father curse John D. Rockefeller, one of the world's first corporate titans. By the late 1800s, Rockefeller's Standard Oil controls the majority of America's refined oil sales through an organization called a trust (similar to what we call a holding company today). Standard Oil achieves its dominant position early on through ingenuity, and later, through brutal manipulations aimed at securing cost advantages based on its giant size. Many of its smaller competitors are run out of business—Ida's father being one of them.

In the early 1900s, Ida seeks revenge on her family's giant, even though her father fears for her life. Now a journalist for *McClure Magazine*, Ida writes a series of articles that will forever stand as a testament to thoroughly researched and brilliantly presented investigative reports.[71] The object of her scathing and daring exposé: Standard Oil.

Through exhaustive interviews and diligent document-gathering, the journalist cuts through the fog surrounding Rockefeller's practices and gets readers buzzing—including US President Teddy Roosevelt—who smells blood as a formal Coercer. The reform-minded leader reads every word of Ida's series, sending along his congratulations in writing. He then goes after Standard Oil under the Sherman Antitrust Act, claiming the Goliath has clearly used its monopolistic market position to the detriment of Americans. To Rockefeller's chagrin, Standard Oil is broken into 34 companies, which must now compete.

Ida Tarbell's bold journalism successfully undermines her father's arch-enemy.

Magnify your impact through words and images—by creating and sending a message that is easily spread, targeted, sender-proofed, striking, supported, humorous and sent right.

TAKE ADVANTAGE OF YOUR WEAKNESSES AND THEIR STRENGTHS

The cabinet minister smiles at me, leans back in his chair and begins to chuckle. "So, Mr. Johnston, if I understand you correctly, you're saying that because we *don't* have the money to pay our large bills, we're well positioned to negotiate?"

"That's right," I respond to the minister and a dozen other senior officials gathered in this small, hot conference room for a hastily arranged meeting. Their developing Asian nation is engulfed in a regional economic crisis and bills worth hundreds of millions of dollars are rapidly coming due to giant corporations and governments around the world.

These officials haven't mismanaged anything, nor are they hiding money. A big drop in their country's currency has just made their US dollar debts unaffordable. If they raise taxes dramatically, there will be riots, putting expensive infrastructure owned by their giants at risk, something their giants definitely wouldn't want. The hands of these senior decision-makers are tied, and they'll soon make this clear to their giant counterparts.

An hour later, we have a plan for moving the country forward. Heads are nodding positively. Everyone in the room understands now. In certain situations, to get what you want, you have to take full advantage of your weaknesses.

STORY: CREDIT WHERE CREDIT'S DUE

Jamie Hodge lives on the edge, funding his small start-up publishing venture on the back of his only personal credit card, issued by a large bank.

Most months, the 40-year-old businessman pays only the interest on his card, which usually has a balance close to its credit limit. Whenever he can afford to, Jamie pays down his card as much as possible to give himself some breathing room.[72]

One day, when Jamie goes out for lunch with a client, he experiences a horrible moment—the kind not mentioned in credit card commercials. The time comes to pay and his VISA card is declined. This is embarrassing, especially when the waiter processing the card cannot seem to control the loudness of his voice. After paying with a check, and saying goodbye to his client, Jamie calls his bank's VISA center, but is told the matter is out of their hands. The manager at his branch canceled Jamie's card earlier that day.

Jamie heads to the bank. He wants to know what screw-up has led to his card being declined. His usual calm demeanor and charm are gone.

"I'd like to speak to your manager."

"Unfortunately, Mr. Bavari is in a meeting. You'll have to make an appointment."

Jamie forces a smile for the benefit of the young woman behind the desk. "No, I'd like to see Mr. Bavari right now, please." Jamie hands over his business card with the title CEO embossed on it, gently adding, "Tell Mr. Bavari that Jamie Hodge is here to see him. I've been a client of this branch for a long time, and if he doesn't come out to see me immediately, I'll close every account I have with you."

The assistant nods, rises from her seat and disappears into a maze of dividers. A couple of minutes later, the bank manager emerges. He motions Jamie to follow him into his office. The two have never met. Bavari goes onto his computer, checks his client's VISA account and confirms the card has been canceled.

"Mr. Hodge, on three separate occasions in the past year, you've missed a minimum payment by one month. In addition, you are over your $20,000 credit limit by $3,000. Our policy is clear in this respect. Your credit privileges have been revoked."

"Mr. Bavari, I've been a client of this branch for a decade. Yes, I've made late payments, and yes, I sometimes go over my limit. But I'll bet I'm easily one of your best clients, even if your policy book may not say so. I've paid you tens of thousands of dollars in exorbitant interest payments. At the same time, I'm a very low risk. I've never defaulted on my obligations, only postponed them briefly—and on rare occasions."

The manager smiles, seeing humor where none was intended. "This is not to be taken personally, Mr. Hodge. And I do apologize for any inconvenience."

Jamie pauses. "On the contrary, Mr. Bavari, I apologize for the loss this branch is going to endure on your watch."

"I'm sorry?" counters Bavari, staring through his gold-rimmed spectacles.

"Well, I seem to have nothing to lose here. Why would I pay you any of the outstanding amounts when you've taken my credit card with no apparent ability to get it back?"

"Well," says the slightly flustered manager, "you, of course, will pay this amount back. There's your credit rating to consider, and your reputation."

"I'm guessing both went out the window when you canceled my card. Isn't that right?" inquires Jamie, suddenly drawing calmness from Bavari's growing discomfort.

"Well, perhaps, but not indefinitely…" stammers the bank manager.

"Long enough, Mr. Bavari, so that an extra little note on my credit record saying I defaulted on the entire amount probably won't make much of a difference in seven years or so. Wouldn't you think?"

"I don't control what you do, or how these things are treated, Mr. Hodge. Now, I must get back to my meeting."

"You do control what *you* do, Mr. Bavari. If I leave here today without my card being re-instated along with a $3,000 increase in my limit, I swear on my mother's life to never pay you back one cent of the $23,000 balance currently outstanding."

"You wouldn't."

"I will," says Jamie, rising up from his chair. "Just watch me."

Bavari hesitates, and finally asks Jamie to sit down. The manager excuses himself, explaining he wants to review the account more thoroughly with one of his team members. Ten minutes later, he re-enters the room and picks up the phone.

"Hello, this is Mr. Bavari at branch 6204. Can I give you a VISA card number? Yes, that's right, Jamie Hodge. Good. I'd like Mr. Hodge's card re-instated please." He glances sideways at Jamie. "And we will be increasing his credit limit to $23,000."

Bavari hangs up and turns to Jamie. "As a longstanding client of our branch, Mr. Hodge, you've obviously persuaded me. Is there anything else I can do for you today?"

"No, that's it, Mr. Bavari. I got what I came for. Thanks for your time."

Take Advantage of Your Weaknesses and Their Strengths

Jamie Hodge's gambit was not for the faint-hearted, nor would I generally advise it, but it proved effective here.

The debt racked up by the entrepreneur away from the negotiation table created a *mutual* dependence with part of his giant, turning Jamie's weak finances into an unexpected source of strength (also ensuring, by the way, that he won't ever want to repay too much at any one time). Magnifying the manager's concern about Jamie's threat to pay nothing back was the fact that Mr. Bavari would have to record any acknowledged loss on the account as a loss for his branch, weakening his own financial results in reports to the giant bank's head office. A loss in the tens of thousands of dollars obviously wouldn't sink a small branch, or be more than a blip for a giant bank, but with a decent argument to be made for not claiming the loss at all, at least for now, Bavari was convinced.

Size Wizards like Jamie remain highly aware of both their actual and perceived weaknesses, converting them into strengths:

- **From weakness—*you're too dependent on your giant*—to strength.** Your giant may also be too dependent on you, as in Jamie's situation. In other cases, your giant may feel they have no choice but to help you because it's clear you have no alternatives to their support. This is in part the dynamic between Israel and the United States, as Israel continues to require significant financial and diplomatic assistance from its giant North American partner.

- **From weakness—*you've been crushed or could be crushed by a giant*—to strength.** Others may be attracted to help you, including non-profit groups, friends, family, and lawyers who are outraged or wanting to further raise their profile through precedent-setting cases. The media, the public and reform-minded politicians love a "David and Goliath" story and could feel compelled to take up your cause. Ralph Nader sprang to prominence because General Motors—GM— tried to crush his credibility after he'd written *Unsafe at Any Speed*. A journalist discovered the car giant had hired detectives to dig up dirt on Nader. Politicians reacted, calling the corporation's president to testify before a senate sub-committee, and making him apologize. GM's powerful attacks propelled Nader's book onto the bestseller lists and enshrined him as a leading consumer advocate.

- **From weakness—*you have nothing of value and won't for a while*** **—to strength.** You can take bigger risks with bigger rewards while not fearing your giant because you have nothing to lose, just like Jamie. As well, payments due are often adjusted based on perceived resources, meaning you might pay lower giant prices if you cannot afford to pay more. And finally, if you're not creating value right now, you may have more time to focus on your giant negotiation than your giant does, yielding stronger results.

- **From weakness—*you've been strong-armed or misled by a giant*—** **to strength.** If you didn't receive counsel from a lawyer or another informed individual, a judge may conclude your giant has unfairly taken advantage of your *genuine* lack of sophistication, especially if you receive little or nothing in return for what you've given. Likewise, if a giant in an extraordinary position of trust or power breaches your trust through bad faith, or through poor agreements reached on your behalf, courts will consider intervening. Relationships affected include parents and children, trustees and beneficiaries, lawyers and clients, doctors and patients, or church representatives and their followers. Finally, if a giant has forced you to sign one of its "standard agreements" and it is unfairly onerous, or its ambiguous terms are being used against you, a judge may also rule in your favor.[73]

- **From weakness—*you're viewed as flighty, unstable or mercurial*—** **to strength.** Your giant may be less likely to anger you and may even placate you if they think you might do something irrational to hurt their interests, without any apparent logic or regard for your own interests. This is clearly a high-risk approach that could get you what you're after in the short term but often undermines your credibility in the long run. Kim Jong-il in North Korea benefits from this approach, as do many dictatorial bosses inside giant corporations. One client of mine used his up-and-down behaviors to keep giant buyers in line, managing to stay on their good side by delivering product as promised and being charming—most of the time.

- **From weakness—*you're viewed as someone who can't control your side*—to strength.** You simply point to those raising a fuss in your own ranks and make it clear that some of their interests will need to be addressed—giving you additional leverage. You may even find your giant is suddenly pushing for a deal, because its looks like you're no longer in full command. When Prime Minister Yitzhak Rabin decided to begin nationhood talks with Yasser Arafat's Palestine Liberation Organization—the PLO—in the early 1990s, part of Israel's rationale was that Arafat appeared to be on the verge of losing control of the Palestinian side, with the arch-rival Hamas group on the rise. Rabin knew the Palestinians would continue to splinter into rogue factions if he put off serious talks with Arafat any longer, giving Arafat and the PLO a much-needed boost.[74]

- **From weakness—*your run-ins with a giant leave you dejected and isolated*—to strength.** You have time to gather up your energies, reflect on any shortcomings, improve yourself, and figure out what really matters to you before setting out again. While imprisoned, Nelson Mandela told his wife how he could ignore less meaningful external measures of success and instead focus on internal measures related to his honesty, humility and generosity. "If for nothing else," he said, "the cell gives you the opportunity to look daily into your entire conduct to overcome the bad and develop whatever is good in you." He further assured Winnie, "Difficulties break some men but make others." [75]

We can also turn some common giant strengths into distinct strengths of our own:

- **From giant strength—*their total resources and clout make them formidable*—to your strength.** Sometimes, giants react without thinking, using their resources inappropriately or arrogantly, leading them to overreach, exposing you to new opportunities. Or your giant may be so focused on big-picture issues that ground-level details elude it, details that could prove critical to what you're after. CBS fell into this trap early in 2002 when its executives assumed that David Letterman's existing contract gave them the right to match any offer their star received elsewhere after their own exclusive renegotiation period with him expired. The late-night talk show host went on to negotiate a near-deal with ABC, only backing away from it at the last moment when giant CBS realized its mistake and upped the ante, offering Letterman a much more attractive deal—which he accepted.[76]

- **From giant strength**—*their high profile puts them in the spotlight*—**to your strength.** If you can somehow direct part of their spotlight toward you during your giant dealings, you can satisfy your interests in ways that might have been impossible otherwise, even if you'd hired a top public relations firm in New York. As Microsoft's lawyers went after Mike Rowe in 2004 for using the domain name MikeRoweSoft. com, the surprised high school student raised his own profile through media coverage of the story, garnering new leads for his website design business and thousands of dollars in unsolicited donations from people wanting to lend a hand. He also managed to sell the legal papers used against him on EBay. Thanks to Microsoft's strong spotlight, Mike has more money to pay for college. Between classes, he can play with the expensive Xbox system and games he received from the Seattle Goliath in return for his controversial domain name.[77]

- **From giant strength**—*they're part of a "giant club" with powerful allies*—**to your strength.** You can use your giant's own allies as Coercers or Convincers, acting on *your* behalf to favorably influence your giant. In the 1970s, Malta asked for increased fees from Britain for leasing the island nation's strategic Mediterranean port facilities. When Britain balked, Malta made sure the US and other NATO allies knew that if talks failed, Malta would likely lease the facilities to the Soviet Union. Britain's allies could not believe that it would risk the turnover of such a strategic asset to their communist enemy, leading them to pressure Downing Street into a sweetheart deal for Malta. The deal included a three-fold leap in the annual payments being received by the tiny nation.[78]

- **From giant strength**—*they run a tight ship, moving solidly in one direction*—**to your strength.** Tight controls inside a giant organization can result in slower, inflexible responses that keep your giant moving in one direction while you come at them from another direction that favors you. Tight controls can also be a sign of iron-fisted, dictatorial management, meaning some members of your giant's team will be unhappy. These potential Cracks may see themselves as losers and you as an ally, leading them to share useful information. When journalist Ida Tarbell exposed Standard Oil and its antitrust violations in the early 1900s, she benefited greatly from Cracks inside the Goliath who resented Rockefeller's controlling character and centralized decision-making.[79]

I'll tell one last story here. It's about two unlikely Size Wizards who take full advantage of their weaknesses and their giant's strengths, bringing a huge corporation to its knees.

McLibel. Most people ignore them.

But the pair persists, despite the cold, damp weather.

Helen Steel, a part-time gardener, and Dave Morris, a single father and unemployed postal worker, keep handing out pamphlets. The two activists and friends want the world to know what they believe lies behind McDonald's slick, family-friendly ads. On this particular day, they've planted themselves outside one of the chain's busiest restaurants in London, England. Without a penny to spend of their own, Helen and Dave want to change the fast food industry—one restaurant at a time.

Their six-page pamphlet asks: *What's wrong with McDonald's? Everything they don't want you to know.*[80] It claims the US-based food giant sells unhealthy food, exploits its workers, unethically markets itself to children, treats animals cruelly, pollutes the environment, destroys rainforests, and contributes to poverty in the developing world by forcing peasants off their land so farm exports can be shipped to McDonald's restaurants.

Although these accusations reach a limited audience, McDonald's doesn't like them one bit. The chain moves to defend its reputation. In

1990, it sues Helen, 24, and Dave, 35, confidently asserting *all* the claims in their pamphlet are completely false.

Under American law, to win a libel case like this, McDonald's would actually have to prove the claims being made against it are false, which is why the corporation focuses on these critics. In Britain, as we saw earlier in *Defend Yourself from the Start*, the burden of proof in libel cases is reversed, so the two activists must prove *their* claims are true. As another challenge, defendants in British libel cases cannot receive public financial assistance to hire lawyers. Since Helen and Dave can't afford legal counsel, they'll be forced to defend themselves. With neither working full-time, the duo will at least be able to carefully research and plan for their trial. Several sympathetic lawyers provide free counsel here and there, but as things stand, no lawyer deems their complex case worthy or strong enough to donate around-the-clock support.

Amid huge media coverage, the case goes to trial. Without any education beyond high school, Helen and Dave team up in court to take on some of Britain's top legal talent. It quickly turns out to have been a huge gaffe for McDonald's to maintain the pamphlet's contents are entirely untrue. This gives the activists an opportunity to revisit each of their claims—one by one—effectively, and painfully, putting the McDonald's corporation on trial for how it runs its worldwide business.

Slowly but surely, Helen and Dave learn the formalities of the courtroom, such as how to present evidence and query witnesses. They prepare each day in the cheapest, most efficient office space they can afford: the subway train on the way into the courts. They will call dozens of witnesses, directly questioning some of their giant's most senior people as they probe issues ranging from McDonald's treatment of livestock and its employees, to its recycling efforts.

McDonald's executives regard the proceedings as a time-consuming embarrassment. Meanwhile, Helen and Dave are in their glory, with an unprecedented platform for voicing concerns about their giant and challenging its executives face-to-face, as a global audience follows their every word.

McDonald's moves to settle. It offers to pay Helen and Dave money that will be donated to a charity of their choice, *if* they accept a gag order that forbids them to discuss the case publicly. The pair says they won't have their right to free speech muffled. McDonald's points out that they'll still be able to speak freely in private. Helen and Dave say they'll consider this possibility if, in return, McDonald's agrees to stop advertising and promoting itself publicly. They add, "Of course, this agreement wouldn't prevent you from privately recommending McDonald's to your friends and neighbors."[81] Settlement talks come to a halt.

The trial keeps going, exceeding 300 days of courtroom hearings, becoming the longest trial in British history. McDonald's legal fees in the end will total around ten million pounds, or $16 million.[82]

In 1997, Judge Rodger Bell delivers his final ruling. He concludes that McDonald's has fostered cruelty to animals, served food that could endanger regular customers, exploited children through ads and paid its workers unreasonably low wages.[83] But he also says that Helen and Dave are guilty of libel because they have not proven everything in their pamphlet, and a number of their statements are either untrue or exaggerations. The judge orders them to pay 60,000 pounds to the corporation. Of course, since neither activist has any money to lose in the first place, and McDonald's knows this, the penalties don't mean much.

McDonald's is the trial's big loser, making changes to its practices even as the trial unfolds. The giant chain looks even worse when it's discovered that in a zealous effort to defend its reputation, it has used spies and its connections with law enforcement officials to uncover information about Helen and Dave. The duo sues Scotland Yard, settling for 10,000 pounds and a formal apology.

In 1999, upon appeal, three judges find there is indeed something to Helen and Dave's claims about McDonald's poor working conditions and links to heart disease. The original penalty is reduced from 60,000 to 40,000 pounds.

In 2005, the European Court of Human Rights goes one step further. The court agrees with Helen and Dave: the British law denying the twosome legal aid deprived them of their right to a fair trial. It orders the British government to offer the activists a retrial and to pay them 57,000 pounds for damages and costs. The court also says that if Britain continues to allow big corporations to sue individuals for libel—where government organizations are barred from doing this in the interest of free speech and open debate—then the nation needs to provide proper support to those being sued. "Hopefully, the government will be forced to change the law, and that will mean greater freedom of speech," Helen tells reporters afterward.[84]

To celebrate, Helen, now 39, and Dave, 50, return to their roots, standing outside McDonald's in central London, handing out pamphlets similar to the one that got them sued 15 years earlier. What's different is that most people stop, smile and take their offering. Both are celebrities after all, courtesy of McDonald's. It's estimated that upward of three million people have read Helen and Dave's famous pamphlet, which has been translated into dozens of languages. Tens of millions of others have heard about their cause through television coverage, a documentary film about them, and their website—McSpotlight.com.

Take advantage of your weaknesses and their strengths—especially when you're at your weakest and they're at their strongest.

HAZARDS TO AVOID

As you make yourself bigger and stronger, here are some traps to sidestep:

Ignoring context and timing as you sequence your deal-making. If conditions don't favor you at crucial times, you risk undermining your credibility and efforts by plowing ahead. After years of maneuvering, escalating protests and deal-making in pursuit of women's suffrage in Britain, Emmeline Pankhurst faces a big decision. World War I has broken out in 1914, but many of her female supporters want to keep pushing aggressively for the right to vote. Emmeline worries they might undercut the war effort and look irresponsible. Instead, she puts their cause on hold, joining hands with the British government to win the war, while continuing to build her movement in a different way. She reaches a deal with the government to jointly promote women working in factories, freeing up men to fight. Women flood into the workplace, becoming such an integral part of the nation's economy that new voting rights for women are inevitably granted—beginning in 1918.[85] America follows in 1920, France in 1945 and Switzerland in 1971.

Bringing the wrong people into a coalition. You can get into trouble by allowing others to join your extended team without considering their impact on your existing or potential supporters. Vermont Governor Howard Dean is the frontrunner for the Democratic Party nomination in the lead-up to the 2004 presidential election—before he loudly announces that he has Al Gore's backing. As Dean will put it two months later, "I actually do think the endorsement of Al Gore began the decline." [86] Dean ends up making many mistakes, but his first may well have been letting Gore come aboard. Why does Gore hurt Dean, whose supporters soon desert him? Dean loses his maverick status as a Washington outsider by hooking up with a prominent insider, the former vice president. Also, attracting such powerful support confirms that Dean is the candidate to beat, creating an anti-Dean movement that will help propel John Kerry to his party's nomination.

Thinking your alternatives are better than they are. If you've been single a long time, unintentionally, you may have fallen into a trap that also plagues some smaller players in giant negotiations. When faced with committing to one woman or man, we often unconsciously blend together the best traits from all of our different dates or partners in the past and compare this wonderful alternative to the person standing in front of us. The problem is that if we walk away, there's actually no one person who meets our interests in so many ways. We've compared a real option on the table to a phantom alternative, and we may be forever single as a result. If we do this when assessing our alternatives to a giant deal, we risk over-estimating their value. This can lead to our pushing too hard for a better giant deal, or to our walking away to an alternative that doesn't meet our interests as well as we'd hoped. Instead, we need to focus on just one concrete back-up plan, improving it and using it as a point of comparison.

Overlooking symbols to help send your message. Without simple symbols, messages can be missed or stop spreading. The Apostle Paul wouldn't fall into this trap, building momentum for a new religion called Christianity by using the cross as a distinct symbol to spread the message that Christ had sacrificed himself for the sins of others. Emmeline Pankhurst's efforts to get women the vote in Britain saw supporters by the thousands wearing purple, green and white broaches, badges and clothes to symbolize growing momentum for their cause. New England Patriots coach Bill Belichick buried a football to show his giant, 53 players, that they could bury their losing ways—a symbolic act that began an unexpected turnaround on the way to their first Super Bowl Championship. Awareness of breast cancer achieved new heights through an elegantly folded pink ribbon first introduced by the Susan G. Komen Breast Cancer Foundation in the early 1990s—a decade after Susan, while dying of the disease, asked her sister Nancy to help find a cure.

Letting pride keep you from using your weaknesses as strengths. Deciding if it's smart to reveal our weaknesses—which ones, when and to whom—requires a clear-headed review of pros and cons, but pride alone should not hold us back. Our weaknesses remain weaknesses until we unleash them. Smaller players are often surprised by how liberating and empowering it can be to let others know about their vulnerabilities and flaws. Doing so can lead to empathy, others sharing their own weaknesses in return, and unexpected sources of support. Britain's Princess Diana is an example of a smaller player revealing her weaknesses to galvanize worldwide support, as she dealt with her giant, Britain's Royal family. Diana's eating disorders, marital woes, suppression and mental anguish endeared her to the masses. The Royal family's own support suffered badly because of its pride, stoicism and projection of strength *without* weakness, which few of us can relate to. Nor do we tend to trust those who claim, improbably, to be perfect.

FINAL THOUGHTS

To make yourself bigger and stronger, carefully sequence your deals like Jesse Rasch did. Remember Nelson Mandela's success against the odds and build up your extended team through coalitions. Follow the example of Ben Franklin and Tom Droog and walk away, or at least plan to. Send a fiery message with words and images that would make Harriet Beecher Stowe proud. Or use your weaknesses and their strengths to turn the tide in your favor, claiming what's rightfully yours, whether it's a credit card or free speech.

Prepare for success. Ahead of all other size and strength enhancements, the Size Wizards prepare their walk-away plan because no matter what happens, feeling like you have an alternative is often the ultimate source of power. If you're looking at building coalitions or a series of deals to bulk up, it's usually best to start with smaller coalitions or deals to lower your risks and gain experience. One benefit of coalitions: they can add to your size and clout without costing you a dime. Finally, whether you're in dire straits or not, list your weaknesses and your giant's strengths, figuring out how you might benefit from one or more of them.

Follow these broad steps as you grow bigger and stronger. As the Size Wizards bulk up, they manage their growth thoughtfully, bearing in mind three best practices of top-performing giants: 1) Within their growing organizations, they stay in smaller working units, maintaining collegiality, a sense of belonging and the positive emotions that created early successes. The Hutterite religious community, many armies, and companies such as Gore Associates—makers of Gore-Tex fabric—follow *the rule of 150*, breaking into new units when a team or division approaches 150 members.[87] 2) They remain humble, knowing any arrogance belies a lack of focus and will be paid for one way or another. 3) They are frugal, remembering the financial disciplines that made them who they are, and that money wrongly spent can undermine creativity, urgency and what really matters.

Be a peacock. The Size Wizards sometimes make themselves look bigger and stronger than they actually are through what I call the Peacock Effect. Just as male peacocks expand their feathers to attract worthy mates, smaller players can puff themselves up to impress their giants during critical periods: they name-drop; they borrow or rent expensive furnishings, clothes or jewelry; they take over someone else's office space for a day and act as though it's theirs; they employ friends to sit at otherwise unoccupied desks; or they use phone systems with menus that make it sound like you've called a huge multinational. These may be smart tactics, assuming you can perform as promised once a giant deal is in place, there are no significant misrepresentations that could put your deal at risk—and you don't kid yourself: *nothing* produces results like real efforts to grow bigger and stronger, through deal sequencing, coalitions, back-up plans, and sparkling messages, drawing on *your* weaknesses and *their* strengths whenever needed.

5

CRAFT GOLDEN DEALS

Transform weak deals or no-deals into big opportunities that glimmer like gold.

REMEMBER MOFFETT FORKING OVER $250 TO ROOSEVELT'S CAMPAIGN TEAM in 1912 so his photo would be used in their pamphlet, when in fact Moffett was the one who should have been paid handsomely—up to $3 million based on copyright laws at the time?

Imagine the deals Moffett might have reached if he'd simply dug for more information and managed to level the playing field before arriving at his final arrangement with Roosevelt's team. There would have been countless possibilities to consider, covering everything from a big royalty payment to Moffett or an investment in his business, to his earning a princely sum as the official photographer for the White House.

The opportunity to create and claim value in giant negotiations is often immense, in keeping with a giant's size. The challenges, as Moffett learned, can also be immense.

So far, we've focused on stories where the dominant strategy involved defending ourselves or leveling the playing field, without looking closely at how we create meaningful and lasting value for ourselves. Now, we turn our attention to stories about deal-crafting, and the ageless pursuit of a formula for turning lead into gold.

The Size Wizards bring their golden deals together in ways that far surpass how well they could have satisfied their interests on their own or with a non-giant counterpart. They tend to create and claim most of the value available to them well before going to the negotiation table, though as we'll see, they sometimes involve their giants early on—usually indirectly or informally. The Size Wizards also build their core activities in a deliberate manner, weaving them into their negotiation activities to attract their giants and generate more value. Moffett's excellent core photography activities managed to attract his giant, he just didn't have the faintest idea how to negotiate golden value.

The value we generate for ourselves depends on how well we can satisfy our interests—including interests related to wealth, strategic positioning, stable relationships, peace of mind, credibility or legacy—all of which can be uniquely satisfied through our negotiations with giants.

The Size Wizards draw on one or more of these approaches to breathe value into their deals:

- They benefit from big differences between themselves and their giants.

- They fully exploit what they have in common with their giant.

- They bring in third parties to help out.

- They involve their giant early on.

- They make their deals bigger, or smaller, to fit the situation.

Highlighting these approaches, a Dutch matriarch structures a fake deal that will allow her real deal to go through. Virgin's Richard Branson gives us a flying lesson. A weakened union leader goes to a doctor to save his dying deal. A British music producer reaches a revolutionary agreement with CD buyers. Canadian Prime Minister Brian Mulroney engineers a whopping trade pact with US President Ronald Reagan. Two actors, Matt Damon and Ben Affleck, use an award-winning approach to break their deadlock with a giant moviemaker. And we discover how the smaller American states secure their rights in 1787, barely averting another bloody conflict—this one with the giant states surrounding them.

USE DIFFERENCES TO CREATE VALUE

When it comes to eating lobster, I have different tastes than an old friend of mine. I love savoring the lobster's meaty white tail; what gets my pal Jonathan's taste buds going more than anything are the green guts that come from inside the female lobster's thorax. So if we're dining together, he gladly gives me his lobster tail and in return, I wince in disbelief as I hand over a lobster part that I'd never eat anyway, because frankly it makes me queasy.

Instead of conflict, our differences here create an ongoing opportunity for mutually joyous eating: we each get twice the value for the same money. The benefits of this culinary lesson in using differences to our advantage can be easy to exploit—and magnified many times over—when we negotiate with giants. Why? Because giants are so different than smaller players, and in so many ways.

STORY: YOU SAY "*TOM-AY-TO*," I SAY "*TOM-AH-TO*"

"It's time to put an end to this silliness," proclaims Christine Hinken to her family.

The Hinkens and an American giant, SuperTech Corporation, have reached an impasse in their negotiations, deadlocked over what price the US Goliath should pay to acquire Hinken Software, based in Holland. After three months of back-and-forth negotiations, it now looks like everyone's time has been wasted on a deal that simply isn't meant to be.

From the beginning, Christine has made it clear that she isn't in a rush to sell. If her family were to sell, however, she says the huge potential for growth in Europe and Asia would justify valuing their "little gem" at $300 million. This is exactly $100 million more than SuperTech has in mind, and a whopping 50% premium over valuations for similar software companies—astounding when you consider how this family-controlled company started out. Hinken Software began as a three-person, manually-driven accounting firm at the end of the Second World War, only evolving over the last 25 years into its role as a producer of leading-edge accounting software for small businesses.[1]

The Hinkens believe their accounting software could yield strong results for SuperTech, rounding out its own small business offerings which already include security, payroll and scheduling software. The family also believes that SuperTech can afford $300 million from its cash reserves, and doesn't want any SuperTech stock as part of its payment. True to their conservative roots as accountants, the Hinkens view holding stock in anyone else's company as a risky undertaking, no matter how big the company.

As her family's elder stateswoman, 67-year-old Christine Hinken has heard enough. She decides to call Maureen Lang, one of SuperTech's senior vice presidents, who oversees the giant's explorations in Europe. Spurred on by their deal being at risk, the two women have a heart-to-heart chat about their interests.

Maureen says she is concerned about three things: first, paying such a premium for Hinken Software would mean giving up a good portion of the deal's future financial benefits; second, while SuperTech does have cash to spend, it has other bigger deals to pursue and is worried about dropping so much money on one smaller company; finally, the giant believes that paying so much will set a bad precedent for its other deals—potentially costing it billions of dollars as other sellers argue that they, too, should receive 15 times their earnings as a selling price, instead of the current industry standard of eight to ten times earnings. This "deal inflation" could attract negative attention from Wall Street analysts and SuperTech's vocal shareholders.

Christine Hinken pauses, reflecting on Maureen's comments. This isn't the first time these concerns have been voiced, but before she had viewed them as a negotiation ploy aimed at wrestling her price down. Christine probes a little more. She then tells Maureen, "Look, I can't help you on price because in light of our growth, we'd prefer to keep running the business rather than give it away for less than we believe it's truly worth. Your other concerns, however, may have simple solutions." Christine now puts forward some ideas for closing the gap between the two sides.

A week later, a tentative deal is made public, subject to final due diligence by SuperTech. The deal is announced in a way that makes the giant look savvy, stressing all the benefits of the purchase from its perspective, downplaying the profile and accomplishments of the Hinkens. The media unanimously conclude that SuperTech has scored a coup.

The price paid to the Hinken family is widely reported to be $200 million—exactly what the giant wanted. And the Hinkens don't mind having the world think they received $100 million less than what they actually received—$300 million—exactly what they wanted.

Sure, Christine says, it might feel good to have the real acquisition price known by others, but the deal wouldn't have gone through that way. The sleight of hand she proposed, having the public amount of the sale differ from the private reality, meets both her family's main interest and the very different interests of her giant buyer.

Legally, SuperTech must somehow record the unannounced $100 million in its formal financial statements but the corporation won't make it easy for casual observers to trace the true amount paid. The Hinken deal may get lumped together with other deals so it's harder to detect, or the extra money may be disclosed separately under "contingent" payments, deal-related costs or consulting fees. If the $100 million is indeed framed as consulting fees, as Christine first suggested, the Hinkens will likely "consult" with SuperTech representatives as they play golf together four times a year in the Swiss Alps.

Whatever the case, the extra money above the market norm is a boon for the Hinkens, and despite Maureen's objections, just a tiny amount for SuperTech whose annual sales run into the tens of billions of dollars.

USE DIFFERENCES TO CREATE VALUE

Sometimes, differences can make all the difference.

The deal we've explored was driven to a successful conclusion by a host of differences, most of which were connected to the huge size gap between the Hinkens and SuperTech. These differences can be placed in one of three buckets: differences in core expertise; differences in profile; and differences in resources. Underlying these differences were different *but* compatible goals, needs and concerns that could come together like pieces of a jigsaw puzzle—forming a highly valued outcome for both sides.

Here's an inventory of the differences that will allow the Hinkens to live like royalty:

- **Difference in core expertise #1—depth versus breadth.** The Hinkens focused in-depth on one thing only: accounting software for smaller businesses. SuperTech made a broad range of small business software but had a strong need for expertise in the area of accounting. This was an opportunity for the giant to have its long-standing need met by Hinken Software.

- **Difference in core expertise #2—geographic imprint.** The geographic roots of the Hinken business were in Europe and Asia, where their people had expertise in understanding these distinct markets, including how customers think and make their buying decisions. SuperTech was US-centric, looking to improve its understanding of foreign markets in Europe and Asia. This was another giant need for core expertise satisfied by the Hinkens—a need that extended well beyond this deal's focus on small business software, boosting *all* the giant's other offerings to individuals, larger businesses and governments around the world.

- **Difference in profile #1—volume of deals.** The Hinkens would not be doing any more deals after this one. SuperTech, on the other hand, planned to continue executing dozens of deals each year to meet its growth targets, leading to a natural concern over precedents, where the Hinkens had none. This difference meant the Hinkens didn't mind announcing a price that made them look less aggressive while setting a helpful precedent for their giant's future deals.

- **Difference in profile #2—constituencies.** SuperTech's stakeholders and interested parties included employees, customers, partners, shareholders, regulators and the media. The giant's Controller here, Maureen, made the call on the Hinken deal but she was accountable to her superiors for her results. As for the Hinkens, they had only a few minority shareholders to deal with, while wanting to ensure their customers didn't raise any fuss that might threaten the deal. This difference in constituency size and composition allowed the Hinkens to remain quiet as SuperTech crowed about its deal in a one-sided way. Crowing created value for the giant, as buyers of its stock were impressed by the shrewdly priced deal and its wide-ranging impact, bidding up share prices as a result. More value in SuperTech's pocket meant it could fork over more cash to the Hinkens.

- **Difference in profile #3—future plans.** SuperTech planned to stay involved in the software industry, aspiring to be number one in all its markets. The Hinkens planned to get out of the software industry, retiring to enjoy life and pursue philanthropic activities. This difference in their basic goals meant that a deal between our giant and the Hinkens would not fall apart over contentious issues related to non-competes and what business activities might be deemed competitive or not.

- **Difference in resources #1—deal size.** The value of this deal was relatively small for our giant compared to its assets, sales and earnings. By contrast, the value of this deal was huge for the Hinkens who had their wealth tied up in their business, with only a dozen individuals sharing in the proceeds of this sale. This difference in the size of the deal from each party's point of view meant that SuperTech had greater flexibility to meet the financial interests of its much smaller counterpart.

- **Difference in resources #2—cash requirements.** The US giant had a lot of cash on hand, but told the Hinkens it needed this money to keep expanding through acquisitions. In theory, the Hinkens preferred to receive all their cash right away because they didn't know what might happen to SuperTech in the future. In reality, the Hinkens knew it was very unlikely their giant wouldn't be able to pay them relatively small amounts of cash in the years ahead. From a taxation perspective, the family benefited by receiving cash payments over time. It was agreed the $300 million would be paid in equal installments over a five-year period, with 5% interest on outstanding amounts. This difference in cash needs between the cash-hungry giant and the suddenly cash-rich, tax-sensitive Hinkens contributed to the deal being sealed—again meeting the interests of both parties.

If Christine Hinken had generated a checklist of differences in core expertise, profile and resources at the outset of talks between her family and SuperTech, she might have pre-empted the concerns that almost torpedoed her agreement with Maureen. In your own planning, brainstorming potential differences in advance of discussions can help you identify giants that might be interested in a deal and better prepare you for talks.

On top of the differences that allowed for the deal between the Hinkens and SuperTech, you can include on your list any differences over assumptions. The Hinkens and their giant had different assumptions about future sales growth if the Hinkens continued to operate their business, and differed over what value to place on Hinken Software. This didn't prove to be a critical issue because SuperTech was so big, had so much upside from the deal, and the payments to the Hinkens could be made over time.

But what if the actual amount to be paid had been an issue?

Let's look at an example where another company figures out a favorable deal based on different assumptions:

DIFFERENCE IN ASSUMPTIONS—RISK AND VALUE. A young, cash-strapped software company, Zirox, needs $100,000 to market its products and break even. It has a giant investor on the hook, Sheila Morgan, who believes Zirox is worth $1 million once she puts her money in. This is just 1/3 of the $3 million valuation assumed by the company's founders, Saul and Lisa Bloom, who see Sheila owning 3 1/3% of Zirox—not the 10% she expects. Sheila's concern: she thinks the fast-growing company is well positioned over the next two years, but at risk in three to five years due to competition. Here's the deal they reached: Sheila puts in $100,000 and gets *no* shares. Instead, since she's so bullish on the shorter term, she'll get a 10% royalty on all sales until she receives a return of 300% within 18 months, or 500% at any point after that. This is easy money from Sheila's perspective, with much lower risk. Saul and Lisa are thrilled, believing they'll generate this cash payout quickly, while not giving up any ownership. Different assumptions about risk and value get this deal done—a superior deal to the one first envisioned.[2]

Here are four other brief examples where differences can create mutual value in everyday deal-making—whether you're a professional sports team, a non-profit organization, a giant employee or a smaller nation:

DIFFERENT EXPERTISE—DEPTH VERSUS BREADTH. As a tiny nation, you reach a mutual defense agreement with your giant. You'll provide highly specialized anti-terrorism expertise which your elite teams excel at, operating on the ground in six languages. These are skills your giant covets given a worldwide increase in terrorist attacks. In return, with its overwhelming military capacity, your giant agrees to protect you against any attacks on your territory by other countries, meeting your broad national security interests in an effective, low-cost way.[3]

DIFFERENT PROFILES—TASTES. Your employer, a pharmaceutical corporation, prefers to develop drugs with large potential markets. As a researcher, you're looking for a change, bored where you are and wanting to make more money. You stumble onto a drug that will serve a relatively small market. Your employer decides to go along with your proposal to spin off a completely separate venture to develop this non-strategic drug, while letting you and your venture's investors keep 50% of the profits.

DIFFERENT RESOURCES—SPACE. You're a non-profit group looking for a low-cost space to host meetings during the weekdays. The area you work in is mainly Catholic but church attendance is way down. You approach a priest at one large local church, reaching an agreement to lease a big space there. You pay a much lower amount compared to other alternatives you've explored. In return, the church gets some money to fund its youth program. Your giant supports a good social cause, while giving up something it's not using, other than on weekends.

DIFFERENT ASSUMPTIONS—RISK AND VALUE. You're the general manager of a losing, low-budget professional soccer team and you believe that one of your young stars is too injury-prone to serve your longer-term needs. You trade this 22-year-old player to a wealthy winning team in return for a 32-year-old veteran player that your giant believes is "washed up." You believe this older player simply needs a new environment to re-ignite his career, surrounded by younger players who will look up to him and learn from him. Your giant is aware of its new player's ongoing medical problems, but believes its deluxe, high-priced conditioning program can lower the young man's risk of recurring injuries.

Use differences to create value—systematically focusing on differences in expertise, profile, resources and assumptions.

USE SHARED INTERESTS TO CREATE VALUE

In 1996, Peru and its much smaller neighbor, Ecuador, come together to try to negotiate an end to armed fighting over a contested region along their shared border.

Before formal talks begin, two of the negotiators—one an admiral from Peru, the other a university president from Ecuador—happen upon a shared concern that will bond them together, ultimately helping the two sides reach an unexpected agreement. Their shared concern has nothing to do with the dispute between their nations.

Both have severely handicapped children.[4]

As the two South American representatives discover, the interests we share with our giants on a personal level can improve our working relationship, so we open up about other interests and get creative to structure better agreements.

Other times, the deal-related interests we share can, on their own, provide all the ingredients we need for giant deal-making—as Richard Branson discovers while breaking into the unfriendly skies of the airline industry.

STORY: VIRGIN MARKETS

When British entrepreneur Richard Branson announces he is going to build on his success in the music business by moving into air travel, there are plenty of skeptics. Even some of his board members think he's crazy.

After all, Branson's Virgin Group will be a tiny, inexperienced entrant into a market in the United Kingdom that has always been dominated by one giant—British Airways. On top of this, Virgin will have to negotiate buying or leasing its airplanes from some tight-fisted, highly experienced giants.

Defying his doubters with the same brazenness that turned Virgin into one of the top recording industry players in the 1970s, Branson pursues his new quest with zeal. On June 22, 1984, just months after declaring Virgin will enter the airline business under the name Virgin Atlantic, Branson's lone aircraft, filled with a gaggle of friends, celebrities and media, takes off from London bound for Newark, New Jersey.[5]

Ahhh. Success.

But having only one craft means Virgin Atlantic is an airplane—not an airline.

Branson's next step is to put together a fleet, requiring intense negotiations with aircraft suppliers. Boeing of America and Europe's Airbus are among a small handful of Goliaths worldwide with the ability and resources to assemble intercontinental airliners. Rather than worry about negotiating with these savvy industry players, Branson believes the two giants might share one critical goal with him: seeing Virgin Atlantic succeed.

Why would Boeing and Airbus care about Richard Branson's wild ambitions?

The United Kingdom is a huge market in which British Airways, or BA, is dominant. Suppliers feel pressured by BA's demands whenever they negotiate with the airline. If you can't sell to BA, you have no other major player to sell to. Having one airline in control means the UK market isn't being serviced with a full range of routes, flights or low-priced packages. A new entrant challenging BA will not only give aircraft sellers another buyer to offset BA's might, it will also stimulate more people to travel, in turn leading to more planes being needed in general.

"We found that people who were selling us planes were desperate to get a competitor in the marketplace," Branson would later say. "With our first 747, Boeing sent their chief salesman over to England, and he stayed there for nine months while he tried to do the deal with us. Having got the feeling that we might stay around, they made an enormous effort to look after us in order to have a company to play off against British Airways."[6]

Virgin Atlantic's early success draws on support from its Goliath suppliers and their longer-term goal of broadening the UK market for their planes beyond one huge buyer. This allows them to overlook their shorter-term interests in profitability. Boeing, in particular, will do everything possible to propel the rookie entrant forward, structuring deals that take into account Virgin Atlantic's limited financial means and its need for flexible terms. As an example, the first plane Branson leases—the Boeing 747 he uses on his inaugural flight to New Jersey—could be returned after a year and *at a minimum*, he'd get all his money back.[7]

Based on his experiences as both a smaller player and a giant, Branson says, "If you spot someone you think can go a long way, you invest time in them no matter how small they are."[8]

Virgin Atlantic has obviously come a long way itself: its passengers now number in the tens of millions each year, its fleet boasts dozens of jetliners purchased from both Boeing and Airbus, and it flies to more than 30 destinations around the world.

USE SHARED INTERESTS TO CREATE VALUE

In Richard Branson's case, a shared long-term goal with aircraft makers— Virgin Atlantic's success as a new entrant to Britain's airline marketplace— helped to forge a number of mutually beneficial deals.

Following in Virgin Atlantic's path, when you think about negotiating with giants, ask yourself if one or more of them might have strong shared interests with you, making for robust agreements in any setting:

- **Shared goals.** Pursue a common end-goal such as profitability, safety and security, or a positive change for everyone involved. In Rwanda, efforts aimed at ethnic reconciliation involved a small but meaningful step after genocide in 1994 led to the deaths of an estimated 800,000 people, most of whom were Tutsis. Years later, the minority Tutsis and majority Hutus came together, agreeing to form a national soccer team with the *shared goal* of healing the deep scars between them while rebuilding their country's image internationally.[9]

- **Shared needs**. Fulfill a common need such as the widespread acceptance of helpful standards, more clout with suppliers or greater credibility in general. On the heels of America's Revolution, a new war brewed in 1787—this one internal, between smaller and larger states. While heavily populated states wanted population size to determine every state's say in national matters, smaller states argued this smacked of the tyranny they had just defeated. They wanted parity. In the end, an over-arching *shared need* to save face and appear united to outsiders, including Great Britain, led to the acceptance of a compromise suggested by Ben Franklin: smaller states would maintain their equality through a Senate, to which each state, regardless of size, would send two senators—counter-balanced by a House of Representatives where size alone would dictate stately clout, ensuring an ongoing, healthy tension between big and small.[10]

- **Shared concerns**. Collaborate to counter common concerns such as the fear of a Goliath competitor, a disease like AIDS or a growing social problem. John Walsh was a real-estate developer in Florida when his 6-year-old son, Adam, was kidnapped from a Sears department store and murdered. John turned his focus to solving crimes, especially those involving children. As a concerned citizen, he teamed up with Fox Television in 1988 to launch *America's Most Wanted*, a show that has tracked down hundreds of criminals by soliciting tips from the public. Most recently, John worked with the US government to tackle a *shared concern* about child predators, resulting in "The Adam Walsh Child Protection and Safety Act." This law was enacted by President Bush on July 27, 2006—exactly 25 years after the abduction of John and Revé Walsh's son, whose abductor has never been found.[11]

In any giant negotiation, we'll find both shared and different interests to help or potentially hinder our deal-making. The key is to identify either dominant similarities—like Virgin did with Boeing—or dominant differences that can move us forward, as the Hinkens found in breaking their deadlock with SuperTech.

 *Use shared interests to create value—surfacing shared goals, needs and concerns.*

USE THIRD PARTIES TO ADD VALUE

As they look to revive dead deals, or turn lead deals into gold, the Size Wizards know how to involve third parties who can contribute value when it matters most—often in unexpected ways.

STORY: A DOCTORED AGREEMENT

"Dick, what the hell are you talking about?" Union leader Mike Murphy is furious. Dick Pall has just dropped a bombshell.

"Mike, take it easy. We're fine with all the other terms," says Pall, management's lead negotiator. "This is the only remaining issue. We're not playing games here. We need a 20% cut in your current health benefits or we're all headed for another impasse."

Six years earlier, management at Copperlink Ltd. had locked out the 1,750 members of Mike's local union, saying that worldwide competition called for lower wages. In a large northern town with one copper mine, and 35% of the local economy dependent on that mine, the impasse had been devastating for both miners and non-miners. Copperlink threatened to shut down their mine and move production elsewhere. The workers finally succumbed, feeling battered by their hard-hitting global giant.[12]

Mike rolls his eyes at the memory. Two contracts later, bad feelings still linger, and management's new position on health benefits could trigger a strike. These benefits cover medical professionals not paid for by the government: dentists, pharmacists, opticians, psychologists, chiropractors and physiotherapists.

The union leader pauses, calming himself. "Dick, if I understand correctly, your major concern here is that all of our healthcare providers are going to keep getting more expensive in the years ahead, right?"

"Exactly," Pall says. "We've no reason to believe there won't be *at least* another 20% increase in these costs over the next three years. We just can't do it. Copper markets are soft again and unlikely to turn around for a while. Unfortunately, a pre-emptive 20% cut in health benefits is the only answer."

The union leader tries to keep listening, but he is suddenly distracted. He has an idea that needs testing. He excuses himself from Pall's offices. "I have to think about this, Dick. I'll get back to you next week. Let's keep this issue between us for now."

At home, Mike talks with his wife about the situation and his idea. She points out that no one has ever attempted anything like this before, but says it's probably worth a try.

Mike quietly lines up separate meetings with key healthcare professionals in the community. He starts with those he thinks will be open to his proposal, providers whose prices have spiked the most of late. He doesn't want Pall involved. Mike wants the focus on his workers, their predicament and their relationship with these providers. He knows a stark choice must be presented, not one muddied by the perception that management might still pay out more money to help cover rising healthcare costs.

Each of Mike's meetings goes something like his first one: "Dr. Martin, my members will have to strike if management insists on this 20% cut in our healthcare benefits. The impact of a strike wouldn't be good for anyone in this town. Your charges have gone up a lot recently. We're requesting a general freeze from you on any further increases in your fees for three years, so we can keep our current coverage levels."

Mike waits. Dr. Martin swallows hard. The union leader continues. "Given the amount of business we send you, are you willing to commit in writing that you'll go along with this price freeze for the term of our next contract? If so, you'll have to figure out how to keep your own costs down while absorbing any additional costs you're charged by others. In return, however, we can guarantee you roughly the same number of union patients that you have now—if not more."

As he moves from one provider to another, Mike makes it clear he will have his members seek services only from those who agree to the freeze. In this way, he brings onside more than a dozen of the main service providers in town. This will make it easier for him to get most of the others on board before the weekend.

From each healthcare provider, Mike obtains a standard two-page agreement, with some deals noting exceptional circumstances where costs could rise slightly, while encouraging preventative measures that union members can follow to keep their health costs down.

The following Monday, six days after their previous meeting, the smiling union leader walks into Dick Pall's office. Pall is relieved to see him, though his 20 years of labor dealings make him wary anytime a union leader seems happy.

Mike sits down, pulls out a checklist, and begins to move through each of the major issues in the new contract where he believes tentative agreement has been reached. He and Pall confirm their understanding of all the terms, point by point. "Well, Dick, that leaves us with healthcare. What if I could guarantee you that the costs related to our current benefits will not go up in the next three years?"

Pall chuckles, then turns serious to signal he's not inclined to entertain fantasies at such a decisive juncture. "Mike, if that were possible," he says, "it would be great. But you and I know that reality dictates otherwise."

Mike opens up his briefcase and pulls out his stack of signed agreements committing to the freeze. He passes one to Pall, who reads it carefully. Pall leafs through the others. He cannot believe his eyes.

A couple of weeks later, Mike's union members unanimously endorse their new three-year collective agreement, which retains all their healthcare benefits while delivering a small increase in wages.

Dick Pall is still shaking his head in amazement. Mike Murphy really pulled a rabbit out of his hat on this one.

USE THIRD PARTIES TO ADD VALUE

Faced with a situation where new value had to be brought to the table to close the gap between union and management, Mike Murphy looked to a third party for a side deal. The healthcare community provided the extra value that enabled the main deal with Copperlink to be completed. The alternative for everyone was not attractive.

In other deal-making environments, any number of third parties can be called upon to add missing value—whether they're initially approached by a smaller player, a giant, or both working together. Sometimes, a distinct side deal is involved, while other times, third parties play a critical and integral role in the central deal itself.

To complete the value equation in your own deals, you should routinely consider:

- **Parties that affect your deal, benefit from it, or might help it happen.** You want to think carefully about this, like Mike Murphy did before involving his town's healthcare providers. Another example: Norfab, a small Canadian building supplier, agreed to sell its products to a giant buyer in the southern US, knowing it could lower its trucking costs by hauling pipes and machinery back to Canada for a number of third parties.[13]

- **National, regional and local governments**. Whenever payments are structured to allow for tax deductions by any party, the invisible third party bringing value to the table is the government allowing these deductions.[14] That's why the Size Wizards consider tax implications before putting their deals together. They don't want to undermine the government's involvement in the value creation process. They also consider the potential for government grants, financial guarantees or subsidies to help get a deal done.

- **Financial institutions**. Banks add value by replacing your cash with their debt to finance a deal, debt whose interest is deductible from your taxable income. Banks can also guarantee performance by one or more parties to a deal, supplying the value of security to you or others. If you need to make or receive payments in a foreign currency over time, a currency dealer can lock in fixed exchange rates so you're not hurt by fluctuations in the value of your currency. Or an insurance company can provide coverage for valued individuals and assets involved in a deal.

- **Charities**. Good causes can provide a face-saving way out of conflicts between smaller players and their giants. Part or all of a contested payment can be donated to charity, putting the money to use in a positive way—without one party being forced to pay the other. This approach once again has the government coughing up a contribution through a tax deduction.

- **Tie-breakers**. Third parties can create or preserve value by acting as Coercers—arbitrating, enforcing deals or playing the role of a jury. Sometimes, disputes are settled by informal juries, without incurring huge legal costs. The film *Good Will Hunting* benefits from a jury of sorts. Miramax is deeply concerned because unknown actors Matt Damon and Ben Affleck are adamant that Gus Van Sant direct their screenplay. But the studio wants a mainstream director to ensure box office success. After going back and forth, the solution evolves: Van Sant will direct, showing his final cut to an impartial focus group. If the film does not attract strong ratings, Miramax can re-edit.[15] This avoids haggles over each edit, maintaining the film's raw appeal, while striking a positive tension between Van Sant's artistic needs and Miramax's financial goals. Indeed, the director's version draws rave reviews from its advance audience, going on to collect nine Academy Award nominations in 1998. Young actors Matt and Ben quickly learn the truth—great films don't get made, they get negotiated.

Here's one last example, this time from the world of sports. The New York Yankees will be called upon as a third-party to help another baseball team unload a player it can no longer afford:

TRIPLE PLAY. It's 2003, and the cash-poor, tiny-market Montreal Expos want to trade their expensive star pitcher, Bartolo Colon, to the Chicago

White Sox—a team with much deeper pockets in a much larger city.[16] When the two teams realize they can't fully satisfy each other's needs on their own, they bring in the New York Yankees to help out. Why? Because a Montreal-Chicago deal would guarantee the heralded Bartolo Colon *won't* be traded to New York's arch-enemy, the Boston Red Sox—a distinct possibility otherwise. New York happily goes along with the scheme, sending veteran pitcher Orlando Hernandez and cash to Chicago for two lesser-known players.[17] Chicago then ships Hernandez, two other players and cash to Montreal for Colon and a minor leaguer. In all, seven players change teams in this three-way swap, meeting each team's unique interests.

Use third parties to add value—including those who might be adversely affected by a non-deal, governments, financial institutions, charities and tiebreakers.

INVOLVE YOUR GIANT EARLY ON

I rip open the thin envelope: *Your application has been denied.* Not good, but not the end of the world either. I know I am just one of thousands of applicants in early 1987 who have received the same message from the Harvard Business School.

Can I negotiate my way into the world's best-known business program? Unlikely.

The next day, I pick up the phone. My first call goes to a Harvard alumnus who plays the role of a Connector, hooking me up two calls later with the School's Admissions Director, Mr. James Foley. Acting as a Counselor, Convincer, Controller and Crack, Foley eventually tells me— over the course of two conversations—exactly how committee members have voted on my file, where their concerns lie (thankfully, there's no mention of my stealing Lumpy's sofa), and what I need to do to change their minds.

The following year, after taking several accounting and statistics courses, visiting the school and re-applying during a period when I've been told my acceptance will be more likely due to fewer applicants, I am indeed admitted—as negotiated with Mr. Foley.

By being in contact with my giant long before applications were due in 1988, I learned plenty about Harvard's concerns and the influence process that governs applications, allowing me to improve my credentials and my approach the second time around. As for Harvard, my second application got them a candidate more geared to their specific needs. Most importantly, the team at Harvard learned some things about me that my first application could not reveal: I am persistent; I do what I say I'll do; and I *really* wanted to attend their Business School.

In some situations, smaller players can create better results by involving their giants sooner rather than later. While I discovered this the hard way through my failed application to Harvard, Britain's Simon Fuller was smart enough to figure it out for himself—through a phenomenon called *Pop Idol.*

STORY: IDOLIZING VALUE

As a record manager and producer, your dream is to sign young singers who will go on to fame, making you a fortune as you reap a small percentage on every song or CD sold online and in stores.

To see your dream come true, even once, five magical things must happen. You need to: 1) Stumble across rare talent, which is like panning for gold. 2) Sign this talent to a contract amid competition from thousands of other record managers. 3) Sign a deal with a record company that's willing to publish and distribute your client's CD. 4) Hope your artist also has the rare ability to thrive under intense pressure from today's mass media. 5) Cross your fingers that your giant—masses of music buyers—will listen to, and like, both your singer and their music.

The odds of achieving all five of these outcomes are low.

Unless you're Simon Fuller.

In the late 1990s, the 40-ish British record manager and producer ponders how he might improve his odds in the industry. Up to this point, random talent searches have typically occurred behind the scenes, and are based heavily on gut feel. A record company will abruptly present the public with a new artist and CD. Attempts to negotiate sales of this CD begin upon its release, and revolve around image, promotion, tours, pricing and the CD's availability in stores.

Fuller wonders what would happen if he were to turn this talent-selection and sales process on its head. What if he involves his giant, millions of fickle music buyers, six to 18 months earlier than the norm? What if he not only exposes these potential buyers to his talent searches, but makes them active participants through new technology?

The music maverick's reflections lead to the creation of a television show called *Pop Idol*, which Fuller quickly sells to a British television network.

In 2001, *Pop Idol* announces its search for singing talent in Great Britain. The winner will be crowned a "pop idol" while receiving a recording contract and the right to be managed by Simon Fuller and his company, 19 Entertainment.

Open try-outs are held, with 10,000 wannabes showing up around the country for their shot at fame. A team of four judges including one of Fuller's partners, Simon Cowell, grimaces at times as amateurs sing their hearts out. The deliberations of the judges are taped, edited and televised for a public that grows more fascinated each week.[18]

Cowell's scathing reviews become infamous as the singing contenders are narrowed down to 50 finalists by the judges, at which point the public begins to vote via phone and the Internet, further reducing the number of potential winners to ten. All the finalists sing in live, televised auditions, and after comments from the judges, the public continues to vote weekly, sending home the least popular singer.[19]

In the end, two singers remain—a good-looking theater student named Will Young, and Gareth Gates, who suffers from a severe speech impediment that melts away when he sings. The British public is addicted, and confounded: they have helped shepherd both young men to the final of Simon Fuller's new-age talent contest and they are suddenly being asked to choose between their two favorites.

Before the last segment revealing the winner, almost nine million votes are registered in a nation of only 60 million people. Viewers finally choose their beloved Will over charming Gareth, but not by much.[20]

With *their* winner announced, do you think members of the public might now be more willing to shell out good money for a CD by Will, and maybe even one by Gareth, instead of buying music by a new artist they don't know?

You bet—and Simon Fuller knew it from the start.

Will Young's debut CD goes on to become the fastest-selling single in British history, surpassing one million copies in the first week alone. Runner-up Gareth Gates also sells an extraordinary number of CDs. Both are managed by Fuller.

The *Pop Idol* concept has since been sold to networks around the world, with dozens of spin-offs including *American Idol, Canadian Idol, Australian Idol, Second Chance Idol* (for losers), *World Idol* and *American Juniors* for kids.

Simon Fuller has discovered how to create value for his giant and himself in an industry that continues to be a game of chance for most managers and producers. At last count, in the United States and United Kingdom combined, his artists are approaching a total of 100 "number one" singles *and* 100 top albums.

The man who once managed acts such as the Spice Girls and Annie Lennox has multiplied his wealth many times over in recent years. "My business is creating fame and celebrity," Fuller says, "and I'm one of the best in the world. I know it to the finest detail." [21]

INVOLVE YOUR GIANT EARLY ON

Our record manager and producer draws his giant into the value creation process at least six months before potential music buyers might normally decide whether to buy a CD by one of his new artists.

Value for buyers is music they love. Value for Simon Fuller is a growing bank account and reputation. His stunning results show that sometimes it makes sense to involve giants earlier than expected in our core activities and the influence process. In these situations, the risks of involving our giant early on are outweighed by one or more clear benefits:

- **Uncover interests earlier than usual and tailor your offerings accordingly.** In an industry where high risk is assumed, Fuller weeds out any significant risk that Will Young's new CD will be rejected by the buying public. He assures Will's success by letting giant buyers identify who best meets their music listening interests long before Will might otherwise be rejected by a manager or a record company through traditional approaches. The more an artist is liked, the more money buyers will pay to listen to that artist's CD, especially when it's been methodically filtered to their specific tastes.

- **Use distinct approaches to attract bigger giants or more giants, creating greater value.** Fuller brings a larger number of potential buyers to the table than he would be able to target through a standard CD release. He does this through the broad reach of television, capitalizing on the medium's ability to convey emotion as well as his show's dramatic format. Many watching would never be interested in buying this type of music if it were not for *Pop Idol*.

- **Get your giant hooked as they help you generate value for you and them.** Fuller's audience members feel fully engaged in the selection process. As such, they are even more psychologically committed to pay for recordings by singers they have repeatedly supported at home, at the office or with their votes.

- **Develop a value creation process that creates *and* confirms value.** The rigorous nature of *Pop Idol*'s value creation process over a condensed period of time and in front of millions of viewers on a live basis is confirmation for Fuller. He knows that the winning pop idol he'll get to manage has traits like persistence, level-headedness and magnetic appeal, all of which are much harder to identify early on through common industry approaches to selecting talent.

- **Claim more value as a natural outcome of your agreed approach.** Fuller increases the value he'll claim for himself from giant buyers through the context and contracts he establishes prior to formally signing any winner. He's clearly the main contributor to value creation through the show he has developed and the record deals he has in place. Where emerging stars sometimes walk away if their manager wants too big a share of their earnings, this won't happen with *Pop Idol*. Participants commit in advance to the terms of their deal with Fuller should they happen to win. Fuller, no doubt, takes a hefty percentage of Will Young's profits.

If you ever shop at IKEA, you're aware that just like Simon Fuller, the Swedish furniture company also involves its mass market giant earlier than usual in order to create greater value for itself and its giant. IKEA knows that most consumers who shop there have the expectation they can pay less money if they're willing to contribute a little of their own elbow grease to the building process.

IKEA saves money by not paying laborers to assemble its furniture: this means it can keep its mass giant away from competitors who sell more expensive assembled stuff, allowing IKEA to benefit from a greater volume of business. More business means more discounts from IKEA suppliers, which translates into greater margins and more value on the company's bottom line. As a consumer, getting involved in furniture-making keeps more value in your pocket, assuming you can spare a few hours figuring out how to put your new crib together!

Here are other examples, based on my work in the technology industry, of how you can get to your giant early and create mutual value:

GIANT REQUESTS FOR PROPOSALS (RFPs). Beth Hubbard befriends a government official, Manny Ortiz, gaining his respect and shaping his views on potential improvements to the state's tax collection systems.[22] When Manny issues an RFP asking for new technology to improve these tax systems, Beth's young software firm already knows the interests in play and has a solution in mind. But Beth also knows the state will favor more established bidders unless a smaller player can provide superior solutions along with performance protections. Since Beth has listened carefully to Manny and quietly influenced the RFP's contents from the start, her bid ends up being the best, taking advantage of her small firm's low overhead costs, flexibility and local resources. She provides protections to guarantee the win, including co-ownership of her firm's software code should non-performance issues arise or if her firm folds for any reason. Beth benefits from Manny's early help as a Crack, Counselor, Convincer and Controller.

GIANT BUYERS. You plan to sell a groundbreaking new product to an array of giant buyers, but your product is still not polished enough to go to market.

Even when your product is finally ready, you know it will be hard to hook initial buyers, since it has no track record. Account manager Marie Gagne comes up with a solution: she chooses an existing, open-minded client and gives them a fading opportunity to become her product's inaugural user, much earlier than the norm. What's more, she offers this risk-taker the rights to a small, but material, royalty percentage on *all* sales of the product going forward. Her giant accepts. In return, Marie has a prized first client to spur sales, act as a reference whenever needed, and serve as a committed source of ongoing feedback. Her interests are fully satisfied—and so are her giant's as an early client with upside.

GIANT PARTNERS. If you can't attract or gain access to a giant—either directly or through helpers—but want your giant involved, you can act on your own to raise the odds they will partner with you. At an online start-up in 2002, Paul Mentos decides to use Apple's unique video technology, guessing the California-based giant will be more inclined to provide support later on. Within months, he has attracted Apple's attention, reaching a co-promotion agreement to showcase Apple's video systems. Apple returns the favor, driving high volumes of new traffic to Paul's website—critical currency for a smaller player. By involving Apple's technologies in his company's core activities from the start, even though Apple itself isn't involved, Paul finishes up by landing a valuable agreement.

Involve your giant early on—boosting mutual value by unveiling giant interests, improving communication, getting them to work for you and shaping unique deals.

MAKE YOUR DEALS BIGGER OR SMALLER

As we finish our exploration of how to create value in giant deals, both shorter and longer term, we'll stand side-by-side with a Canadian Prime Minister as he decides whether it makes sense to do a big trade deal with the indomitable Ronald Reagan.

STORY: SO WHAT'S THE BIG DEAL?

It's early 1985. Canada's Prime Minister, Brian Mulroney, has won his first election with a massive majority and faces a seminal decision as his nation's new leader.

Mulroney has pledged to never support a wide-ranging free trade deal with the United States—a country ten times Canada's size in population. He's made it clear that for reasons of national sovereignty, smaller deals will continue to govern limited free trade between certain sectors of the American and Canadian economies. Right now, there are trade arrangements in place to exchange products such as automobile parts, defense weapons and farm machinery.

However, after meeting with US President Ronald Reagan, Mulroney is suddenly weighing the pros and cons of a trade deal that would cover virtually all industries and sectors—instead of smaller, incremental deals. His final decision will have to take into account his past opposition to a bigger deal, developing realities inside the US and his nation's history with its giant neighbor to the south.

Since the beginning of their cross-border relationship, like a younger sibling, Canada has experienced feelings of awe toward America, mixed with scorn. In 1867, Canada became a distinct nation in part to encourage new east-west trade within its own provinces to replace lost trade with the US. The year before, when Canada was just a colony, America had punished it, severing their trade deal after Canada's mother—Great Britain—irked the states in the North by not supporting them during the Civil War.[23]

Fast forward to the free trade deal Brian Mulroney is pondering: many Canadians worry that erasing all protective tariffs, trade quotas and pro-Canada domestic regulations will lead to job losses. Companies might move plants to the US to be closer to major markets and to avoid paying unionized Canadian workers more expensive social benefits. Meanwhile, those staying in Canada may be squashed by new Goliath competitors running at them from across the border. The Prime Minister's past pledges to smaller, limited deals also ring true with those concerned that broader and deeper economic ties with the US could result in negative American influence—even control of Canada's culture, environment and resource ownership.

Yet as Mulroney looks out from his new office on Parliament Hill in

Ottawa, he finds himself on the verge of embracing an all-encompassing trade deal.

Americans are rapidly becoming protectionists, encouraging their law-makers to build trade walls in a bid to protect US jobs. Trying to renegotiate existing smaller trade deals and create new ones might prove difficult, if not impossible, and risked weaker terms for Canada. Reagan says he's confident he can overcome the growing protectionist tendencies in America, *but* says he'll only do so if it's worth his time and effort.[24]

Reagan has made it clear to Mulroney that he wants a comprehensive trade deal: this will help cement Reagan's legacy as a fighter for economic and political freedoms. It could also prompt favorable deals for the US with other nations that don't want to be left out of freer international trade. The President truly seems to believe that free trade can force companies around the world to be at their absolute best as they compete openly with others, allowing winners to jack up their sales volumes, while lowering their per unit costs—leading to more profits and greater wealth creation. In President Reagan's mind, free markets discipline countries to do what they're best at—not simply pump out lower quality goods and services because they can.

Canada's rookie Prime Minister makes up his mind: he'll throw his efforts behind a massive trade deal, which he now believes will best serve his nation's long-term interests.

Those against a big trade deal are enraged by Mulroney's dramatic about-face. They accuse him of selling out Canada and its future. Protestors take to the streets, promising to make this the battle of the century. They paint Mulroney as a flip-flopping con artist whose Irish roots belie his "blarney."

As the complex trade talks progress in 1986 and 1987, Mulroney's developing deal garners thin, widespread support—typical of large deals like this—while facing vocal, concentrated opposition in areas where specific interest groups feel threatened. Finally, agreement is reached on all fronts. To secure the deal and its approval in parliament, the Prime Minister figures he must give a louder voice to the dispersed supporters of free trade, uniting them behind him in his quest.

He calls an election. Mulroney wants Canadians to decide if they support his deal. Muddying the waters is the fact his Conservative Party has been pummeled by scandal, falling to third place in recent opinion polls.

The campaign that unfolds in 1988 is hard-fought, polarized and focused on what it means to be Canadian. Mulroney slowly rises, making his case, cajoling undecided voters to write history. After a roller-coaster campaign, he wins another majority of seats in the House of Commons, again giving his Conservative Party iron-fisted control of government.

Mulroney and Reagan's Free Trade Agreement takes effect January 1, 1989. The deal is to be phased in over a ten-year period, easing the transition on both sides of the border.[25]

Canada loses lower-skilled jobs in areas such as textiles, but it creates an equal number of better paying jobs in other sectors. Productivity rises through competition. Overall trade levels skyrocket. National revenue goes up significantly. Despite these results, critics of Mulroney and free trade continue to voice concerns about culture, softwood lumber and future rights to the nation's vast water resources.

MAKE YOUR DEALS BIGGER OR SMALLER

For Canada, a comprehensive free trade deal with the US had undeniable benefits—all of which can be used in our favor as smaller players, inside or outside the political arena.

If we put ourselves squarely into Prime Minister Mulroney's shoes after he was first elected in 1984, and think like he might think, the arguments for one big deal are compelling:

- **A bigger deal grabs our giant's attention.** *I'll be able to put enough value on the table to make this deal of interest to President Reagan specifically. Based on everything Reagan has said to me, a series of smaller deals or renegotiations won't grab his attention or his support.*

- **A bigger deal can offer us a range of protections.** *1) It protects every sector of the economy, getting all sectors inside the US trade tent before Congress closes that tent. 2) Even though it's a big deal, Canada can, and will, receive protective exemptions in areas such as healthcare, education and culture. 3) If a big deal turns out to be a mistake, I'll* *protect us by pulling the plug, projecting myself as a strong leader who's willing to stand up to our giant neighbor. 4) It's harder for specific interest groups to attack and torpedo a broad deal once it's been reached because the overall interests of each nation must be considered prior to acting on behalf of any single set of players and their distinct interests. 5) One big deal makes it easier to monitor and to remedy any disputes—compared to multiple smaller deals that may have inconsistent mechanisms and leave us exposed.*

- **A bigger deal leverages our time and resources efficiently.** *1) Shorter term, because of the magnitude of a big deal relative to our size, we'll be able to focus our nation's best analysis, people and resources on this one negotiation. 2) Longer term, our time is better spent now on one big deal than a bunch of smaller deals that will no doubt fail to cover off all the issues needing attention.*

- **A bigger deal raises our chances of success.** *1) In negotiations, it gives my negotiation team a wider range of trade-offs to make between different sectors of the economy, i.e., we give a little here, but get something over there—helping to avoid stalemates. 2) After the deal closes, trade on so many fronts means that unpredictable losses are more likely to be offset, and hopefully overwhelmed, by gains in other sectors—creating net gains for both countries. 3) Overall, a bigger deal—while riskier politically right now—is more likely to bring bigger benefits to the nation and to my personal legacy as Prime Minister.*

In some situations as a smaller player, *un*like Canada's Prime Minister in the 1980s, you may not be able to put together a big enough deal on your own. If that's the case, you might want to rely on one or more Coalitionists to contribute value that will attract your giant's attention and create meaningful mutual value. For example, one smaller nation could join up with other smaller nations to form a trading bloc before approaching a giant nation like the United States to propose a big trade deal.

Clearly, big deals can offer us big benefits. Now, let's switch gears and look at the benefits of smaller deals, especially if there's potentially strong resistance to a bigger deal from significant players inside or outside our giant:

- **A smaller deal is easier to negotiate and close.** This saves you and your giant time, while also easing any tensions as you negotiate a new relationship. More importantly, perhaps, it means you'll be able to close a deal before any changes in the context occur, or other players intervene.

- **A smaller deal can be less risky.** You're able to focus on delivering better results, fewer resources need to be involved, and by touching on fewer issues and interests, you're less likely to ignite a powerful coalition against your deal. Should the deal prove to be a failure anyway, you don't tend to lose as much as you would when a larger deal tanks. Former US President Bill Clinton and First Lady Hillary Clinton found out through a sweeping healthcare initiative that "less can be best" in terms of risk and reward. Their broad reform plan in the early 1990s managed to alienate so many players in the US healthcare system that it died from widespread opposition. An ambitious but incremental approach to reform based on a series of smaller legislative and regulatory deals would have been less risky, and in all likelihood, met their interests much better.[26]

- **A smaller deal can secure irreversible steps toward a bigger deal.** If your goal is to grow a giant relationship, generating bigger deals over time, a small deal can get you across the drawbridge and inside your giant's castle—to stay. By pursuing a small joint-venture as a pilot deal, you can learn from this effort, build rapport and expand on the venture if it proves successful.

- **A smaller deal can reduce disclosure requirements.** If one or more public companies is involved, a large and material negotiation may require unhelpful and premature disclosures, whereas a smaller deal can keep it under the radar.

Lastly, here's an example of a smaller deal making a lot of sense, based on some work I did with one of the world's leading management consulting firms:

STRATEGIC CONSULTING. Karen Blanchard at Corden Associates, a management consulting firm, has just landed one of Europe's largest car companies as a client. But as Karen and her team interview executives at the car giant, she receives a jolt: deep skepticism about Corden's ability to come up with practical solutions. One executive says, "I've heard you're all inept, intellectual wankers." Despite initial resistance from her client's surprised CEO, Karen radically scales back the size of the assignment. Rather than a wide-ranging strategic review, she decides to focus on a small online project with big benefits for most of the executives at the car giant. After this proves successful, she moves on to slightly bigger projects, finally tackling a broad strategic review once she is confident its results won't be undermined by wary executives responsible for implementing her recommendations. Her firm ultimately creates much more joint value by taking patient, timely steps toward a robust client relationship—instead of rushing into things.[27]

Make your deals bigger or smaller—weighing the risks and benefits of each approach.

HAZARDS TO AVOID

In putting together golden deals, here are some traps to sidestep:

Confusing different interests with different values. Creating deals based on different goals, needs and concerns makes sense—but not if the deeply held values and principles underlying these interests are diametrically opposed. Some smaller players rue the day they agreed to partner or be taken over by a giant whose differences appeared to mesh well with their own, only to later discover that different values around issues such as loyalty to their employees, community and even clients should have led them to say *no*.

Assuming shared interests lead to harmony. Shared interests can result in great deal outcomes, but having the same goals, needs or concerns as your giant can also lead to ongoing conflicts. For example, if both you and your giant need to be in the spotlight while working together, that spotlight may not be big enough for two. Or if you each have the same goal of dominating a niche, that may cause problems as well.

Bringing third parties into deals inadvertently. Third parties can save deals, but they can also undermine the value in your deals if they remain invisible until it's too late. The wrong giant counterpart or wrong deal can surface: antitrust authorities in the case of over-reaching deals; law enforcement officials if past offenses have been committed by your giant; or hungry creditors looking to make good on major claims against your giant.

Involving giants inappropriately early on. Think carefully before involving giants too early as you create value if there is any significant risk they could derail or block your initiative altogether. When consulting giants, make sure you're clear about expectations as to how their input will be used so they're not disappointed and ready to tear down value as payback. Finally, you do not want giants to think you're consulting them because you don't know what you're doing: no one ever accused Simon Fuller of not knowing what he was doing with *Pop Idol*.

Pursuing big deals when they're not the right answer. Smaller organizations wanting to follow consultant Karen Blanchard's smaller deal approach must avoid a bias toward bigger deals over smaller ones. Of paramount importance: making sure internal strategies, praise and compensation systems reward long-term, value-maximizing approaches to deal-making and relationship-building—regardless of deal size.

FINAL THOUGHTS

Be the Hinkens—using giant differences to create enormous value. Or wing it like Richard Branson, searching for valuable interests you and your giant might share. Think about union leader Mike Murphy when you hit a wall because maybe a third party can add value to your deal. Even if you never buy a CD by a pop idol, never forget Simon Fuller's lessons about how to involve giants earlier than expected. And when you negotiate your next big deal, remember Brian Mulroney's trade legacy—or Karen Blanchard's patience if you believe your next "big deal" should actually be a smaller one.

Prepare for success. Start by deciding if it makes sense to involve your giant sooner or later in your core activities, negotiation activities, or both, to maximize the value you can create and claim. To identify the right giant partners, or the right structure for your deal, list key aspects of your profile, expertise, resources and assumptions, brainstorming partners based on your differences. You can also list your main goals, needs and concerns and seek out giants who share them. If you might need a third party to add value, weigh the benefits of bringing them to the table on your own or approaching them jointly with your giant. Finally, try to gain insights from your helpers—especially Cracks, Convincers, Counselors and Controllers—to decide if a big deal or a smaller deal is the ideal first step.

Follow these broad steps to bolster value. The goal is to create value by satisfying our interests. The more value a giant receives by satisfying their interests, the more likely they will share value, instead of fighting us for crumbs. Since giants are often quick to gobble up the value pie, the Size Wizards work hard at baking in a lot of value beforehand—tracing lines where the pie should be divided *before* any explicit negotiations take place. The Hinkens could have tried to sell their company to SuperTech ten years earlier, but their core activities would have been worth a fraction of their fully-baked value. To further boost the overall value they would receive, the Hinkens turned to their negotiation activities, digging into SuperTech's interests and structuring a deal that met these interests, as well as their own.

Keep the golden goose alive. When David killed Goliath, the giant wasn't contributing much value to society. Today, we usually don't want to destroy the giants who make our golden deals possible, even when they do bad things. If Exxon had been wiped out after the *Valdez* oil tanker spill in 1989, who would have paid the clean-up bill? Sure, Exxon caused the damage, but many mining companies pollute and simply aren't big enough to clean up, so they go bankrupt and the mess is dealt with by taxpayers, if at all. Most giant organizations have golden value to offer us: we just have to make sure they pay up, and in a timely manner—which brings us back to Exxon. The Goliath paid billions toward the *Valdez* spill but kept appealing the punitive damages it owed, finally reducing these damages to $500 million (10% of the jury's original award). Vulnerable smaller players, such as those Alaskans who lost everything in the *Valdez* accident and have waited two decades for this money, believe they deserve better. They want a legal system that protects them from giants who use their golden resources to fund one appeal after another until they get a decision they like—or their tiny adversary goes broke.[28]

6

Stand Tall in Conversations

Increase your stature by what you say and how you say it.

Have you ever been in the presence of a giant who leaves you tongue-tied, making commitments and saying things you later regret? What about giant authorities and menacing, hard-bargaining or uninterested Goliaths? Can you keep your wits when face-to-face with them, remaining respectful while still getting what you want?

Giants naturally tower over us in direct discussions, frequently looking for opportunities to make us feel smaller and weaker than we already are.

But it doesn't have to be this way.

So far, we've focused on stories dominated by strategic undertakings away from the negotiation table, whether we were pre-meditating our defenses, leveling the playing field or creating golden deals. For the most part, conversations in person, on the phone or via email played only a supporting role, if any.

We now turn our attention to the "negotiation table" and situations where the conversation itself is central to getting what we want from giant Controllers.

We'll experience a remarkable range of discussions. In all our stories, everything is riding on what happens during a single conversation. This offers us an opportunity to learn how we can rise and stand tall in any giant encounter based on the following approaches honed by the Size Wizards:

- They respect *and* question giant authority figures who intimidate them.

- They build trust incrementally, even under the most difficult conditions.

- They fend off angry, hard-bargaining giants by understanding their tactics.

- They attract indifferent giants, keep them glued and close the deal.

In pursuing these approaches, the Size Wizards draw on the same habits and helpers we've seen in our three other core strategies. They remain calm as they go about their business, knowing anxiety only undermines their ability to think and risks handing control of a conversation to their giant. They try to listen more than they talk, building relationships that permit more talk. And at best, they watch more than they listen, aware that body language and facial gestures answer more tough questions than spoken words.

In *Stand Tall in Conversations*, the last of our size and strength strategies, we'll meet a patient who turns a delivery table into a negotiation table, with the stakes as high as you can imagine. We witness someone taken hostage by an armed killer negotiating for her life. We see an architect shield herself, her firm and her fees against verbal attacks and relentless efforts to lower her prices. And finally, the conversation becomes lighter as a street busker shows us how to attract busy giants against the odds and get them to pay up.

RESPECT AND QUESTION AUTHORITIES

We have an innate instinct to follow authority—perhaps an ancient tribal tendency that allows us to function in groups, especially when seeking direction amid uncertainty. Like many of our psychological tendencies, however, this one is a double-edged sword.

We can become weak-kneed and unthinking when we see a white lab coat, a police uniform, an impressive title or an accomplished person. Multiple studies and endless real-life scams highlight how we repeatedly bow to authority figures even if they're people simply *acting* the roles of police officers, lawyers, bosses, researchers or doctors. In the extreme, we'll do things for these perceived authorities that we would never do otherwise, such as give up our savings, physically hurt someone or lie.[1] In other situations, we'll silence ourselves, which happens much too often when we're dealing with authorities who are also our giants.

The key, as we're about to learn from a young woman facing an extraordinary choice, is to respect true giant authorities and never forget that we alone as smaller players are responsible for protecting and promoting our own interests.

STORY: A SCARRING EXPERIENCE

"Breathe deeply, Maria—in and out! Push now. Good. And again. You're getting there!" urges Dr. Robert Manse.

The sharp pains came two months early. No one else knew about Maria Mortare's pregnancy because her stomach remained taut and she wore loose-fitting clothes. She had left her friend's house without explanation, rushing by taxi to the emergency room at this nearby San Francisco hospital. Soon after, Dr. Manse arrived, summoned from an obstetrics/gynecology conference. He'd been at a podium, finishing his presentation about a new medical procedure, when his pager went off.[2]

Drenched in sweat, the young, blue-eyed brunette lying on her back rolls her eyes, moaning as she follows Dr. Manse's orders. A nurse dabs Maria's olive skin with a cloth, offering assurances.

But there is a problem: where a head should be beginning to show, there are two small, bloodied feet. Maria stares up at the tall, 58-year-old doctor she's entrusted with both her life and her child's.

"Relax, Maria," Dr. Manse says in a calm voice, masking how quickly he must now move. "Your baby's simply turned the wrong way and having trouble moving down the birth canal. We deal with breech births like this all the time."

Maria smiles weakly, taking comfort in her doctor's confidence, and his resemblance to her grandfather who is about the same age. Both are large men with a gentle manner.

Dr. Manse smiles back, promising to put an end to her misery. "We'll start the pain medication through your lower spine immediately, and take the baby out by caesarean in just a matter of minutes. You won't feel a thing, young lady."

"Caesarean? What do you mean? Cutting my stomach open?" Maria asks.

"We'll be careful, Maria. You'll be back on your feet in no time. I've done hundreds of these operations successfully and this one will be no different."

"No!" she cries, abruptly stopping herself, altering her tone. "I mean, please find another way, Dr. Manse," she begs. She can no longer bear to look at those tiny feet in the mirror above the delivery table.

Dr. Manse knows there's often resistance to any invasive surgery, especially when it's unexpected. But he also knows that, like all his patients who find themselves in this situation, Maria is in no position to refuse a caesarean, and *will* provide her consent. There's no time to waste. The baby may already be in distress.

"Maria, if you're worried about the scar, it will be quite small and should fade." He watches as his patient closes her eyes and leans back, sighing deeply. Now that she's stopped pushing, the pain is less severe but the contractions are still racking her body. She opens her eyes, turning to him.

"Dr. Manse, I said on the form I was 20 years old. But I lied. I'm only 17."

"Oh," he says, his brow furrowing.

"My parents don't know about this baby, and they never will because I'm putting it up for adoption. One day..." Another contraction interrupts.

The doctor hadn't considered his patient's age. He sees young moms all the time. This one acts well beyond her years—poised and well-spoken.

"Maria, I don't want to scare you, but your baby is at risk if we don't get it out. And you will definitely be at risk if we attempt a vaginal delivery. It's not an option at this point. Believe me." He pats her leg, signals to the nurse to prepare Maria for the operation, and turns to go and scrub.

"I can't have a scar, any scar," she says hoarsely, bracing for another jolt. "My parents will figure out I've had a baby, and that I hid my pregnancy from them for seven months. My father will kill me. For real. He's warned me not to have sex, not to get pregnant."

"We'll have to worry about that later, Maria," Dr. Manse says, turning to go once again.

"Please worry about it now!" she counters forcefully. In her desperation, she suddenly gains the strength that accompanies delivery and motherhood. Her next contraction pushes an idea out, one she clings to until she can speak. "If I have the operation, how else can the scar on my tummy be explained?"

"What?" Dr. Manse answers, as though he's misheard his patient.

"How else can we explain the caesarean scar to my parents?"

Maria's giant shows signs of fluster. "Not possible. I mean, yes, maybe but…*we?*"

"Maybe what?" she continues.

"In theory, I suppose the incision is similar to one you'd receive if you had an ovarian operation."

"Why do women have an operation like that?" Maria asks hurriedly.

"To remove ovaries sometimes. Other times, to take out an ovarian growth. Cysts can form," Dr. Manse explains, his mind pedaling furiously for the right approach here.

"Do 17-year-olds get them? The cysts?"

"Yes, it's possible, though rare. We don't know why they develop…but Maria, this isn't, I mean, we're not going to have this conversation. Not now."

"I don't want to risk the baby's life if it comes out between my legs—and I don't want to die, either. But I'm scared, Dr. Manse. You need to help me. I watch TV. I know that doctors take some kind of oath that says you have to help me, and not tell others if I don't want you to." She pauses, wincing, "It's true, isn't it?"

Dr. Manse can't believe his ears.

He doesn't need this teenager to remind him of his Hippocratic Oath, which he swore 30 years ago. He keeps staring at his feet, thinking. He glances at the clock on the wall. The nurse reads out vital signs robotically, fixated on the discussion she's pretending not to hear. Another minute ticks by. The patient is beginning to bleed. Her baby's in the early stages of distress—its heartbeat is slowing. Dr. Manse's head clears, he regains his balance.

"Okay, Maria. Your scar can be from an emergency medical procedure to remove a cyst from your ovaries. Whatever you want," Dr. Manse says with resignation.

Relief spreads across Maria's face. "Thank you, Doctor. And you'll be sure to tell my parents that it's a cyst if they talk to you?"

Another glance at the clock. "No, Maria. Just because I'm bound by patient confidentiality doesn't mean I have to lie to anyone. What you tell your parents is your business. If they come to me, I'll simply say they need to talk to you."

"Okay," she says. "And after the operation, where will you put me?"

"Well, the maternity ward is where…" he begins to explain.

"I can't be there if my parents come to see me, Dr. Manse!" Maria interjects. "Where do you normally put patients who have cysts?"

"The gynecological ward."

"Can you do that for me?"

He pauses. "Yes, Maria. I suppose that would make sense if we're taking this approach," he concedes.

"You have my consent then, Dr. Manse. Please get this baby out of me. I'm ready."

Fifteen minutes later, a tiny baby boy screams with life—life that results from an intense negotiation. The mother is wheeled into a private room, far from the maternity ward.

RESPECT AND QUESTION AUTHORITIES

Maria Mortare did something many adults never do: question a doctor about a chosen path for treatment.

She got what she wanted by knowing what she wanted. Though intimidated by her giant, she clearly communicated her interests. She put forward a standard of behavior—an oath—that caused her giant to pause. She introduced her alternative course of action in a way that was credible, even though it might endanger two lives. And finally, she offered up options for meeting her interests and her doctor's that would see them reach agreement because Dr. Manse believed these options satisfied his interests better than any of his own alternatives.

In her conversation with Dr. Manse, ironically, Maria was the one doing the poking and prodding, as she explored a medical world with which she was unfamiliar. For the most part, our teenager was respectful of her authority figure, subjecting him to tough questions and choices but never attacking him personally or being overtly rude—despite the fact she was stressed both mentally and physically. Her doctor was not wrong about the caesarean, but he had to find a way to do it that was right for his patient.[3]

Like all authority figures, doctors can be wrong. In a number of studies, medical professionals have consistently misdiagnosed or changed their diagnosis, whether it was right or wrong, from one session to another. In an early study, physicians examined 389 boys, judging that almost half of them needed a tonsillectomy. Those determined *not* to need their tonsils out—the healthy boys—were then examined by a different set of doctors. These doctors concluded that almost half of the "healthy" boys needed a tonsillectomy. So the remaining 116 boys, who had seen two sets of doctors and twice been told they were okay, now go on to see a third and final set of doctors. What do these experts declare? You guessed it. Almost half the boys will need a tonsillectomy.[4]

Whenever we're being diagnosed by a doctor, it's worth remembering that these highly trained professionals are still unraveling the truths behind how our bodies work.

Here are some other things to think about as you speak with any giant authority figure—but especially doctors, who influence life and death issues and who can help us better understand all the other authorities in our lives:

- **Stay vigilant.** Guard against our tendency to follow authority without thinking. You can question authority figures until you have answers, first politely confirming—as needed—that they are indeed true authorities. It's often helpful to be explicit in expressing the interests behind your questions, while remaining respectful toward your giant. Don't be afraid to ask what certain jargon means, or clarify something you've found hard to follow. Authorities who are confident of their approach and expertise should fully understand and respect anyone wanting reasonable information and choices before making a significant decision.

- **Provide better personal data.** Doctors are among society's most educated professionals, yet they are dependent on critical preliminary data provided by total rookies in medicine—patients like you and me. If we want to influence the range of doctors we see to give us the best possible treatment for our particular physical condition, we need to give them better information. Some Size Wizards in the domain of medicine keep their own health diary, jotting notes to track past appointments, tests, ailments and any prescribed medicines or prior medical procedures. Special-purpose diaries can also support our interests as we deal with lawyers, accountants and other professionals who must rely on our historical data.

- **Watch subjectivity.** Different experts are going to be anchored by their past experiences, financial incentives and training in terms of their diagnoses and proposed remedies. We shouldn't expect a radiologist, for example, to say surgery alone is definitely the way to battle prostate cancer. Nor is every lawyer specializing in divorce cases likely to say, "You know, maybe your spouse is not as bad as you think. Before spending a lot of money on my services, let's do everything possible to avoid a costly divorce that could really hurt your kids."

- **Use the Internet.** Reliable web resources can help us gather information about an illness, including symptoms, remedies, reference books, support groups and relevant organizations to contact. This information can influence our doctors and the course of our diagnosis, treatment and prognosis. Remember, quality data is usually the most valuable thing we offer up as a patient—not our conclusions. In fact, busy doctors risk misdiagnosing their patients by listening too much to their conclusions, while potentially ignoring important conflicting data. In most other areas of giant authority, good websites can also be used to offset ignorance.

- **Gather more opinions.** Go for a second opinion, or a third opinion, whenever you're uncertain. Make sure the professionals you consult are truly independent and can't collude for any reason. If you feel awkward, remember that your giant ultimately benefits in the end from their assessment being confirmed or corrected.

- **Maintain control.** When dealing with professional giants, you are the client, the one in control of your destiny, the one who has to live with the results of any action taken on your behalf. The Size Wizards act as quarterbacks for their team, never abdicating responsibility for outcomes. Most legal firms, for example, do not hold expertise in relationships or influence, so you have to communicate clearly and firmly with lawyers to ensure they take an approach that meets your *overall* interests, not just certain narrow legal or financial interests.

- **Call on helpers.** Bring along a friend or relative to important meetings as a Counselor, helping to retain and process information if you're off-balance, struggling emotionally and unable to listen well. By getting another person involved, you're also making your giant more accountable.

- **Resolve conflicts thoughtfully.** If you've been mistreated by a professional giant, do your best to resolve the issue with that professional directly, then consider going to their boss or the professional body they belong to—as Coercers. Legal action may be required in more extreme situations, but be clear about your main objective beforehand: is it money, or gaining resolution and making sure something never happens again? These interests can conflict. It's much harder to get honest answers from someone who thinks you're about to sue them.

- **Start a group conversation.** One couple I know in Canada, upset with a doctor about a birth gone awry, decided to get answers and protect others from the oxygen-deprivation that left their boy partially paralyzed. In a collaborative way, not accusingly, they gathered together key players at a single meeting—including the delivery-room doctor, their boss, the anesthetist and the baby's pediatrician—to chart what had happened during delivery. After this group conversation, the hospital adopted new practices and suspended the attending doctor, who had clearly made a series of mistakes. Tighter limits on medical liability suits in Canada helped this conversation happen.

In your workplace, if a giant authority demands you do something extreme or unethical, you can always ask questions focused on standards, *their* interests, other options or appeals to their better instincts and what they might lose:

- "Joan, if you're going to fire Bill just to appease the board, shouldn't we make sure there are no laws or employment rules that might hurt us so the board can't jump on you again, this time for mishandling the firing?"

- "Mr. Martz, if I can get you 75% of that information *without* breaking the rules, would you consider that a success, all things considered?"

- "Jacques, you've spent so much time building up goodwill with these people, have you thought about the concern that doing something like this could undermine *all* your incredible past efforts?"

- "Mrs. Gonzalez, cutting 20% of our costs so quickly is obviously going to create animosity, and some enemies. What if we could increase revenues by 10% so the cost-cutting can be more gradual and less severe?"

Former energy giant Enron is a good example of a Goliath that went astray when no smaller players inside voiced concerns skillfully enough to avoid the corporation's ongoing misdeeds and eventual collapse.

The Size Wizards are careful not to appear like they're passing judgment on giant authorities during difficult conversations, and they pick their spots. They constantly remind themselves of what they value, and question whether their long-term interests are genuinely aligned with those of an authority asking them to do something. The Size Wizards steer clear of the assumption that there is no good way to have a difficult conversation with an authority figure—because there always is.

Respect and question authorities—researching, storing and sharing accurate data, drawing on helpers and framing solutions from their perspective first, not yours.

BUILD TRUST IN UNLIKELY SITUATIONS

When we think about "trusting" someone, we generally mean that a person has gained our confidence because we believe they'll act reliably, and in our best interests, as part of a strong relationship over time.

When we talk to our giants, we need to turn this thinking about trust on its head. That's what Ashley Smith does early one morning in March 2005—and it saves her life.

STORY: A MATTER OF TRUST

As she gets out of her car, Ashley Smith listens as another door opens and closes behind her in the parking lot.

It's past 2 a.m. and the 26-year-old is alone. A chill runs down her spine. She grips the key to her nearby apartment and makes her way in the dark.

Ashley prays that the loudening footsteps she can hear are headed toward someone else's apartment in the complex. Her pace quickens as she approaches her front door; she plans to unlock the door in seconds and slip through it. Her trembling key finds the lock. The door opens. A huge man lunges at her back, grabbing her arm. She screams. A gun goes to her blond head, warning her to stay quiet. She's pushed forward into her home.[5]

Once inside, Brian Nichols takes off his hat. "Do you know who I am?" he asks.[6]

"Yeah, I know who you are," Ashley says breathlessly. "Please don't hurt me. I have a five-year-old little girl. Please don't hurt me." She instinctively personalizes herself to her menacing captor.

By now, everyone in the Atlanta, Georgia area knows who Brian Nichols is: a massive manhunt has been underway since his escape from an Atlanta courthouse the day before. The former college football player was there being tried on rape charges when he overcame his guard and killed a judge, a court reporter and a deputy. He somehow managed to board a train for the suburbs where he killed another man, stealing his truck.

"I don't want to hurt you. I don't want to hurt anybody else," he says to Ashley, as he frantically surveys her new apartment, where she hasn't even put up curtains yet. "You know someone could have heard your scream already. And if they did, the police are on their way, and I'm going to have to hold you hostage. And I'm going to have to kill you and probably myself and lots of other people. And I don't want that."

"Okay, I'll do what you say," she says, her mind and body overwhelmed with fear. Nichols ties her up with masking tape, an extension cord and a curtain. He goes to shower, keeping his guns on a nearby counter. She thinks he may kill her afterward.

As he showers, Ashley calms herself. She knows she needs to stay strong and clear-headed for her daughter. She thinks desperately but deliberately about how she can improve her odds of survival under these circumstances.

Ashley decides she must build trust with her captor, doing nothing to alarm him. She also figures she must let him get to know her so she's seen as a breathing, life-filled human being, not just another body. Finally, she needs to know him, how he thinks, what drives him and what will most influence him as she prepares for her exit. The young mother's overriding goal is to leave her apartment by 9:30 a.m. so she can see her daughter at 10 a.m. as planned—while doing her best to make sure no one else gets killed. Unlike some other hostage situations, this man has already proven that he will kill without hesitation.

Not long after his shower, seeing that his hostage is making no attempt to flee, Nichols decides that Ashley can be trusted enough not to scream or run for help. He unties her.

They sit in the bathroom, far from the apartment's uncurtained front window, and begin to talk.

She says that her daughter is expecting to be picked up hours from now at a church where Ashley and her aunt have arranged to meet. "Can I please go then?" she asks. He says *no*. She shares the details of how her husband was murdered four years earlier. She tells Nichols that if he hurts her, her daughter won't have a mommy or a daddy. She must get to her daughter by 10 a.m. and show her that Mommy is okay. Nichols says *no* again—though less emphatically this time.

The escaped killer says he just wants to relax, watch TV, eat some good food and feel normal. Ashley relents about her daughter, knowing she can help meet these immediate needs of his. She also knows that one wrong move could end her life.

They go to her bedroom.

She asks if she can read him something. He agrees, and she pulls out a book called *The Purpose-Driven Life*, written by Rick Warren.[7]

As hundreds of law enforcement officials scour Atlanta for the killer, Ashley Smith does everything she can to help Brian Nichols find some peace.

"Stop. Will you read that again?" he asks.

She reads once more from a passage in *The Purpose-Driven Life*: "God deserves your best. He shaped you for a purpose, and he expects you to make the most of what you have been given…"[8]

The strange conversation continues, mixed with readings from both Rick Warren's book and the Bible—along with more discussions about life, faith and choices.

Ashley talks openly about her life, her mistakes, her daughter and the devastating loss of her husband.[9] She gently probes her abductor about his family, his background, what he cares about and the series of events that brought him to her apartment. She asks why he did what he did at the courthouse. She listens. He says he's a "soldier," and that "his people" needed him to do this job. She talks to him about being a soldier of God instead, and doing God's will.

He has a picture of the last person he murdered, before taking the man's truck. Nichols says he didn't intend to hurt him. As they look at the photo, Ashley impresses upon Nichols that this 40-year-old victim probably has a wife and children grieving his loss.

Nichols looks at pictures of her family, and wonders what his own family is thinking.

After hours of talking, he turns to Ashley. Eyes wide open, he says she must be an angel sent from God. He admits to feeling completely lost. He now believes that God wanted him to meet her, to show him that he's hurt a lot of people, and to let him know how the families of those who died felt—because she has already experienced their loss.

He asks for her advice. She says he should turn himself in, so no one else gets hurt, including him. He says, "Look at me, look at my eyes. I'm already dead."

She says firmly, "You are not dead. You are standing right in front of me. If you want to die, you can. It's your choice."

They turn on the TV and watch coverage of his rampage. The 33-year-old man cannot believe what he's done.

At 6 a.m., Nichols announces he must get rid of the truck he arrived in, or he'll be found. Convinced that he will let her go so she can see her daughter, Ashley agrees to go with him. She follows him in her car so they can drive back to her place once he drops his vehicle somewhere. She has every opportunity to escape, or to call the police on her cell phone, but she doesn't do either. She understands the nature of her giant at this point and won't take any unnecessary risks. Even if she were to escape, she believes other innocent people would suffer.

When they return to her apartment, she continues to build their relationship. She cooks him pancakes—he's in bliss. They talk more about God and the meaning of life. His guns are lying around unguarded now. The trust is complete.

She looks in his eyes. "You're here in my apartment for some reason. You got out of that courthouse with police everywhere, and you don't think that's a miracle?" She pauses. "You know, your miracle could be that you need to be caught for this. You need to go to prison and you need to share the word of God with them, with all the prisoners there."

Before Ashley leaves the apartment to get her daughter, Nichols puts his guns under the bed and says he won't be using them again. As she walks out the door, he asks if he can do anything for her after she's gone, like hang curtains. She says, "Yeah, if you want to."

Within an hour, Brian Nichols is arrested. He does nothing to resist the police officers, called by Ashley as she drove to pick up her daughter.

BUILD TRUST IN UNLIKELY SITUATIONS

If you think about anyone you've distrusted, did you ever have as much reason to doubt them as Ashley Smith did when she encountered Brian Nichols at gunpoint?

Probably not. Yet Ashley's life and freedom depended on her ability to foster a trusting relationship with her captor during the span of seven and a half hours.

How did she build up this trust so quickly, and then use it to her advantage?

- **Focus on mutual trust as your end goal.** Ashley always kept her objective in mind: to have her captor allow her to walk out the door so she could pick up her daughter on time. Knowing mutual trust was her greatest ally given her predicament, she never flinched, ran, grabbed a gun she might not handle well or railed against her assailant. Nor did she remain silent and petrified. Instead, Ashley engaged Nichols, constantly nurturing their unlikely relationship so he could trust her, and she could ultimately trust him to let her go.

- **Model trust-building behaviors.** Ashley built trust step-by-step, always being the first to show she could be trusted and that she trusted him before looking for Nichols to trust her. Following Ashley's lead, he acted calmly, untied her, shared his story, shared his interests, listened to her, left himself unguarded and treated her respectfully.

- **Redefine trust around your giant's interests.** Ashley instinctively knew she could trust her giant to do what he perceived to be in his best interests. So the key for her was to figure out, and influence, how Nichols saw his interests. As their mutual trust grew, Ashley's captor opened up, sharing his goals, needs and concerns. She satisfied some of these interests, mainly related to basic needs like food and a sense of normalcy. Most importantly, she picked up on his goal of not wanting to kill anyone else, and repeatedly played that back to Nichols as an interest to be respected, not forgotten, as he moved forward.

- **Separate your giant as a person from recent untrustworthy actions.**
  Ashley was credible and firm on the substance of what she said—that
  Nichols had done wrong by killing innocent people. She was soft,
  however, on the man himself, separating him from his horrific actions,
  letting him see rays of hope and allowing their relationship to remain
  positive and trusting. She focused on what was decent about this man
  because that's the side of him that would set her free.

- **Frame choices to bolster trust.** Ashley urged her giant to understand
  that he had choices no matter how bleak things seemed. Giants who
  feel cornered without choices are particularly dangerous and hard to
  trust. Giants with choices, who are not told what they *must* do, behave
  more predictably and tend to trust us more.

- **Uncover meaning as a trusted advisor.** Ashley guided Nichols to
  find meaning that would help shape his interests going forward in
  a way that met her interests. She did this through credible reading
  sources, a gentle, inquisitive approach and some creative thinking as to
  how her captor could serve a clear purpose in life while also serving a
  life sentence. Ashley herself was strengthened by the meaning she gave
  to her own life through God, her daughter and the opportunity to save
  lives if she could persuade Nichols to surrender.

If Brian Nichols had not responded, or suddenly turned on her and
attacked, Ashley would have resorted to her alternatives, trying to scream,
flee or grab a weapon.

Many of us are taken hostage by our giants in much different and less
harrowing circumstances than Ashley Smith. This courageous mother shows
us that we can often get what we want, even in the toughest situations, by
unilaterally pursuing our giant's trust.

Building on Ashley's success, here are some final thoughts on managing
trust and distrust:

- **Consider helpers.** Review the pros and cons of using helpers in
  developing trust. In Ashley's case, the cons may have outweighed the
  pros. A third-party hostage negotiator acting as a Coercer might have

failed given the circumstances. She excelled on her own, connecting with Nichols one-on-one. I usually advise my clients to try talking to their giants directly so they can establish the capacity to cope with differences on an ongoing basis. If called in to mediate, my goal is to develop this critical capacity—and then get out. Other potential helpers in building trust include Connectors, Convincers and Coalitionists.

- **Communicate unambiguously.** The responsibility to be clear is yours, ensuring a giant doesn't misunderstand your intentions and act against you. Don't tell a giant "I'm pretty sure we'll support you" if you are sure of your support. Instead say, "We're behind you 100%." Ambiguity can haunt you.

- **Heal with history.** If useful, jointly chart in writing—and without judgment—negative developments that led to distrust. In this way, each side can better understand the other, initiating a healing process and future steps to avoid past mistakes. You can also focus on positives. My wife, Mary Lue, who has studied girls' conflicts, interviewed an 8-year-old who did what the girl called "back-flips" with her friends, going back in time to talk about positive things they'd done together, to help mend their current differences. So there you have it: depending on the circumstances, try a time chart—or a back-flip!

- **Benefit from trust.** There is power in being trustworthy. At some point, you can credibly say to your giant, "My track record speaks for itself. It's up to you to make the first move now, knowing you can count on me to come through on my end." As mutual trust grows, be sure to explore a wider and deeper range of interests along with better, more creative options for satisfying those interests.

Build trust in unlikely situations—by being trustworthy, trusting your giant to do what's in their best interests, modeling behaviors, framing choices and healing with history.

STAY CALM AMID ANGRY ATTACKS

I once mediated a raging dispute between a menacing company and unionized employees who had been locked out of their plant and replaced with other workers. Tough, hardened leaders on both sides of the table could barely look at each other, let alone suppress their anger when they spoke. The impasse had become a crisis.

One evening, after getting to know everyone around the table, I asked the two teams to step out of their roles. Without prejudice to our discussions, and in the spirit of brainstorming, each person agreed to take on a *completely* different role so we could have a different conversation. They became architects, teachers, doctors, professional sports coaches and even each other. They spent time thinking about the real challenges faced by the company and the union, using the perspectives of their newly adopted roles to reframe problems, interests and potential solutions. If anyone acted in a way that was partial to their real-life roles, they had to pay for their breach, throwing quarters into a "cheap-shot" cup, amid great guffaws from all sides.

The anger in the room evaporated and a meaningful conversation began. Everyone could see things more objectively and creatively after being permitted to step out of their own angry skins, and into the calmer skins of others.

The woman you're about to meet doesn't have to role-play being an architect. Nor does she ever have to be reminded how to stay calm: we'll be invisible spectators as we watch Pria Sahtra negotiate her way through a maze of hidden interests and boiling emotions.

STORY: STANDARD PROCEDURES

"Your fees are ridiculous—beyond belief!" shouts Tom Singer. The stout, ruddy-faced hotel manager stares angrily across the table at Pria.

"Why do you think that, Tom?" responds Pria, her large green eyes exuding calm.

Singer snorts. "Hey, I *know* your rates are way too high because I just finished a much larger project that was one hell of a lot cheaper than what you've proposed."

"What project was that?" Pria inquires impassively.

"I had my house renovated. It's not a small place. The ground floor alone is the size of this restaurant—and that's all you were asked to bid on. Or did we misunderstand each other? Perhaps the $150,000 in fees you've quoted me is to cover renovations for my entire hotel?" Singer smiles sarcastically. "Geez, the fees for my house were a fifth of what you're trying to charge me for re-doing this place," he says, looking up and down at the restaurant they're sitting in.[10]

Pria nods her head. "You want to pay an appropriate amount for the value you receive on this project, Tom. I'd want the same if I were you," she says. She's now framed things from Singer's perspective to help him relax, while subtly anchoring their conversation to the terms "appropriate" and "value"—which will favor her later on.

Pria begins to refine the relevant standards that will drive this conversation over billing levels. She explains the difference between commercial and residential projects in terms of approach, risks and time: one is designed to produce revenues while the other is not, and high-end restaurants, in particular, require specific marketing expertise. She also clarifies with the general manager of the Chateau Brunswick Hotel that he isn't just looking for "renovations" as she understands it—he's asking for a complete overhaul of his restaurant's identity, mood and appearance. "Isn't that right, Tom?"

Singer grunts. Pria assumes he's new to the design game, or he's trying to play dumb to drive down her price. Either way, she remains respectful even as he stares down at his Blackberry. "Look, Pria, I was introduced to you by my boss. Before that, I'd never heard of your firm. If you guys designed the Eiffel Tower, I *might* be willing to pay this price. But you didn't, did you?" He smirks. "No offense, but you look too young to have designed *anything*—except maybe a sandbox!" She ignores his comment.

Pria had fully expected Singer's boss, Rick Mayer, to be at this meeting. She'd met Mayer at a football game ten days earlier. Mayer runs 30 large hotels and mentioned this restaurant re-design work at the Chateau Brunswick, suggesting that the small design firm Pria owns might want to whip together a bid. Pria had jumped at the opportunity since her firm has many leads on new projects, but nothing confirmed. She's anxious, needing to close a deal before her firm's next payroll. Tom Singer had been helpful during their first brief meeting as they scoped out this restaurant project the previous week. But today, without his boss around, Singer is on the attack, and Pria knows that a counter-attack isn't going to get her what she wants.

"Tom, you're right." He looks surprised. "You don't know who I am or anything about my firm," she says politely. She doesn't bother to point out that this background information had been included in the pitch she sent to Rick Mayer. In fact, she relishes opportunities like this one. Pria laughs, pushing her long black hair to one side. She tells Singer she would *never* be chosen to build the Eiffel Tower, or anything like it. Her expertise lies uniquely in the food and beverage industry.

After a waitress refills their coffee mugs, the 34-year-old architect spends several minutes speaking about her experience before and after starting her own firm. She then pulls out her sketches and talks in detail about how the new layout and design her team has in mind for Singer's restaurant will position it for much higher sales.

While Mayer's decision to let Singer lead these discussions is an unpleasant surprise, Pria knows better when dealing with a big organization, where people can be on a project one day and off it the next: her written materials had to be straightforward, her messages clear and easily relayed internally; she always had to ask in advance who she'd be dealing with, while clarifying the decision-making process and making sure at the start of each meeting that everyone was up to speed. She'd been too excited and sloppy on this one, assuming Mayer would be here or at least pass along her credentials. Maybe the stress she's been feeling has finally caught up to her, she thinks.

Tom Singer forces a smile. "Interesting," he says, referring to her sketches. "Clearly, you have the expertise to do this work, Pria—I just don't want to pay so much for it. I have a budget in mind for this project, and the number from your firm is far too high."

Pria reaches into her bag. She hadn't planned to share her detailed budget projections in such an open manner, but she now believes it makes sense to do so. She brings out six pages of pencil jottings and numbers, asking Singer to excuse their appearance, hoping their lack of polish might actually inject some authenticity and trust into this conversation. "What if I walk you through exactly how we estimated our fees?" she asks.

"Fine," says Singer impatiently, looking at his watch and wincing noticeably.

Pria decides not to ignore this gesture. She knows that time must be on her side, not his. "Tom, if you're too busy now, and have to be somewhere else, why don't we get together later today or tomorrow? I'll need about 20 minutes."

"No, I'm fine. Do it now," Singer says, seemingly taken aback by her direct approach.

"Great," says Pria, moving her chair over to his side of the table. She explains the way her firm's hours are allotted and billed. She shows how her firm will end up earning around 12.5% of the project's expected construction costs, well within accepted standards for top firms doing this kind of specialized work. "Anyone doing this for less isn't delivering what we do, Tom. Our expertise equates to much higher, faster and lasting returns on your investment compared to other firms. Our references will confirm this."

"Okay, this helps," Singer says with apparent reluctance. "At the risk of sounding like a broken record though, we still need to get your prices down."

"Is there a reason for that, Tom? Are things slow for your hotel right now? Because we could look at a payment plan that meets your needs until things improve."

"Things are tight, but manageable," Singer says. "I only came into this hotel group and region three months ago, so I'll tell you *what I can't afford*: blowing my brains out on this project. Frankly, I was hoping you'd come up with a really low price to land this contract and open the door for additional work from our other hotels."

Another oversight: Pria didn't know Singer was so new to his job. This explains a lot. She figures his aggression may be hiding a strong need to show Mayer he can handle any project, getting the best possible terms. Pria also suspects Singer may be miffed his boss asked for her proposal without consulting him. She could always go around Singer—one of two Controllers involved in this decision—and try to get her price from Mayer as the more senior Controller, but that might not work. At this point, she'd rather sort things out with Singer directly. For this project to be successful, and for her to earn a chance at others like it from the wider hotel group, she'll obviously need Singer on her side.

"Tom, we have standard hourly rates for everyone working on this type of project. I can't arbitrarily lower these rates for a new client, no matter how big they are, when existing clients have been paying them for years. That wouldn't be appropriate. Clients pay our fees because our work pays for itself—in your case, probably within 15 months at most."

Singer doesn't relent. "I've got a budget, Pria. I hear everything you're saying, and it's convincing, but I can't do it, not based on these other construction and furnishing costs you've outlined."

"Okay, Tom. We could revisit the overall project, maybe scale it down a bit to bring you in on budget. If we end up doing less work as a result, we'll charge less."

"Yeah, but Rick might want it as is, *if* we decided to work with you," he says haltingly.

Pria pauses for half a minute, revisiting her numbers. "Look, we could knock at least $25,000 off our fees if we don't oversee the construction on a daily basis."

"That would help," Singer says. "Who would monitor construction instead?"

"You would. Or you could hire someone else to do it on the cheap," replies Pria.

"What's the downside?" he asks.

"None, necessarily. Our clients just usually prefer us to worry about making sure a project is unfolding exactly as we've designed it—keeping tabs on sub-contractors, keeping the site safe and free of liabilities for you—that kind of thing."

"No, I want *you* accountable," says Singer curtly. "I appreciate all your explanations and ideas. But despite everything you've said, my gut still tells me I'll have to tender this work to other firms." He waits for her reaction.

Pria gazes down, gathering her thoughts, then looks unwaveringly at him. "That would be disappointing to us, Tom. We've done our best to scope, plan and price this project as competitively as possible. We've even put aside our best people resources to start work as early as next week, in keeping with the timetable Rick and I first discussed."

"I'm not saying for sure we'll get other bids," Singer clarifies. "I'll talk to Rick about it."

Pria now presses, gently. "Tom, you should make it clear to Rick that our bid won't necessarily stay the same if we don't have a confirmation this week as hoped. I don't want to pressure you, but we've got several projects on the horizon. I can't keep a hold on my best people if we're not 100% sure your project is going to involve them."

"Well, we'll see what happens," Singer says gruffly as they rise from the table.

"Thank you, Tom. We'd love to work with you on this restaurant and make it the crown jewel of your hotel, which is what it should be. If there's anything else you want to know, please call me. And I'll be sure to send along our references later today."

She extends her hand. He takes it, awkwardly, and thanks her for coming.

Two days later, Tom Singer calls Pria to confirm she's got the business.

STAY CALM AMID ANGRY ATTACKS

After winning this contract, Pria Sahtra was told by one of Singer's assistants that Singer was "blown away" by her calm, measured approach. Never before had he concluded a conversation like this one without achieving a significant discount through his various tactics and outbursts.

Pria calculated correctly that Singer's anger was due to new job stress and her proposal being parachuted in by his boss. But Singer tends to bargain in this manner anyway. Why? Because it works for him—or he thinks it does.

Negotiators like Tom Singer who bargain "hard" at the table try to wring concessions through one or more tactics: they don't listen; they raise their voices; they attack you or your credibility to lower your own perceived value; they don't discuss their real interests, or yours; they stake out an extreme position, without justification and without looking at different options for agreement; they refer to arbitrary numbers, choosing to ignore discussions of real value; they look for you to commit to what they want, not committing to anything themselves; they constantly change what they want; and they boast about what they can do without you, ignoring or downplaying your alternatives.

When faced with these difficult behaviors by a giant, most smaller players cave in, not knowing they could have done better. Others lose their cool, understandably perhaps, counter-attacking with tactics similar to those being used on them, which can result in a bad deal, no deal or being crushed.

So how did our architect defy the odds, defusing Singer's aggression, handling his relentless price pressures and then pushing *him* to give her what she wanted?

Over the years, I've advised Pria on strategies for negotiating client relationships, while always learning something from her as well. She maintains her balance and excels by identifying hardball tactics and their purpose. She counters these tactics with a distinct mindset, a number of proven approaches and preparations away from the table:

- **Focus on the longer term.** Pria stays focused on her longer-term interests, and how she wants conversations and relationships to unfold, never reacting to what others say or do. She knows that as she keeps her eye on the future, having good manners in the shorter term can sometimes mean putting up with a giant's poor manners. That said, if someone's manners aren't meeting her interests at all, like when Singer tried to rush her presentation, she does respond, usually through well-placed questions, polite "push-back" or humor.

- **Look at other perspectives.** Early on, Pria puts herself on her giant's side of the table. She did this figuratively at first, then literally so she and Singer could look at their problem together, focusing less on each other as the problem. She always asks herself how objective players outside the room, including informal and formal Coercers, might see things from a different perspective. To engage a giant and appear reasonable, Pria begins explaining any solution in terms of how well it will meet her giant's interests, not her own.

- **Apply clear standards.** Pria has thought carefully about her fees and why she believes they're "appropriate." She developed her prices based on the general marketplace (10% of construction costs) and tailored this standard to the niche she serves, the strong talent she hires, and the resulting value her firm provides beyond the norm (taking her to 12.5% of construction costs, consistent with leaders in other upscale niches). These prices are fine-tuned by objective factors such as the seniority of project staff, a project's risk profile, seasonal demand, her firm's experience in a particular sub-niche—or any savings Pria can pass along due to efficiencies in handling larger projects. These well-reasoned standards blunt giant attacks and keep Pria on an even keel. If she couldn't attract new clients based on these standards, she would have to revisit marketplace standards, her firm's true value relative to the marketplace, or quite simply, how well she has marketed her firm's unique value.

- **Realize that budgets reflect interests, and are not *independent* standards.** Pria knows a giant's "budget" can be used as an arbitrary means to reduce her pricing. She recognizes, however, that budgets can be a valid concern. So she stays firm *and* flexible, sticking to her market-driven billing standards, while ready to suggest options for meeting a client's budgetary interests by reducing a project's overall costs, increasing project-related revenues or making payments over time.

- **Remain aware of the big downside to arbitrary pricing.** Years ago, Pria learned the hard way that when you come in with below-standard prices to win a contract, you firmly set giant expectations about both your value and your future pricing, no matter how well you may rationalize this short-term, arbitrary discount. In addition, you risk alienating existing clients who have already paid standard rates, or seeing these clients demand the same lower prices when they find out about a non-standard discount given to someone else.

- **Surface ignored information.** When Singer ignored Pria's alternatives to accepting his arbitrary price demands, she delicately applied pressure by mentioning that her alternatives to an immediate deal included releasing her best staff from the project. Without threatening anything overtly, or lying, she also made it clear that she had other potential projects "on the horizon" to keep her busy if Singer did not agree to pay her firm's standard rates in the days ahead. And by suggesting her firm's plans could be scaled back, Pria prompted Singer himself to introduce useful information—that his boss seemed to like the current plans as they were.

Beyond the mindset, approaches and preparations we've just reviewed for dealing with hard bargainers, Size Wizards such as Pria have some distinct ways they handle anger—both their own and anger coming from giant representatives like Tom Singer:

- **Try to understand your giant's anger.** The Size Wizards look to context and timing for clues as to why their giant might be stressed or moody. They wait, watch and listen, knowing they can't pour out their thoughts as smaller players until a giant empties its own glass of emotions and has room for other perspectives. They dig under angrily stated positions, harvesting hidden interests as ingredients for solutions. If they've caused a giant's anger, and it seems fitting, the Size Wizards apologize sincerely and in a timely manner; otherwise, they don't bother.

- **Don't take things personally.** Pria reminds herself of the obvious— giants say what they say to get what they want. One of her jobs is to help them understand there may be better ways to get what they really want *and* need. As well, Pria never forgets that a giant's intent is frequently not the same as its hurtful impact, so we need to test our assumptions before concluding a giant has tried to hurt us.

- **Create back-up plans.** Often, anger for smaller players results from feeling trapped. Instead of exploding from frustration, the Size Wizards channel their anger by developing alternatives they can pursue on their own as needed.

- **Lose your cool—intentionally.** At their best, the Size Wizards follow Aristotle's ancient advice and *decide* why, how, where, when and with whom they'll let themselves become angry. They stay cool *unless* they've planned to get angry with a specific purpose. In expressing their anger, they speak about how they feel, not their giant's intent. They use controlled, factual tones that cause giants to pause and listen. And they take breaks from conversations to collect their thoughts.

- **Look at yourself honestly.** Successful smaller players own up to themselves about any emotional baggage they might be bringing unfairly to discussions with a giant. In particular, they look at their recent conflicts with others, acknowledging if they have pent-up anger that's looking for a target.

- **Be aware of your anger threshold.** Whenever our resting heartbeat goes up by more than ten beats a minute, our bloodstream starts to flood with hormones such as adrenaline, driving our angry responses. These "angry" hormones can stay in our blood for hours after a triggering event, making it more likely we'll lose our cool again. Men tend to "flood out" faster than women, more intensely and take longer to recover. If you might get angry in an unhelpful way, consider rescheduling or involving helpers in a meeting. If you're already angry, speed the cooling process by arguing against your anger, distracting yourself, meditating or using vigorous physical activity to calm your body.[11]

- **Vent smartly.** If they can't calm themselves, the Size Wizards vent to confidantes, knowing that just one or two vents is about right; too much venting can create emotional ruts. Those we confide in need to know what to do with our anger: usually, they should listen first, then take on our giant's perspective to give us insights as to what our giant may be thinking. Other ways to vent include writing letters we never send, and fantasy conversations. The Size Wizards know the difference between fantasy and reality.

Stay calm amid angry attacks—focusing on the long term, getting into their shoes, preparing walk-aways, applying clear standards and releasing your anger productively.

GET THEM COMMITTED

I'm shopping in downtown Boston. Out of nowhere comes an unexpected lesson in negotiating with giants. "This guy's brilliant," I whisper to my wife, Mary Lue. For the next half-hour, we're entranced. When we get home that night, I grab my gnarled negotiation notebook and jot down what I believe to be the secrets of "The Knife Guy." These are secrets we can all use in any situation to attract our giants to conversations and keep them glued, right up until we confirm our deal.

STORY: STREET SMARTS

If you're The Knife Guy, here is your challenge: using only a bunch of knives and your voice, how do you get busy people walking by you to stop, watch, and pay you a pile of money for the otherwise free show you're about to perform?

Today, The Knife Guy is set up in Boston's Faneuil Hall, an open area where people can come and go as they please.

No one comes to this marketplace thinking: *Hey, I wonder if The Knife Guy might be around.* No tickets are sold. No advertising appears. No one knows for sure whether The Knife Guy will come or not. Everyone has something better to do—meet friends, shop, grab a bite to eat or just pass through. These people have plans for how to spend their time and money and The Knife Guy doesn't figure into them.

Yet it is virtually guaranteed on this warm Sunday afternoon that The Knife Guy will quickly have at least 100 people gathered around him in a huge circle. Remarkably, most of these people will commit to paying this busker something tangible for his efforts, much more than they would normally pay entertainers on the street.

Getting a handful of people to watch isn't hard. The stocky, middle-aged juggler flings several two-foot-long knives skyward as an intriguing warm-up. He drops a knife, apparently by mistake, and collects hearty laughs as he hops around on one foot, the other having been struck by the knife's blade. "As you can see, I'm on the cutting edge of my profession," he says with a feigned grimace to a small group that now includes me and my wife.[12]

Eyes twinkling, he asks us if we can do him a favor and yell "ooohs" and "ahhhs" mixed in with some hearty laughs to attract others so he can begin his "big show." We comply because he's asked us to, it's fun and we, too, have an interest in getting the main show underway. Sure enough, more people join in. A young girl to our left even agrees to lend a hand, tossing knives to The Knife Guy. He misses most of them, muttering that her throw is off.

Others walking by become attracted by the shining blades swirling through the air, accompanied by guffaws, a child's participation, more "ooohs" and "ahhhs" and The Knife Guy's gravelly, undulating voice.

With 100 people charmed, The Knife Guy begins his show, juggling different-sized blades with different body parts, escalating his stunts each step of the way. As he continues to perform, those approaching our circled gathering from the outside cannot see much as they walk by—there are too many bodies. They may catch the odd glimpse of a sword, but are more likely drawn in at this point by what *others* are watching and they *can't* see. Many of them inevitably work their way into the crowd, grabbing the remaining spots that offer a decent view.

Ten minutes later, the giant audience around us swells to more than 200 onlookers. The most recent additions are a little fidgety—like we were at first—not sure whether to stay or keep going, prepared to vote with their feet if this juggling joker cannot keep their attention.

The conversation and show continue. The Knife Guy cuts to the heart of his message, mixing sharp humor with brief jabs of sincerity, while still wowing watchers with his physical feats. "Folks, believe it or not, this is how I pay my bills...sad, isn't it?"

We all laugh. Someone starts the crowd yelling, "Ahhh," in mock sympathy.

"Well, thanks for that," he says with a grin. He turns quite serious. "I would only ask that if you're enjoying my show, please put money into the hat being circulated by my fantastic new helper. One buck, five bucks, ten bucks, whatever you can afford, and only if you can afford it." The pretty girl who threw knives at him in the warm-up is moving around with a big hat, her parents gazing on proudly. A few people move forward to toss in contributions.

The Knife Guy drops another sword and seems to prick his hand on it as he picks it up, juggling the whole time. "Ouch! Look, I'm trying my best to give you some good entertainment. I'd only ask in return that you give back to me what you can. By the way, if you're really cheap and not going to pay me anything, please leave right now," he cracks, his head turning deliberately to scan the crowd.

Two hundred people glance around to see who will actually own up to being a cheapskate in this public forum. Everyone laughs at the entertainer's ploy. My wife elbows my ribs as a reminder that this would be a good time to overcome any penny-pinching tendencies.

No one leaves.

The Knife Guy smiles broadly as he catches a wayward sword with his foot and keeps juggling. "Nice to see everyone staying. I guess we now have what you might call a contract!"

More laughter. Each feat of juggling is surpassed by a new one. As the show approaches 30 minutes, The Knife Guy announces it's time for his "grand finale"—the one he's been touting since the start. He slowly mounts a bunch of precariously stacked chairs and juggles half-a-dozen knives while perched there. The crowd gives him a big round of applause. The Knife Guy waves, throws himself off balance and falls to the pavement, knives following. He jumps to his feet, and bows. Our applause grows.

"Ladies and gentlemen, thank you. Thank you very much," he says. "If, by chance, you can't afford to pay anything into my hat, come up, say hi, and introduce yourself. I'd appreciate that too. Money helps a lot—it allows me to earn my living—but I'd love to hear your words of encouragement if that's all you have to offer right now."

One final burst of applause. The giant crowd begins to go its separate ways, back to whatever we were all doing before The Knife Guy's show. Many who have not paid already, do so now. I thank the juggler for his inspiring performance, leaning over to place my $10 bill inside his brimming hat.

The Knife Guy belts out one last request over my head: "By the way, if you didn't like certain parts of the show, please write your concerns down—preferably on the back of a $20 bill! I assure you that I'll look at those comments first!"

Another round of laughter.

Another successful show.

The Knife Guy attracts his giant, entertains it, and sends it away, pocketing close to $500.

GET THEM COMMITTED

The Knife Guy's story makes it easy to see just how important our ability to negotiate with giants can be if we want to realize the full value of whatever it is we do.

The Knife Guy is a good professional juggler—not a great one. He is, however, a great face-to-face talker and influencer who knows how to attract his giant to a conversation even though it's busy and has no immediate plans to see him. He manages to keep his giant's attention by quickly building rapport and meeting its needs. Finally, he creates a whole bunch of potential deals and closes on most of them. All this is accomplished in just over 30 minutes, generating returns on The Knife Guy's time that would thrill a high-priced lawyer, or the head of any sales force pitching services to corporate giants.

Let's look at the well-prepared and deceptively simple approaches that lead our Size Wizard to dazzling success, as he intuitively draws on some of our known psychological tendencies to get what he wants from his giant.

Attract your giant. The Knife Guy started in a straightforward way, choosing conditions that lead to his best outcomes—a sunny day and an area with high pedestrian traffic. Next, his skills and glimmering swords easily attracted some curious bystanders. These early members of his giant audience enjoyed special benefits: an excellent vantage point for watching the show, and an ability to communicate directly with the entertainer.

The Knife Guy reached across the divide between himself and these dozen-or-so crowd members, creating an impromptu Trojan-Horse Coalition. This one-time coalition not only quickly attracted more giant members with its orchestrated hoots, hollers and laughter, but as "insiders," original members—including me—felt like we were part of our performer's show and were much more likely to stick around.

After 100 people joined in, the attraction of early membership went away, since newcomers had to strain to see. However, to the The Knife Guy's benefit, a different form of attraction now made his value proposition appeal to late-arriving audience members: spaces to stand and watch were scarcer, making them more attractive based on our tendency to value things that are in short supply, or at least that appear to be.[13]

Keep them glued. What can a juggler possibly do for half-an-hour to keep people not just hanging around, but riveted? Unlike some dull presentations we're all exposed to, this performer varied his tone and pace, always speaking so we could hear him, but pausing for effect, raising his voice, then lowering it, even shouting loudly at times to keep us on our toes.

We were also glued because the danger of the swirling knives contrasted with the juggler's hilarious inadequacies, making his mistakes twice as funny and dramatic.

The Knife Guy gave us a choice, a chance to become "unglued" if we weren't going to pay him anything, but he made our alternative look so bad—admitting to 200 people you were cheap—that no one dared walk away. Psychologically, when you looked around and saw others similar to you weren't leaving, your tendency to stay was reinforced.

Despite this ploy, and others, The Knife Guy remained highly likeable through his self-deprecating humor, his unique form of entertainment and his flashes of warmth, like when he spoke tenderly with the girl helping him out. He didn't undermine this favorable profile by overusing his serious voice.

Most importantly, The Knife Guy escalated his show, introducing more exciting stunts as he neared his grand finale (there could be no denouement after the climax, unlike stage shows, or people would have left prematurely). He met our interests well enough to keep us around and entertained, but never met them fully, until the end.

Close the deal. To encourage his giant to pay up generously, The Knife Guy was straightforward and firm about his interests. He needed to make money because this was how he paid his bills. So he'd entertain us in return for our paying him, drawing on our deeply engrained tendency to reciprocate. He didn't request any money until we were completely engaged in his show, and then he asked, openly and politely. Since we'd already publicly committed to paying him something by the fact we'd chosen to stick around, those of us who like to think of ourselves as reliable followed through.

The only remaining issue was the amount to be paid. The juggler anchored our expectations early on, referring to specific numbers we might pay—$1, $5 or $10. He also introduced the standard of what we could afford, which seemed reasonable given the diverse range of onlookers. People watched as others contributed, often spurring them to contribute as well.

Lastly, to close multiple deals and ensure as many people as possible paid up, The Knife Guy kept entertaining us, even during the collection process, constantly building the perceived value of his show. He let someone else do collections on his behalf, someone much cuter and harder to say *no* to—his little blond helper. She acted as a compelling Convincer, informal Coercer and Coalitionist, influencing many giant Controllers in the crowd to pull out their wallets, when they wouldn't have otherwise.

As you reflect on The Knife Guy's show and lessons it might hold for your own giant conversations, here are some questions and thoughts to consider:

- To attract your giant, how can you take advantage of: optimal conditions and timing; eye-catching visuals; striking helpers; your core activities; special benefits for those first-in; a Trojan-Horse Coalition; or the element of scarcity?

- To keep your giant glued, can you vary your tone and pacing? Show you're good-natured, self-deprecating and not too serious? Escalate your offerings over time so they want to stick around? Use extreme contrasts to heighten your impact, or the psychology of imitation so your giant unwittingly follows the favorable lead of another player similar to themselves? What might be done in a subtle, humorous or helpful way to worsen your giant's perception of their alternatives?

- To close deals, how will you anchor expectations early on and introduce relevant and favorable standards to act as a guide for discussions? Can you bring into play your own interests or reciprocity to get what you want? If you're not comfortable closing a particular deal, who among your helpers might get the job done? What natural, credible deadlines related to either your core activities or your negotiation activities can you use to prompt closure? These might include your own deadlines related to walking away, quarter-ends, year-ends, seasonal commitments, legal requirements or important internal meetings. If your deadline is not anchored by a tangible event, it will be seen as arbitrary by your giant and won't work.

• The Size Wizards move gently but firmly in closing their deals, ending any giant discussion by agreeing on next steps to move things forward one way or another. They know that common closing tactics can encourage closure in some situations, but are most helpful when the transaction size is low. The higher the stakes, the less these pressure tactics work. They can even backfire. So if you're trying to get a giant to sign a trade treaty before they've fully reviewed it, think twice before saying to them, "Should we sign this today or tomorrow?" or, "Sign by midnight tonight and we'll give you a free pen set."

Get them committed—through psychology and three distinct stages aimed at attracting giants, keeping them glued and finalizing your deal.

Hazards to Avoid

To stand tall in conversations with your giant, here are some traps to sidestep:

Falling into a conversation. If you pick the wrong time, place, people, issues or forum for having a particular conversation, you'll end up with the wrong results. The Size Wizards know that how and when a conversation unfolds will have a positive or negative impact. If your giant catches you off-guard by beginning a conversation you're not fully prepared for, delay somehow, or listen without committing to anything. Be explicit as needed, saying you haven't thought through the issues in any detail and want more time.

Letting conclusions go untested. If a significant and faulty conclusion by your giant goes unchecked, it can be assumed to be correct, or worse, that you agree with it. The Size Wizards are effective at inquiring politely about: supporting data and its sources; data that is possibly being ignored; interpretations of chosen data; and underlying assumptions and beliefs that may be driving their giant to the wrong data, interpretations and conclusions.[14] If you're ever on a jury and your giant is made up of 11 jurors who see things differently than you, start by gently asking questions along these lines—just as Henry Fonda did in his role as a hold-out juror in the classic film *Twelve Angry Men*.

Relying on conversations with one giant source. Smaller players leave themselves exposed by focusing all their efforts on one Controller inside a giant organization. Should this Controller turn on them, change jobs or shift responsibilities, they can find themselves on the outside looking in—a trap Pria Sahtra almost fell into by catering to Tom Singer's boss, Rick Mayer, instead of Singer. The Size Wizards develop relationships with helpers surrounding their main contact, and they make sure a giant's organizational interests stay front and center, not just the interests of one individual. They also use the approaches we discussed earlier— in *Defend Yourself from the Start*—to protect their deals and keep their giants honest so any existing agreements are respected after a key contact has moved on.

Expecting a giant to say "sorry." Even if a giant authority like a doctor has made a serious mistake, you'll rarely hear them apologize, especially if they practice in America. Professional pride can get in the way, but so can the law. Many giants think you'll be able to use their apology—or any empathy they show—against them in a legal suit, regardless of whether they're truly liable. Ironically, their stonewalling can make you feel so poorly treated that it actually raises the chances you'll sue for physical and emotional damages. These dynamics are leading many state and national jurisdictions to adopt "I'm sorry" laws, explicitly making it okay for giant authorities and corporations to say they're sorry without having to fear their words alone will be used against them.[15]

Being uncomfortable with silence. Giants can use silence to their advantage, hoping smaller players will be intimidated and awkwardly fill in voids with revealing statements or concessions. The Size Wizards use silence to either let their giants jump in and do the talking, or they take the opportunity to gather their thoughts.

Being someone you're not. If you act uptight, cavalier or cagey, you may influence your giant to react the same way, meaning you'll be less likely to achieve strong results. Breakthroughs happen when smaller players relax, presenting their best selves to their giants, with suitable deference being paid in formal situations. In teaching seminars, I sometimes "freeze" a group of negotiators so they can step out of their role-playing and talk about the rut they're in. Invariably, they all lighten up, start chatting across the table and openly assess their stalemate—quickly identifying opportunities they've missed. I always ask why they feel it's necessary to be so reserved and serious during "the negotiation," instead of relaxing and making progress like they are now. The participants laugh, go back to their roles, lose the attitude and typically surge ahead.

FINAL THOUGHTS

In talking to giant authority figures, you want to inquire like our teenager Maria did when negotiating with her delivery-room doctor. If your giant is untrustworthy, learn to trust *their* interests and actions, not them, consistent with Ashley Smith's approach as a hostage. If your giant is playing hardball, remember architect Pria Sahtra's calmness, using arm's-length standards to help blunt calculated, angry attacks. And if your giant is tough to attract, keep glued or close on, bear in mind The Knife Guy's vibrant approaches so you, too, can make a living—any way you want.

Prepare for success. One way to prepare for giant conversations is through *active preparation*, all those initiatives you can undertake away from the negotiation table to defend against attacks, level the playing field and lay the groundwork for golden deals. As part of this type of preparation, most of which occurs long before you head to the negotiation table, you'll want to make sure you've researched everything there is to know about your giant and any specific giant representatives acting on their behalf.

The other way to prepare is through *mental preparation*—efforts to preview and plan conversations in your head—working on your own or with your team just before a meeting. This includes: 1) Going over your prioritized goals, needs and concerns. 2) Reflecting on your giant's interests and what mission or meaning may be guiding those interests. 3) Brainstorming a range of options to satisfy both your interests and your giant's interests. 4) Focusing on standards to guide which options are most appropriate. 5) Deciding on your best back-up plan while assessing theirs. 6) Thinking about how you'll build rapport with giant representatives. 7) Generating answers to tough questions. 8) Knowing what additional information you'll want to surface with your questions. 9) Forecasting steps you may discuss with your giant at the end of the meeting to move things forward. 10) Role-playing any parts of the negotiation that might prove difficult.

I once worked with a group of teenage convicts, including murderers, preparing them for their release at age 21. Together, we re-created some of the conversations and crime scenes that had landed them in jail, role-playing what they might have said and done differently to better satisfy their interests as they dealt with their giants, many of whom were gang members, drug lords or abusive parents. These juvenile offenders made amazing strides forward. Sure, they weren't being subjected to actual pressures just yet, but if possible, I think we all need to practice in low-risk situations as a stepping stone to real-world success. Before going into a new situation, or one where you've experienced past failure, I'd recommend you find the right Counselor for guidance, conjure up scenes and practice until you get it right.

Follow these broad steps at the table. Start by building relationships to ease your way into discussions. In formal settings, establish an agenda and a time frame. One of the first things to discuss can be interests, spending a lot of time on those. With interests as your core ingredients, talk about options and guiding standards for agreement, circling back to interests to clarify what people care about. The last step is to move toward commitment on a particular deal, usually after a series of meetings, making sure you commit *tentatively* to pieces of a deal before seeing how well the deal as whole meets your interests. If you hit trouble spots, take a break, possibly returning to relationship or communication issues that keep getting in the way. Consider mentioning *your* back-up plans if they are being under-estimated, and *their* back-up plans if you think they are being over-estimated.

Rethink your conversations. There is no inevitable way to have conversations. They end up with very different results depending on how and when we choose to have them. If you can't envision a conversation turning out the right way, you're probably thinking about having it the wrong way. Keep thinking, drawing on the insights of the Size Wizards, while remembering that your approach to a conversation not only affects your immediate outcomes, it can also establish expected patterns of behavior that will govern all of your future discussions with a giant.

Conclusion: What If?

What if early in his term as US Secretary of State, Colin Powell had been more effective in negotiating with others inside the Bush administration, significantly altering plans for the invasion of Iraq and maybe stopping it altogether?

What if Mark Felt at the FBI had chosen to remain a loyal soldier to Richard Nixon when the President was undermining his nation's laws and democratic institutions? Or, instead of gradually leaking information to *The Washington Post*, Felt had bypassed his historic role as Deep Throat and chosen a less effective approach to influence change inside the White House?

In other giant negotiations, what if Baron Robert FitzWalter hadn't taken London, pushing King John to sign Magna Carta? What if Ben Franklin hadn't gained support from France as America tried to negotiate its independence from Great Britain? What if Bill Gates hadn't promised to supply IBM with an operating system? What if Nelson Mandela had slaughtered thousands, fracturing his coalitions and never negotiating his way to power? What if Rosa Parks had quietly moved to the back of the bus?

Smaller players and their choices have played a defining role in shaping our history. The choices *you* make in your next giant negotiation may not be the stuff of legend, but may well determine your future. That's why I wrote this book.

GETTING WHAT WE WANT AGAINST THE ODDS

We've always been told to follow our dreams. Today, however, there's often a giant standing between us and our most ambitious goals.

Merely wanting something *really* badly and working *really* hard to get it isn't good enough—not anymore. You can have an exceptional skill-set and still not make the big-time. You can have a breakthrough idea for eradicating a killer disease and never attract the funding you deserve. You can know that a war is wrong, and watch helplessly as fighting takes the lives of your nation's youth. In the end, if you don't know how to negotiate with giants—understanding the full range of choices at your disposal—your hopes and dreams are unlikely to come true.

The Size Wizards offer us a bridge between our biggest dreams and their achievement.

At a minimum, we've learned through the stories and successes of others that we don't have to accept that one-time, "take-it or leave-it" ultimatum being forced on us by our giant. Nor do we have to put up with abusive giants or being ignored. And at best, if we plan carefully, applying the right habits, calling on the right helpers and executing the right strategies, we can turn the tide of influence in our favor and get what we want.

When beginning your own quest, it's vital to remember the Size Wizards' habit of staying firm *and* flexible. You need to firmly apply their habits and execute their strategies in order, staying flexible enough to realize that your giant negotiation may call for improvisation. If need be, you can skip less relevant strategies and approaches or circle back to a strategy. For example, you might go to the table and then move away from the table to further promote and protect your interests.

What you cannot do—ever—is ignore your helpers. Keep in mind Nelson Mandela's tribal saying: *You can do nothing if you don't get the support of other people.* As we followed Mandela through his lows and highs, we saw him use Coalitionists as the catalysts in freeing South Africa from apartheid. But Mandela also drew on support from many others: a Controller named de Klerk; a Crack who revealed the government's links to Zulus; Convincers and Coercers promoting greater freedoms; white and black Counselors offering strategic guidance; and Connectors introducing the helpers needed to round out the ANC's arsenal of influence.

I mentioned early on that my clients sometimes draw a people map, highlighting a giant Controller and the helpers required to influence that decision-maker. If you create your own map, consider adding (in a different color perhaps) all those potential helpers who could be used *by your giant* when they look to influence you as *their* Controller. With this human chessboard set up, you'll be better prepared—particularly in complex negotiations—to anticipate where "pieces" might move, even using some giant pieces to your benefit. For instance, a Crack that your giant may access inside your organization could be fed information that works to *your* advantage.

If Bill and Hillary Clinton had drafted a people map prior to their failed attempt at sweeping healthcare reform in the 1990s, they would have seen—issue by issue—attacking players appear on their map: distinct Cracks who would leak their plans to the media; Convincers, Coercers, Connectors and Counselors who, as "friends" of the Clintons, would act for displaced insurers, anxious hospitals and big tobacco companies upset about new taxes; Coalitionists from the business community who would fight costs to be borne by corporations and taxpayers; and congressional Controllers who would fear lost donations or votes.

In surveying these players *before* they rose up as a united force, the Clintons could have surmised their government team was surrounded and headed for defeat, *unless* they chose to unveil one or two major issues at a time. An incremental approach would have allowed them to concentrate on each issue, making sure they had adequate support and fresh helpers every step of the way, while splitting their giant opponent into manageable pieces.

As smaller players, we must constantly build, nurture and treasure our relationships with potential helpers—especially Connectors who link us to other helpers—so that whenever we find ourselves in a giant negotiation, our people maps can spring to life.

FINDING THE RIGHT BALANCE BETWEEN BIG AND SMALL

Although we need to focus on our own negotiations, I think it's important we not lose track of much broader negotiations that are determining the size of our giants and the clout they wield.

National and international lawmakers have frequently looked the other way in recent decades, letting powerful Goliaths bend the rules, break the rules or create new rules that allow them to grow bigger and more dominant in their dealings with smaller players.

Some areas we need to watch over globally in business, politics and governance include:

- Campaign financing laws that make it too expensive for smaller players to run for office, or that let giants exert too much influence with the public officials they finance.

- Media consolidation that allows giants to decide which issues make the news.

- Legal systems that move slowly and permit giants to appeal decisions for years—even decades—working against smaller players who regularly settle for a fraction of a court's award because they can't afford to go on.

- Anti-demonstration laws that make it hard for critics to be heard.

- Market structures and taxation policies that encourage indiscriminate corporate growth, compounded by antitrust laws that don't prevail when the costs of size outweigh its benefits.

- Practices that treat incorporation as a right rather than a privilege that can be revoked, just like a driver's license.

- International bodies such as the UN that are dominated by giants, without the same wise decision-making balance Ben Franklin struck between America's big and small states.

Like the steroids that created giant home run hitters in baseball and then ripped their bodies apart, undermining America's favorite pastime, societies favoring giants can produce inflated short-term results that eventually lead to breakdowns. If the playing field becomes too lopsided, nimble smaller players who've played such a critical role in our history will find the odds against them even tougher to overcome, risking an imbalance that threatens smaller players and giants alike.

Smart giants, the ones who thrive over longer periods, understand the grand balancing act that is required. They know smaller voices must be heard, even if the messages they carry are sometimes jarring. Of course, the Controllers inside giants usually can't argue openly against rules that favor them; they tend to fight changes or they wouldn't be doing their jobs. But this doesn't mean they don't realize that certain rule changes could prove to be in their long-term interests either professionally or personally, with respect to protecting the environment as one example, assuming their rivals must also abide by any new rules.

Smaller players concerned about rules that silence them—rules that bubble up from the Hidden Infrastructure of our giants—will need support from enlightened giant corporations, governments and individuals. They will also need help from other smaller players like you and me, so that together we can strike the right overall balance between big and small.

MAKING MISTAKES AND LEARNING AS WE MOVE FORWARD

Whether we are trying to change the rules that govern our societies or land our dream job with a giant organization, we are going to make mistakes.

Since the odds are stacked against us from the start, failing to get what we want from our giants doesn't label us as failures, nor does it necessarily indicate we've made mistakes. But more often than not, even when we achieve success as Size Wizards, we *will* make mistakes because there are so many decisions and risks in every negotiation—most involving the imperfect science of predicting how other human beings are going to act.

The key is to have a framework that points us in the right direction, telling us what we're supposed to do in our giant negotiations so we can compare our efforts against something, figuring out what we've done wrong when things do not turn out as expected. The Size Wizards—with their habits, helpers and strategies—provide this framework.

It is *not* a mistake, by the way, if you've done everything to meet your interests and your giant's interests, and one of you walks away. The Size Wizards work to arrive at an informed choice for what best meets their interests, asking: *Should I say yes to what's on the table with my giant, or should I walk away?* It is definitely a mistake, however, if you say *yes* to a giant deal when you could have better satisfied your interests in other ways.

One of the benefits of being surrounded by giants today is that we have an ongoing opportunity to make use of the habits, helpers and strategies of successful smaller players, learning from our own efforts—and mistakes— in a wide range of settings. The Size Wizards we've met have exposed us to negotiations in business, consumerism, politics, education, health, sports, entertainment, violent conflicts and personal relationships. If we continue to view the world through the lens of all these types of giant negotiations, we will keep improving each time we negotiate.

So as you listen to one of the thousands of songs on your iPod and climb into your splendidly engineered Honda Odyssey while sipping from your delicious cup of Starbucks brew, you can revel in some of the amazing things our giants do for us. But as you pick up speed along your journey, and you turn a corner into an unknown neighborhood, what if you run headfirst into a giant negotiation?

Well, now you can smile to yourself, even laughing under pressure like Nelson Mandela, knowing you're not alone as you draw on the timeless lessons of the Size Wizards who have traveled this same road—many times before.

ACKNOWLEDGMENTS

NEGOTIATING WITH GIANTS WOULD BE LIFELESS IF IT WEREN'T FILLED with the stories of successful smaller players who had the courage and smarts to defy the odds against them. I thank my clients and everyone else who shared their stories through this book.

If Harvard hadn't let me through its doors, these pages would never have been written. It was there I met Professor Howard Raiffa, author of the *The Art & Science of Negotiation* and a pioneer in both decision-making and negotiation analysis. Like his contemporary, John Nash—profiled in the film *A Beautiful Mind*—Howard is brilliant at using mathematics to solve complex problems. During the Cold War, he extended his problem-solving into the international realm by helping set up and run IIASA—an Austrian-based institution that would bring together leading thinkers from the Soviet Union and the West to attack common challenges, including global warming issues. Howard's passion for negotiation and his relentless efforts to improve approaches and results, even in the most extreme conflicts, inspired me to enter the negotiation field and, ultimately, to write.

Where Howard found many of his answers in numerical patterns, Roger Fisher found answers through his legal training and through the destruction of the Second World War. Roger also decided that we had to develop new ways to handle our conflicts. His commitment to this goal and his ability to grab simplicity from the clutches of confusion are reflected in the bestseller he co-authored, *Getting to Yes*. Roger taught at the Harvard Law School and it was there that he co-founded the Harvard Negotiation Project (HNP). I worked for two HNP off-shoots at one point, testing HNP theories through practice. Many of the intellectual pillars that support *Negotiating with Giants* come from my links to HNP and Roger—who was tireless, even in his seventies. I remember emailing him a long document just before midnight as we worked on a client file together, only to find that document back in my inbox with detailed comments by 7 a.m. the next morning.

I met some tremendous people and influences through Roger, HNP and the Harvard Law School, including: Scott Brown, Chris Cervenak, Maria Choi, Monica Christie, Paul Cramer, Mark Gordon, Ken Hyatt, Stu Kliman, Liz McClintock, Michael Moffitt, Bruce Patton, Steve Reifenberg, Rob Ricigliano, Paul Rocklin, Don Thompson and Jeff Weiss.

At the Harvard Business School, they continue to work hard at how we think about negotiation. My former colleagues David Lax and Jim Sebenius, who also cherish Professor Howard Raiffa as a mentor, influenced my early thinking about negotiating away from the table to create and claim value. Their Harvard Negotiation Roundtable is a signficant forum and I'm thankful for having been asked to participate along with leading faculty members when I was first exploring "giant negotiations" as a distinct field.

As I began to draft *Negotiating with Giants*, I benefited from the support and input of many friends, colleagues and family members: Barbara Emmerson, Jamie Fraser, Pat Johnston, Evan Jones, Gordon Mackay, Bill McGee, Michael Sachter, Michael Watkins and my amazing wife, Mary Lue. Marketing guru George McTaggart went beyond the call of duty with his early support, stressing the potential for a book that could help readers tackle their most challenging negotiations through stories.

As drafts evolved, the circle of readers commenting on the book expanded to include: Heather Adam, Jules Bloch, Eric Blumenschein, Lisa Blumenschein, Andrew Brooks, Kathryn DaSilva, Mark Edwards, Melissa Edwards, Dr. James Filbey, Brian Fraser, Rachel Greenwald, Sandra Hamilton, Kim Hanen, Annette Humphries, Dr. Kristen Korol, Pierre Levesque, David Malone, Duncan McTaggart, Colin Mercier, Matt Mazzotta, John Norwood, Phil Richmond, Dave Schneider, Jim Soame,

Hai Tang, Peter Wilson, Albert Wocke and Ian Wright. I thank all of these people for their insights. I am grateful to Derek Emmerson in particular for working ridiculously late hours as we finalized these pages—one by one.

In closing, I have three people to recognize for their unique contributions:

- When I met Ian Taylor, he said he'd heard about **Negotiating with Giants** through our common friend Dave Schneider, and loved the concept. Ian then told me that his foreign exchange firm, Custom House, would support the book's global launch. For their belief in this book's importance, I thank Ian and Custom House—an innovative, rigorous smaller player that serves smaller organizations worldwide, working hard to out-hustle giant competitors on all sides.

- Jonathan Ferguson is an old friend I met at Harvard, where he'd traveled as a Nieman Fellow because of his superb journalistic mind. Jonathan has been an ardent supporter, offering detailed feedback on my writing, while attacking my ideas, making them sharper and stronger. His "keep-it-simple" approach has influenced me since the day I first sat down to structure my thoughts.

- I arrive at the incomparable Warren Lang, a friend, educator and one of the smartest people I've ever met. Warren immersed himself in this project in early 2006, and more than anyone else—including me— believed in its premise and its potential. He pushed me to tighten my thinking, think differently and cut stories or whole sections. He was ruthless, relentless and passionate about getting this book to market.

As the author of **Negotiating with Giants**, despite the wonderful help I've received over the years, I take sole responsibility for the content within these pages, including any mistakes or omissions.

Back-of-the-Book Summary

Definition of *Giants* and *Giant Negotiations*: Our giants gain their status through resources and social or emotional clout many times larger than our own. We're negotiating with them anytime we try to influence them to do something—or not do something—and most objective observers would rate our odds of success between zero and 40 percent, often believing it's more likely we'll be crushed.

Secrets of Success: Successful smaller players—those I call the *Size Wizards*—have consistently overcome the odds against them across hundreds of years. They get what they want by applying *the right habits*, calling on *the right helpers* and executing *the right strategies*. You might think of their habits as the foundation for our influence efforts, their four size and strength strategies as the structure for these efforts, and their helpers as the people who assist us in building our influence.

Secrets of Success: The Right Habits

Habit	Key Story	Page
The Size Wizards **think differently** about what it means to negotiate, staying away from the "negotiation table" as long as possible.	Nelson Mandela	2
They are **grounded dreamers**—figuring out what they want and focusing on it.	Bolivian Orange Woman	3
They **weave** together their negotiation activities and their core activities.	John D. Rockefeller	4
They remain **firm *and* flexible** on their interests, approaches and relationships.	Prime Minister Diefenbaker	5
They take advantage of the **context** that most favors their interests.	Husband for an Hour	6
They are **information hounds**, digging for facts and interests.	Taxi driver polling	7
They understand the one interest that most giants obsess about—**growth**—and the Hidden Infrastructure that fosters the growth of giant organizations and individuals.	The Wright brothers & Standard Oil	8

SECRETS OF SUCCESS: THE RIGHT HELPERS

Helper	Description	Page
Controllers	*The decision-makers:* they control the final decisions inside your giant's castle.	10
Convincers	*The influencers:* they subtly or openly *pull* giant Controllers toward what you want.	11
Coercers	*The arm-twisters:* they are informal or formal authorities who *push* giants your way.	11
Connectors	*The networkers:* they connect you or your message to Controllers and other helpers.	11
Coalitionists	*The allies:* they add to your resources and clout as extended team members.	11
Counselors	*The advisors:* they advise you on strategy, giant-thinking and the helpers you'll need.	12
Cracks	*The informants:* they let you see things inside a giant's castle that you're not supposed to see.	12

SECRETS OF SUCCESS: THE RIGHT STRATEGIES

Defend Yourself from the Start	Key Story	Page
Guard your information—either by protecting it carefully or sharing it openly.	Michael Schiller's meat	19
Preserve your reputation—by moving quickly to set the record straight, sticking to the verifiable truth and not inappropriately attacking the reputation of your giant.	Vic Feazell & WFAA TV	26
Shield your core activities—by sticking to the rules, keeping key contributors happy, installing invisible defenses, naming their game or showing them on the attack.	Sheldon Breiner & Apple	32
Protect your deals—by prioritizing your interests, embedding these interests in your deals, and running through a checklist to make sure you've covered off key clauses.	A&M Records, PolyGram & the Bronfmans	38
Fend off broken promises—by capturing deals memorably, making deals realistic, and including smart compliance mechanisms with monitoring and meaningful penalties.	Susan Marx & her cheating husband, Ken	45
Shelter your time—by valuing your time, staying organized, creating time rules, modeling timeliness and being ready to walk away from a giant deal if it's taking too long.	Jill Turney & her venture capital investors	56

Level the Playing Field: Make Them Smaller and Weaker	Key Story	Page
Get out the rulebook—research relevant standards, follow the silence, and question your most basic assumptions about your giant and the rules at hand.	Linda Cramer & her marina deal	69
Change the way the game is played—change rules or referees, or just ignore the rules.	Lucia Pacifico & Brazil's supermarkets	76
Wear their team jersey—gain insider influence as a Controller and Convincer, access giant resources and insights, or tip your giant's boat over.	Guy Adams & the board of Lone Star Restaurants	82
Worsen their ability to play without you—claim one of your giant's significant assets or remove valuable players from their team.	Baron Robert FitzWalter & England's King John	88

Level the Playing Field: Make Yourself Bigger and Stronger	Key Story	Page
Sequence your deals inside-out—starting with the end in mind, avoiding disruptive conflicts and saying *no* to deals that risk undermining your long-term interests.	Jesse Rasch sells, then buys InQuent from SBC	102
Grow the size of your team—through an All-Small Coalition, a Big-Player Coalition, a Giant Coalition, a Mass Coalition or a Trojan-Horse Coalition.	Nelson Mandela & white South Africans	113
Plan to walk away—by applying clear criteria while improving and testing one of these alternatives: operate on your own; hook up with a smaller player or another giant; say *yes* to your giant when you mean *no*; walk away from some giant parts but not others; escalate things inside your giant; or pursue a plan that meets other, very different interests of yours.	Tom Droog & Wal-Mart	133
Magnify your impact through words and images—by creating and sending a message that is easily spread, targeted, sender-proofed, striking, supported, humorous and sent right.	Harriet Beecher Stowe & white Americans	145
Take advantage of your weaknesses and their strengths—especially when you're at your weakest and they're at their strongest.	Jamie Hodge & his bank manager	157

Craft Golden Deals	Key Story	Page
Use differences to create value— systematically focusing on differences in expertise, profile, resources and assumptions.	The Hinken family & SuperTech	175
Use shared interests to create value— surfacing shared goals, needs and concerns.	Richard Branson & Boeing	182
Use third parties to add value—including those who might be adversely affected by a non-deal, governments, financial institutions, charities and tiebreakers.	Union representative Mike Murphy & Copperlink	186
Involve your giant early on—boosting mutual value by unveiling giant interests, improving communication, getting them to work for you and shaping unique deals.	Simon Fuller & *Pop Idol* music buyers	191
Make your deals bigger or smaller— weighing the risks and benefits of each approach.	Prime Minister Mulroney & President Reagan	197

Stand Tall in Conversations	Key Story	Page
Respect and question authorities— researching, storing and sharing accurate data, drawing on helpers and framing solutions from their perspective first, not yours.	Maria's special delivery & Dr. Manse	208
Build trust in unlikely situations—by being trustworthy, trusting your giant to do what's in their best interests, modeling behaviors, framing choices and healing with history.	Ashley Smith & hostage-taker Brian Nichols	217
Stay calm amid angry attacks—focusing on the long term, getting into their shoes, preparing walk-aways, applying clear standards and releasing your anger productively.	Pria Sahtra & Tom Singer's hotel restaurant project	224
Get them committed—through psychology and three distinct stages aimed at attracting giants, keeping them glued and finalizing your deal.	The Knife Guy & his crowd	234

CHAPTER NOTES

THERE ARE TWO MAIN TYPES OF STORIES COVERED BY THESE NOTES:

- There are *true stories* which to the best of my knowledge unfolded as described, recognizing that even facts are limited by subjective observations and human memory (my own included). At times, I've had to fill in missing information or dialogue in these true stories but I've done my best to do so without changing the nature of a story or its lessons. In some of these stories—as described in the notes below—I've had to change names and identifying circumstances so the Size Wizards involved are not adversely affected. *Unless I've indicated otherwise in the text itself or in these notes, you can assume the stories you're reading are true stories.*

- There are stories *based on true stories*. I've included these stories borne of actual events because I believe they hold valuable lessons for all of us. They don't gain the designation of simply being true stories because I've had to change the circumstances enough to protect others or because I can only confirm certain core elements of these stories due to restrictions on my sources. In a limited number of situations—again as noted below—I've changed some circumstances in these stories to enhance the depth or breadth of learning for readers.

Any names created in either *true stories* or those stories that are *based on true stories* are *not* intended to bear any resemblance whatsoever to the real-life names of people, companies or groups.

While I am constantly dealing with legal issues on behalf of my clients, I am not a lawyer. Any of my stories or thoughts that touch on legal issues should be treated accordingly. Also, remember that laws often vary from one country to another, and even among states or provinces within the same nation.

INTRODUCTION

1. My references to "giants" and "smaller players" in connection with these types of extreme, size-imbalanced negotiations evolved over time, along with all the related terminology I use.

2. Estimates aren't adjusted for inflation. US GDP in 1980 was almost $3 trillion, rising to roughly $14 trillion in 2006. The "90 times" divide refers to an article by Walter Shapiro, "Hope and Glory," *USA Today*, 26 November 2004. Shapiro put this "rapidly increasing" divide at "88 times" in 2004.

3. See my explanations concerning name or circumstance changes at the outset of these chapter notes.

4. According to the Bible, David used a sling, which is an ancient ancestor of the slingshot. A sling was often made of just a leather pouch connected to two long strings on either side. The sling's user would swing it rapidly in a circular motion, releasing one string to send the stone flying from the sling's pouch.

1. SECRETS OF THE SIZE WIZARDS

1. This is a true story as recounted by Lawrence C. Bacow and Michael Wheeler in *Environmental Dispute Resolution* (New York: Plenum Press, 1987), 73-74. Most professional photographers lived a precarious existence in 1912. I make the assumption that Moffett was no exception and would have benefited hugely from a positive outcome to this negotiation with Roosevelt—who's a former President at this point, running on an independent ticket with Governor Hiram Johnson. My former Harvard colleagues Jim Sebenius and David Lax have also written about Moffett, which is how I first heard about his story.

2. Amar Bhidé writes about risk-taking and entrepreneurs in *The Origin and Evolution of New Businesses* (New York: Oxford University Press, 2000). I met Amar through the Harvard Negotiation Roundtable.

3. Ron Chernow, *Titan: The Life of John D. Rockefeller*, 1st Vintage Books ed. (New York: Vintage Books, 1999), 110-112.

4. H. W. Brands, *The First American: The Life and Times of Ben Franklin*, 1st Anchor Books ed. (New York: Anchor Books, 2002), 463.

5. Roger Fisher, Bill Ury and Bruce Patton, *Getting to Yes: Negotiating Agreement Without Giving In,* 2nd ed. (New York: Penguin Books, 1991).

6. This story has been rumored for decades, but I'd never known of Galbraith's role before speaking to him.

7. Jeff Cottrill, "Husband for an Hour," *DivorceMagazine.com*, 22 September 2003. Accessed 29 April 2004 at www.divorcemag.com/news/husbandforanhour.html.

8. Chernow, 430.

9. This is a true story. Names have been changed.

10. Malcolm Gladwell delves into a different but related type of "connector" in *The Tipping Point* (New York: Little, Brown, 2000). If you're into networking online, websites such as Linkedin.com, Xing.com, Visiblepath.com and Facebook.com may be able to hook you up with connectors and other helpers.

11. Anthony Sampson, *Mandela: The Authorized Biography* (London: HarperCollins, 1999), 10.

2. DEFEND YOURSELF FROM THE START

1. This story was relayed to me by a son of "Michael Schiller" many years ago. I jotted down rough notes at the time and I make a number of assumptions in retelling the story since I haven't been able to track down his son since. As such, the names in this account—which is based on a true story—have been changed along with some circumstances.

2. If Michael Schiller had a new and unique way to execute his floating fridge idea, such as technology he'd developed that made the meat freezing process possible for extended periods of time on a freighter, he may well have been able to receive patent protection. But as an idea alone, one that others could easily execute without inventing anything new, Michael's idea had to be defended through other approaches.

3. If you create a unique text or art form, you're automatically covered by copyright laws in most legal jurisdictions. Likewise, any distinct shorter phrases or symbols you consistently use to sell a product or service automatically receive legal protection as trademarks. The reason to consider formal filings is to clarify in a central registry that you were the first to develop your creation, which can speed up the legal process in your favor if you're ever challenged. Also, in the case of trademarks specifically, successful filings allow you to claim your trademark over a broad geographic area, whereas when relying on prior usage alone, you're only covered in those geographic areas where you can prove people associate a certain trademark with your product or service. On the other hand, patents—to protect new and concrete ways of doing or making something—must always be filed and formally approved. Today, you can make many legal filings online, without a lawyer, and at a reasonable price—certainly helpful for smaller players. Even provisional patents can be filed cheaply online. However, you may well be better off using legal counsel on more complex filings or filings with high stakes. Smaller law firms that come recommended on intellectual property matters are often the best avenue for smaller players because they tend to receive more attention at these firms and pay less than they would at big law firms focused on big clients. Finally, if you're pursuing any kind of filing, be aware that depending on where you'll have a presence, you may need to file in multiple jurisdictions.

4. NDAs can be one-way or joint, with examples found online. As a smaller player, signing a weak NDA or a poorly worded NDA can be worse than no NDA at all because you're giving your giant the right to learn your information, while formally acknowledging the real risk they may be able to use this information.

5. Unless noted otherwise, all dollar amounts cited are American.

6. I'm drawing here on an article by Tony Wong as my main source, "Architect Settles Disney Suit," from *The Toronto Star*, 26 September 2002.

7. I quote Voltaire in connection to Vic Feazell based on an article written by Rick Young, "The Wade-Feazell Comparison: Part I," *The Vidor Vidorian*, 25 August 1988.

8. Barry Silachter, "Plaintiff Played David to Win Goliath Award," *Fort Worth Star Telegram*, 28 April 1991. I also draw on this article for general background information.

9. Rick Young, "Benefit for Wade Family Nets More than $2,800," *The Vidor Vidorian*, 9 August 1988.

10. Silachter.

11. Karen Blumenthal, "A.H. Belo Ordered to Pay $58 Million in Libel Lawsuit," *The Wall Street Journal*, 22 April 1991.

12. Defamation laws can vary not only by country but by state or province as well, and they're constantly evolving, particularly as they relate to electronic communication.

13. If you say something negative about someone in good faith, as part of a job reference for example—believing you have an obligation to tell the truth and that a potential employer contacting you needs to know this truth—then your protection against defamation charges in many countries is stronger because of *Qualified Privilege*. You're also allowed to give evidence at trial, or talk freely in a legislative body like congress or parliament, due to *Absolute Privilege* which encourages people to speak out through their justice and political systems. Finally, media players in America can make good-faith mistakes in their reporting and not be guilty of libel, whereas that's not necessarily the case in nations like England.

14. I haven't used the café owner's real name.

15. I draw significantly here on an article by Steven Levy as my main source: "A Suit in Time," *Macworld Magazine*, November 1992.

16. John Markoff, "Company News: Broader Use of Macintosh Software Set," *The New York Times*, 21 January 1992.

17. Levy.

18. Even though Sheldon Breiner experienced success here, legal issues like those raised by his giant can undermine the momentum of any early-stage company—and should be side-stepped whenever possible.

19. Refunds or rebates—worth up to five times what clients had paid for PeopleSoft software—took effect if a takeover led to reduced product support in the following four years. PeopleSoft finally agreed to be acquired by Oracle in late 2004 for $10.3 billion, twice the amount of Oracle's first offer in 2003. For more information on the history of this deal, see Lisa DiCarlo, "The Oracle of Oracle-PeopleSoft," *Forbes.com*. Accessed 20 September 2007 at www.forbes.com/2004/12/13/cx_ld_1213oraclepsft_print.html.

20. This is a true story according to an executive who no longer works for the food giant. Names and some circumstances have been changed.

21. This is based on a true story, relayed to me by a member of the farmer's extended family. Names and some circumstances have been changed.

22. I've changed my acquaintance's name.

23. For some of this background and biographical information, I draw on Herb Alpert's official page at *MySpace.com*. Accessed 7 April 2007.

24. Andrew Cave, "Herb's on Song as Vivendi Goes Off Key," *Telegraph.co.uk,* 2 May 2002. Accessed 20 September 2007 at www.telegraph.co.uk/money/main.jhtml?xml=/money/2002/05/03/cnviv03.xml.

25. Geraldine Fabrikant, "Vivendi Universal, with its Complex Balance Sheet, Meets Distrust from Investors Shaken by Accounting Scandals," *The New York Times,* 11 February 2002.

26. John Carreyrou, "Vivendi's Woes a Taste of Honey for Herb Alpert," *The Wall Street Journal.* This article appeared in *The Globe and Mail* on 3 May 2002.

27. This payment of 8.8 million shares and $100 million are outlined in a Vivendi Universal press release issued 11 March 2003. Accessed 15 January 2005 at www.vivendiuniversal.com. I've confirmed the general terms of the price protections that Herb and Jerry received, but not the precise mechanisms or the exact amount they earned by selling their shares—which is only estimated here, at $180 million. Herb and Jerry declined to comment on my numbers or any other aspects of this story.

28. Brian Milner, "Broken Spirits," *Report on Business Magazine,* September 2002, 26.

29. Under the common law "indoor management rule," if you sign a deal with corporate representatives, you can assume they have the authority to bind their organizations (unless you obviously should have known otherwise). As a result, if your counterparts *didn't* actually have the right to commit their corporations, your deal should still be deemed valid by most courts in nations such as the US, Canada, England and India. Other nations and jurisdictions that do not follow common law may or may not have protections similar to the indoor management rule.

30. This story is based on two different situations where I was involved as an advisor, with the circumstances adjusted to highlight best practices in keeping our giants to their word. Names have been changed.

31. Putting assets in "escrow" means they're formally put aside and only released if certain agreed conditions are satisfied.

32. This is based on a true story. Names and some circumstances have been changed.

33. For more information on the Kyoto Protocol, refer to www.unfccc.int/kyoto_protocol/items/2830.php.

34. The percentage of rebates actually paid out to consumers is a secret that's guarded closely by most giants. Depending on the manufacturer or store, this percentage seems to range from the single digits to well over 50%. If you're like me, you may have sent in for a rebate and never heard back or been told more information was required, and you gave up—adding further to the percentage of rebates never claimed.

35. This is based on a true story that unfolded in Massachusetts. Names have been changed, with some circumstances adjusted to highlight the key lessons here about timing.

36. Portum was apparently in the process of raising another fund and planned to focus its partners on these efforts beginning early in the new year.

37. In the upcoming quarter, based on experience, she can estimate sales with some accuracy: she figures there's a 40% chance she'll run up $300,000 in new sales, a 35% chance she'll reach $400,000, and a 25% chance she'll hit $460,000. By multiplying each of these three probabilities, which must total 100%, by their potential gains, and adding up the three results, Jill arrives at her "expected" net gain in new sales: $375,000. These are the new sales she can expect, on average, given her situation. Her calculation: (.40 x $300,000) + (.35 x $400,000) + (.25 x $460,000) = $375,000.

3. LEVEL THE PLAYING FIELD: MAKE THEM SMALLER AND WEAKER

1. This is a true story, as relayed to me by "Linda Cramer." Names and some circumstances have been changed.

2. This is a true story. Names have been changed.

3. This is based on a true story. Names and some circumstances have been changed.

4. Amanda Ripley, "The Night Detective," *Time Magazine*, 30 December 2002, 40.

5. Ripley, 40.

6. This is a true story as relayed to me by my client "Michael." Names and some circumstances have been changed.

7. Miriam Jordan, "Brazil's 'Housewives' Pinch Nation's Pennies," *The Wall Street Journal*, 7 January 2003. I draw on this article for background information as well, along with a Bloomberg article, "Shrinking Toilet Rolls Spark Consumer Rebellion in Brazil's Troubled Economy," published online in the *Taipei Times*, 1 September 2001. Accessed at www.taipeitimes.com/worldbiz/archives.

8. Names and some circumstances have been changed.

9. This is based on a true story. Names and some circumstances have been changed.

10. "Skinny Models Banned from Catwalk," *Reuters/CNN Online*, 13 September 2006. Accessed 13 September 2006 at www.cnn.com/2006/world/europe/09/13/spain.models/index.html.

11. This quote is from a 1992 National Public Radio interview with Lynn Neary.

12. Any shareholder, large or small, can usually put forward proposals in advance of a corporation's annual meeting. Many proposals are defeated in voting through management's influence, often because they're not well-crafted and presented. Proposals put together thoughtfully, and that strike a broader chord, can help to initiate change in the right circumstances.

13. Sourced from a Lone Star news release issued 26 June 2001.

14. Gretchen Morgenson, *The New York Times*, 24 June 2001.

15. Sourced from a Lone Star news release issued 22 May 2002.

16. I spoke with Guy Adams on 11 July 2007.

17. I'm not making the case here that TD knew its merger with CIBC would help prompt an end to all bank mergers in Canada. But the impact of TD's additional merger had to weigh on the government at the time.

18. Notions of left and right are subtle here; the "right-leaning" National Party Prime Minister, Robert Muldoon, was apparently an interventionist as finance minister, and

his party had the most attractive policies on women's issues at the time, according to Waring.

19. Marilyn Waring, *Three Masquerades* (New Zealand: Auckland University Press/Bridget Williams Books, 1996), 11. Waring says this specific quote comes from Katherine Mansfield's Journal.

20. I spoke with Pam MacKenzie about this story not long after these events unfolded in 2000.

21. Names have been changed in this story.

22. Magna Carta is Latin for "the Great Charter." In Latin, the original language of the document, there is no "the" so the Great Charter is referred to only as "Magna Carta" by scholars.

23. Danny Danzinger and John Gillingham, *1215: The Year of Magna Carta* (New York: Simon & Schuster/Touchstone Books, 2004), 250-251. I also draw on this fascinating book to create or confirm many aspects of the background information in this story.

24. At various points in this story, I've dramatized the thoughts of real people based on what I know of their mindsets and interests.

25. Four copies of Magna Carta have survived some 800 years. Two copies are in the British Library.

26. Michael Wheeler and Georgia Levenson, "Tobacco Negotiations," *Harvard Business School Case 9-899-049*, revised 17 April 2002.

27. Nathaniel C. Nash, "Oil Companies Face Boycott Over Sinking of Rig," *The New York Times*, 17 June 1995.

28. After several weeks, the four Greenpeace activists were removed from the oil platform, but two activists returned by helicopter.

29. Nash.

30. "Brent Spar Gets Chop," *BBC News Online*, 25 November 1998. Accessed 22 April 2004 at www.news.bbc.co.uk/1/low/world/europe/221508.stm.

31. "Brent Spar Gets Chop," *BBC News Online*.

32. Leslie Scrivener, "Goliath Strikes Back at David," *The Toronto Star*, 12 April 1998. I draw on this article for this quote and general background information.

33. Laws related to primary and secondary picketing vary by country, state or province.

34. "Free Speech the Winner in Consumer Boycott Case" (Editorial), *Financial Post* (Canada), 16 April 1998.

35. When I contacted Ed Bianchi, he told me formal negotiations between the Lubicon Cree and Canada's federal government continued until 2003, coming to a halt at that point over two key issues—self-government and compensation. The issues in land settlement cases like this are often emotional ones, and complex, since the relevant historical context dates back generations and valuable natural resources are usually involved.

36. Scrivener.

37. Salman Rushdie, "Mohandas Gandhi," *Time Online*, 13 April 1998. Accessed 21 August 2007 at www.time.com/time/time100/leaders/profile/gandhi4.html.

4. LEVEL THE PLAYING FIELD: MAKE YOURSELF BIGGER AND STRONGER

1. A former colleague and fabulous raconteur, Don Thompson, passed a version of this story along to me many years ago.

2. SBC and Jesse signed confidentiality clauses that bar them from speaking about their dealings. The information in this story comes from a range of confidential and reliable sources. I've had to fill in some blanks in Jesse's story from newspaper accounts and by making educated guesses based on my own experience in similar circumstances. Certain numerical estimates may be off, but not by much.

3. Vito Pilieci, "How to Make Millions Before You're 25," *The National Post* (Canada), 9 August 2000.

4. SBC grew even bigger in 2005 by acquiring AT&T as a long distance carrier. The newly combined entity took on the better-known AT&T name. For sake of clarity, however, given that the *old* SBC is our focus here, I'll continue to refer to SBC by its historic name—the name it held when these events unfolded.

5. Presumably this loss is further reduced in significance by US taxpayers picking up roughly $70 million of the tab—assuming a 35% corporate tax rate at the time—since SBC remained taxable and its pre-tax earnings were lowered by approximately $200 million.

6. James Wallace & Jim Erickson, *Hard Drive: Bill Gates and the Making of the Microsoft Empire,* 1st HarperBusiness ed. (New York: HarperBusiness, 1993), 182.

7. Zaire was renamed in 1997, becoming the Democratic Republic of the Congo.

8. Anthony Sampson, *Mandela: The Authorized Biography* (London: HarperCollins, 1999), 61. I dramatize Sampson's description. I also use his book for general background information.

9. Sampson, 47.

10. The ANC had loosely allied itself with Indian groups in 1947. Albert Luthuli, president of the ANC in the 1950s—and winner of the Nobel Peace Prize in 1960—was a firm believer in the use of coalitions.

11. Sampson, 65.

12. Nelson Mandela, *Long Walk to Freedom,* 1st Paperback ed. (New York: Little, Brown and Company, 1995), 139-140. I also draw on Mandela's autobiography for general background information.

13. Mandela, 174. The Freedom Charter would serve as the ANC's manifesto and as a rough draft for South Africa's Constitution in the 1990s.

14. Mandela, 282-283.

15. Mandela, 293-302.

16. Sampson, 193. The ANC was a highly democratic organization. Members could influence and debate any decision and even the ANC's president was bound by the final decisions of his peers.

17. In the late 1980s, Winnie becomes increasingly volatile and is accused in connection with several assaults and deaths, most notably that of Stompie Seipei. She and Mandela will divorce in the mid-1990s.

18. "Case Studies in Sanctions and Terrorism," Institute for International Economics. Accessed on 9 November 2003 at www.iie.com/research/topics/sanctions/southafrica.htm.

19. Sampson, 338.

20. Sampson, 359.

21. Mandela, 556.

22. To appease its supporters and send a signal to the government, the ANC had to break off public talks at times, with Ramaphosa and Mandela continuing talks in secret so they could keep moving things forward.

23. John Mossman, "Kariya and Selanne Reunited in Colorado," *Associated Press/Post-Gazette.com*, 4 July 2003. Accessed 17 September 2003 at www.post-gazette.com/penguins/20030704lanchepens.asp.

24. This brief example is based on advice I provided to a software entrepreneur. His name has been changed.

25. Barbara J. Falk, *The Dilemmas of Dissidence in East-Central Europe* (New York: Central European University Press, 2003), 44-45, 176-177.

26. Michael Fumento, "Letters to the Editor," *The Wall Street Journal*, 10 April 2000.

27. Elisabeth Bumiller, "Evangelicals Sway White House on Human Rights Issues Abroad," *The New York Times*, 26 October 2003.

28. Mitchell Bard, "US Aid to Israel," *The Jewish Virtual Library*. Accessed 23 May 2007 at www.jewish virtuallibrary.org/jsource/US-Israel/U.S.Assistance_to_Israel.html.

29. Dana Kennedy, *The New York Times*, 18 August 2002.

30. Some information here was accessed 18 September 2003 at www.opec.org/About_OPEC/History.html.

31. Daniel Yergin, *The Prize: The Epic Quest for Oil, Money and Power*, 1st Paperback ed. (New York: Free Press, 2003), 792. The prices referenced are nominal prices, not indexed for inflation.

32. Charles Olivier, "What if…OPEC Collapses?" *Worldlink Magazine*, January 1999. Accessed 26 September 2003 at www.backissues.worldlink.co.uk/articles/19021999195259/90.htm.

33. H. W. Brands, *The First American: The Life and Times of Benjamin Franklin*, 1st Anchor Books ed. (New York: Anchor Books, 2002), 538.

34. Brands, 573-574.

35. Walter Isaacson, *Benjamin Franklin: An American Life*, 1st Simon &Schuster Paperback ed. (New York: Simon & Schuster Paperbacks, 2004), 67.

36. This is a true story I've pieced together through sources. Names have *not* been changed, with the exception of "Jack Higgins," who is no longer the head of sales at Spitz.

37. Barry C. Lynn, "Breaking the Chain: The Antitrust Case Against Wal-Mart," *Harpers Magazine* (July 2006), 32.

38. Joe Ashbrook Nickell, "Mayberry DSL," *Business 2.0*, August 2002, 17.

39. I spoke with Jake Langley in 2006.

40. Larry Collins & Dominique Lapierre, *Is Paris Burning?*, 6th ed. (New York: Simon and Schuster Pocketbooks, 1966), 222-224.

41. Nick Cafardo, "The Improbable Dream," *The Boston Globe*, 5 February 2002.

42. Belichick had been an assistant coach with the team years before, returning to the New England Patriots as head coach.

43. I spoke with Will McDonough on the phone in February 2002. He was a writer for *The Boston Globe.*

44. This is based on a true story involving a client of mine. Names and some circumstances have been changed.

45. I've changed the names of the folks from Sears.

46. "Carl Brewer Joins McMaster Grid Camp," *The Globe and Mail,* 10 September 1960.

47. "Carl Thomas Brewer," *LegendsofHockey.net,* accessed 13 June 2003.

48. Some information here comes from former Vice President Al Gore's introduction to Rachel Carson's book: *Silent Spring* (New York: Houghton Mifflin, 1994).

49. Noel B. Gerson, *Harriet Beecher Stowe* (USA: Praeger Publishers, 1976), 87.

50. Gerson, 81.

51. I make an assumption here about Harriet's mindset based on the tough publishing context and how she had reacted so modestly just a couple of years earlier when selected as a "distinguished woman." See: Joan D. Hedrick, *Harriet Beecher Stowe: A Life,* Paperback ed. (New York: Oxford University Press, 1995), 198.

52. Apparently, Harriet's publisher was reluctant at first, according to www.PBS.org/wgbh/aia/part4/4p2958.html, accessed 8 December 2003.

53. Gerson, 88.

54. Gerson, 88. Gerson's estimate of 350,000 books sold in year one is conservative. Given the royalty checks Harriet received early on, first year sales may have reached as high as one million copies, or more—once international sales were factored in.

55. Gerson, 194. This particular quote attributed to Lincoln has many variations and interpretations.

56. Gerson, 195.

57. Gerson, 88.

58. Later public perceptions of the characters in *Uncle Tom's Cabin* were altered through distortions and extreme stereotypes introduced by unauthorized traveling shows that dramatized the book.

59. Review from *The Independent,* 15 April 1852. I've modernized punctuation from this review which can be found at www.iath.virginia.edu/utc/reviews/rehp.html, accessed 12 December 2003.

60. This information on Douglass and white reaction comes from www.PBS.org/wgbh/aia/part4/4p2958.html, accessed 8 December 2003.

61. Harriet Beecher Stowe, *Uncle Tom's Cabin,* 1st Aladdin Paperbacks ed. (New York: Aladdin Paperbacks, 2002), 123.

62. Review from the *Boston Morning Post,* 3 May 1852, which can be found at www.iath.virginia.edu/utc/reviews/rehp.html, accessed 12 December 2003.

63. Review from the *London Times,* 3 September 1852, which can be found at www.iath.virginia.edu/utc/reviews/rehp.html, accessed 12 December 2003.

64. Jeffrey Kluger, *Splendid Solution: Jonas Salk and the Conquest of Polio* (New York: Putnam Books, 2002), 204.

65. There is a fine but important line to be drawn here. In identifying both your giant and your primary Controller within your giant, test whether they can decide to reach an agreement with you and, in all likelihood, are well-placed to see this agreement

through to implementation. Rarely do governments in free nations physically force organizational giants to do anything, even in antitrust cases. As a result, government leaders usually find themselves acting as arm-twisting Coercers and not decision-making Controllers when they influence organizational giants. In criminal cases, the government as a drafter and enforcer of laws can often act as a Controller. Also, in the case of war, where US Presidents have the broad capacity to act unilaterally and forcefully on an issue as Commander-in-Chief, they're viewed as the Controller—just as Lincoln was with respect to emancipation. Similarly, governments act as Controllers more frequently in societies where standard freedoms are restricted through force. South Africa's pro-apartheid government was one example of this, and in Iraq, Saddam Hussein was another.

66. *Super Size Me*—released in 2004 by The Con Production Company—was written and directed by Morgan Spurlock.

67. This quote attributed to the former head of the NCLC comes from an article by Jody K. Horn, interim director of the Lore Degenstein Gallery at Susquehanna University in Pennsylvania (August 2000). Accessed 20 May 2005 at www.susqu.edu/art_gallery/hine/hine.htm. The current president of the NCLC, Jeffrey Newman, told me his group continues to honor Lewis Hine each year by presenting the Lewis Hine Awards to ten unheralded Americans in recognition of their work on behalf of children and youth.

68. David L. Marcus, "Indonesia Revolt Was Net Driven," *The Boston Globe*, 23 May 1998. More recently, in 2007, text-messaging was used by Chinese protestors to successfully coordinate protests against a planned chemical plant near Xiamen. And in Venezuela, a TV station shut down by the government resorted to broadcasting through YouTube.com as a way to be heard and counter iron-fisted tactics.

69. Allen Jones, "Canadians Take Fight to End Death Penalty Stateside to Arizona," *The Tomball Potpourri*, 6 August 2002.

70. Siri Agrell, "Scott Peterson's Virtual Voice," *The National Post*, 2 August 2005.

71. Ron Chernow, *The Life of John D. Rockefeller, Sr.*, 1st Vintage Books ed. (New York: Vintage Books, 1999), 443. Ida Tarbell's magazine reports would later be published as a two-volume book.

72. This is a true story as relayed to me by my client "Jamie Hodge." Names and some circumstances have been changed.

73. Under a concept known as contra proferentem, those drafting a deal can be held responsible for ensuring its clarity, with their counterpart benefiting from any ambiguity. For a discussion of other legal issues related to power imbalances, see: Robert S. Adler and Elliott M. Silverstein, "When David Meets Goliath: Dealing with Power Differentials in Negotiations," *Harvard Negotiation Law Review*, Spring 2000, 28.

74. Thomas L. Friedman, *From Beirut to Jerusalem*, 1st Anchor Books ed. (New York: Anchor Books, 1995), 532-546.

75. Sampson, 252-253.

76. Bill Carter, "How ABC's Full-Court Press Almost Landed Letterman," *The New York Times*, 18 March 2002.

77. This is sourced from two articles: Sandra McCulloch, "Teen's Web Dispute Files Attract High Bids on EBay," *Times Colonist*, 30 January 2004; Todd Bishop, "Where Are They Now? Mike Rowe, of 'MikeRoweSoft' Fame," *Seattle Post-Intelligencer*, 15 March 2007, accessed at www.blog.seattlepi.nwsource.com/microsoft/archives/112571.asp.

78. W. Howard Wriggins, "Up for Auction: Malta Bargains with Great Britain, 1971," from *The Fifty Percent Solution*, I.W. Zartman, Editor (Garden City, New York: Doubleday, 1976), 229.

79. Chernow, 442.

80. Helen and Dave distributed the pamphlet as members of a small environmental group, "London Greenpeace," distinct from Greenpeace International. When five members of London Greenpeace were sued for libel by McDonald's, three decided to back off and apologize; Helen and Dave decided to fight. The pair didn't write the pamphlet, nor did the three others who were sued.

81. Sarah Lyall, "Big Mac Attack," *The New York Times*, 16 November 1997.

82. "McLibel Pair Back in Court," *ManchesterNewsOnline.co.uk*, 7 September 2004. Accessed on 3 November 2004 at www.manchesteronline.co.uk/news/s/129/129601_mclibel_two_back_in_court.html.

83. Eric Schlosser, *Fast Food Nation*, 1st Perennial ed. (New York: HarperCollins, 2002), 247.

84. Heather Timmons, "Britain Faulted Over McDonald's Libel Case," *The New York Times*, 16 February 2005.

85. Alan Travis, "Big Brother and the Sisters," *Guardian Unlimited*, 10 October 2003. Accessed 24 November 2003 at www.guardian.co.uk/humanrights/story/0,7369,1060014,00.html.

86. Elisabeth Bumiller, "Endorsement from Gore Became a Dubious Prize," *The New York Times*, 8 February 2004.

87. Malcolm Gladwell talks about this "150" phenomenon in *The Tipping Point* (New York: Little, Brown, 2000), 179-187.

5. CRAFT GOLDEN DEALS

1. This is based on a true story relayed to me by a former colleague. Names have been changed. Some circumstances have also been changed to highlight lessons related to building deals around differences.

2. This is based on a true story. Names and some circumstances have been changed.

3. This example and the three others that follow are examples across different contexts based on my experience in general, and are not based on any particular real-life stories.

4. This story was relayed to me by a former colleague and long-time friend, Steve Reifenberg. The final agreement gave Ecuador a small piece of private land inside Peru at the heart of the fighting, where it could erect a monument and its flag. The deal also created a "bi-national park" in the mountains and jungles of the disputed border area in the Cordillera del Condor region.

5. This information and some of the other background information in this story comes from Virgin Atlantic's website at www.Virgin-Atlantic.com/our_story_history.view.do, accessed 9 August 2004.

6. Peter Kafka, "Davids and Goliaths," *Forbes*, November 1997. Accessed 14 September 2007 at www.members.forbes.com/forbes/1997/1103/6010020a.html.

7. Richard Branson, *Losing My Virginity* (New York: Three Rivers Press, 2004), 159. According to Katie Francis in Virgin Atlantic's communications group, the company's first 10 planes came from Boeing.

8. Kafka.

9. "Come Together," *Associated Press/SportsIllustrated.com*, 23 January 2004. Accessed on 23 January 2004 at www.sportsillustrated.cnn.com.

10. H. W. Brands, *The First American: The Life and Times of Ben Franklin*, 1st Anchor Books ed. (New York: Anchor Books, 2002), 682.

11. The source here is www.amw.com/about_amw/john_walsh.cfm, accessed 28 August 2007.

12. This is a true story where I was involved as an advisor. Names and some circumstances have been changed.

13. Rick Spence, "The IKEA Factor," *Corporate Knights Forestry Issue 2005*, Volume 4.4 (Toronto, Canada), 14.

14. As a case in point, in many countries—including the US—an "intangible" premium paid by a larger player to acquire a smaller player can often be deducted from taxable earnings over time as a "goodwill" expense. If the tax rate applied to giant earnings is 35%, for example, then every dollar of goodwill that can be deducted from these earnings for tax purposes saves the giant 35 cents that would otherwise be paid to the government.

15. The main source here is "The Making of Good Will Hunting (D)," *Harvard Business School Case*, N-X-098-000, 1998.

16. The Montreal Expos have since become the Washington Nationals.

17. The Yankees publicly denied their intent was to keep Colon away from the Red Sox but many sports commentators looking closely at the three-way deal concluded otherwise. See ESPN.com—15 January 2004—"Three-way Deal Includes Yanks' Hernandez to Expos" with commentary by Dave Campbell. Accessed on 18 February 2004 at www.sports.espn.go.com.

18. Helen Bushby, "What's All the Fuss About?" *BBC News Online*, 23 January 2002. Accessed on 22 September 2007 at www.news.bbc.co.uk/2/hi/entertainment/1775716.stm.

19. The format of subsequent *Idol* shows varied in terms of when the audience started to vote.

20. "Will Is Your Pop Idol," *BBC News Online*, 9 February 2002. Accessed on 22 September 2007 at www.news.bbc.co.uk/cbbcnews/hi/tv_film/newsid_1811000/1811896.stm.

21. "Simon Fuller: Guiding Pop Culture," *BBC News Online*, 18 June 2003. Accessed 22 September 2007 at www.news.bbc.co.uk/1/hi/entertainment/music/2999872.stm.

22. This example and the two that follow are based on real situations and advice given to dozens of my technology clients, large and small. Names have been changed, apart from Apple.

23. William A. Niskanen, "Policy Analysis: Stumbling Toward a US-Canada Free Trade Agreement," *The Cato Institute*, 18 June 1987, 5. Accessed 21 September 2004 at www.cato.org/cgi-bin/scripts/printtech.cgi/pubs/pas/pa088.html.

24. Niskanen, 6-7. Refers to the US wanting a broader deal as confirmed by the Mulroney-Reagan 1985 meeting at the "Shamrock Summit" in Quebec City.

25. In the early 1990s, the Canada-US Free Trade Agreement (FTA) was extended to include Mexico and re-christened the North American Free Trade Agreement (NAFTA).

26. Dana Priest and Michael Weisskopf, "Health Care Reform: The Collapse of a Quest," *The Washington Post*, 11 October 1994.

27. This single story is based on a number of real situations and advice given to this leading management consulting firm. Names have been changed here along with some circumstances.

28. Background here from: Andrew Gumbel, "Betrayed by an Oil Giant," *The Independent*, 25 March 2004.

6. STAND TALL IN CONVERSATIONS

1. Robert B. Cialdini, *Influence: The Psychology of Persuasion*, Revised ed. (New York: William Morrow, 1993), 208-236.

2. This is based on a true story as relayed to me by an operating room source. I've changed names and some circumstances.

3. The age of medical consent varies by state or country, and differs depending on the type of procedure and circumstances. Most US states are like California, where even the youngest woman deemed to be competent can decide *not* to tell her parents about an abortion or a birth, respecting her right to choose.

4. J. Edward Russo and Paul J. H. Schoemaker, *Decision Traps: The Ten Barriers to Brilliant Decision-Making and How to Overcome Them*, 1st ed (New York: Fireside Books/Simon & Schuster, 1990), 122.

5. Ashley was forced into her apartment under unique circumstances. In other situations, if you're accosted in public, most experts recommend you keep screaming and try to get away, no matter what your assailant says. You usually *lower* your odds of escaping unharmed by going into a closed space farther from public view.

6. Many quotes that I use in this story are drawn from a news conference held by Ashley Smith, "Ex-Hostage: 'I Wanted to Gain his Trust,'" *CNN Online*, 14 March 2005, accessed 15 March 2005 at www.cnn.law. Ashley has written a book, *Unlikely Angel*, (with Stacy Mattingly) detailing her time as a hostage, which I draw upon in re-creating portions of her negotiation with Nichols (New York: William Morrow/Zondervan, 2005). I also spoke with Ashley in the summer of 2007 about her experience, confirming certain facts as well as my understanding of how she influenced Nichols to release her. She had recently re-married, taking her new husband's last name: Robinson.

7. Rick Warren, *The Purpose Driven Life: What On Earth Am I Here For?* (Grand Rapids, Michigan: Zondervan, 2002).

8. Warren, 249.

9. Ashley's past mistakes involved drugs. By her own admission, she makes a related mistake with Nichols by giving her captor "meth" (methamphetamine) to help build their relationship. The drug risked making him more aggressive, but it apparently had no significant impact on his personality or their interactions.

10. This is based on a true story involving our architect "Pria Sahtra" and a client of hers. I've changed names and some circumstances.

11. Daniel Goleman, *Emotional Intelligence: Why it Can Matter More than IQ* (New York: Bantam Books, 1995), 139-141. Of particular interest, Goleman talks about the physiology of anger and how to manage it. The reference here to men "flooding out" faster than women is based on research related to couples and how they handle their conflicts.

12. I'm recounting this based on memory and my notes at the time, improvising some of the dialogue and details. I refer to our performer as The Knife Guy. He didn't call himself by any name as far as I can recall.

13. See Cialdini's *Influence* for a highly accessible discussion of psychological tendencies and influence.

14. For more on these matters, see Chris Argyris and his writings about "The Ladder of Inference."

15. For more on this topic from a medical perspective, see "Sorry Seems to Be the Hardest Word, but Admitting Fault Is Gaining Popularity," *Arkansas Democrat-Gazette* (Little Rock), 17 April 2007.

ABOUT THE AUTHOR

PETER JOHNSTON IS AN INTERNATIONAL NEGOTIATION EXPERT whose groundbreaking results have been formally recognized by the US government for their positive economic and social impact.

He's a pioneer in helping underdogs negotiate against the odds with giants who tower over them in size and clout. His folksy, concrete advice to smaller players—entrepreneurs, athletes, struggling organizations, embattled political leaders and individuals seeking change—is driven by his experiences with clients and ongoing research into the best practices of successful smaller players across hundreds of years. Peter's insights also come from his extensive work with giants, including governments, global institutions and some of the world's largest corporations.

He quietly advises clients of all sizes on significant negotiations and conflicts; goes to the table as needed on their behalf; enhances the effectiveness of their organizations in negotiating both internally and externally; mediates disputes; and teaches tailored negotiation seminars. His ideas emphasize efforts away from the negotiation table that better position negotiators once they're at the table. As Managing Director of NAI—a boutique consulting firm founded in Cambridge, Massachusetts—he has developed the discipline of integrated negotiation, an approach that builds value by seamlessly weaving together core operating activities with negotiation activities.

Recent examples of Peter's client engagements include helping a renowned gallery negotiate the return of stolen artwork; guiding a small company in its successful efforts to get a giant retailer back as a customer; supporting the Founder and Chairman of a high-profile fashion group in negotiating the sale of his company; advising a group of municipal leaders on a sustainable regional development and governance plan; speaking at a global M&A conference about the advantages of being a smaller competitor; training the board of a large union in best negotiation practices and then counseling its executive team on critical issues; mediating a rights dispute between a national government and its aboriginal people.

The early foundations for Peter's distinct approaches to influence were formed by working closely with founders of the Harvard Negotiation Project, the Program on Negotiation and the Harvard Negotiation Roundtable. He is a Harvard MBA, trained journalist and former corporate and investment banker. Peter is Canadian and divides his time between Canada and the US, as well as the East and West Coasts. Dynamic and entertaining, he often lectures at universities and speaks at conferences.

Peter has been featured in media around the world, talking about his work and commenting on newsworthy negotiations, volatile conflicts and successful influence strategies related to politics, economics and personal relationships. Dozens of news groups have interviewed or quoted him, including *CNN*, *ABC's "America This Morning,"* *FOX Business News*, *Oprah & Friends*, *US News & World Report*, *Business Week*, *Wired Magazine*, *Embassy Magazine*, *The Globe and Mail*, *The National Post* and *The Wall Street Journal*.